THE RIGHT SPOUSE

THE RIGHT SPOUSE

PREFERENTIAL MARRIAGES IN TAMIL NADU

ISABELLE CLARK-DECÈS

STANFORD UNIVERSITY PRESS
Stanford, California

Stanford University Press
Stanford, California

Printed in the United States of America on acid-free, archival-quality paper

Library of Congress Cataloging-in-Publication Data

Clark-Decès, Isabelle, 1956– author.
The right spouse : preferential marriages in Tamil Nadu / Isabelle Clark-Decès.
pages cm
Includes bibliographical references and index.
ISBN 978-0-8047-8806-9 (cloth : alk. paper) — ISBN 978-0-8047-9049-9 (pbk. : alk. paper)
1. Tamil (Indic people)—Marriage customs and rites. 2. Tamil (Indic people)—Kinship. 3. Marriage—India—Tamil Nadu. 4. Kinship—India—Tamil Nadu. 5. Endogamy and exogamy—India—Tamil Nadu. 6. Tamil Nadu (India)—Social life and customs. I. Title.
DS432.T3C63 2014
954'.82—dc23

2013040995

ISBN 978-0-8047-9050-5 (electronic)

Typeset by Thompson Type in 10/14 Times New Roman

To my late husband Jim Clark, my role model and closest kin

CONTENTS

ACKNOWLEDGMENTS

It is impossible to thank individually the many people who have contributed directly and indirectly, in ways large and small, to this project. I am grateful to them all but want to mention some in particular.

Fieldwork in Tamil Nadu and the Union Territory of Pondicherry during 2007 and 2008 was generously supported by a grant from the Fulbright Foundation. A small faculty research grant and travel funds from Princeton University allowed for two follow-up visits in 2010 and 2011. Much of this book was written during my tenure in an Old Dominion Professorship from the Council of the Humanities of Princeton University in 2011–2012. I presented earlier versions of various chapters of this book in the Anthropology Department and the Society of Fellows of Princeton University (2008, 2011, 2012), at the London School of Economics (2011), the Association for Asian Studies in Honolulu (2011), the annual Tamil Conference in Berkeley (2010, 2011, 2012), and the AAA meetings in San Francisco in 2012. I thank Larry Rosen, Rena Lederman, Jim Boon, Chris Fuller, Laura Bear, Alpa Shah, Mukulita Banerjee, Indira Arumugam, Craig Jeffrey, George Hart, Kausalya Hart, Ann Gold, and many others for their invitations, encouragement, and critical feedback. Condensed versions of Chapters 6 and 7 appeared in *A Companion to the Anthropology of India*, which I edited for Wiley and Blackwell (2011).

It is hard to imagine how this book could have come into being without the warm hospitality and collegiality of Susan Stewart, Carol Rigolot, Mary Harper, and the fabulous Cotsen fellows of Princeton University. Gabriela Drinovan helped me with the literature research, and Leo Coleman edited the manuscript. Frederick Smith's curiosity and deep knowledge of India inspired me. I take this opportunity to offer him my profound thanks for enriching my work and my life.

In an act of collegiality for which I am most grateful, Chris Fuller read an earlier draft of the present text, and his sound advice and detailed comments on all the chapters guided the revising process. I heartily thank Dennis McGilvray and the other reviewer who read the manuscript for Stanford University Press. Dennis's careful reading and critical suggestions were invaluable, and I hope he sees his imprint on this book. Michelle Lipinski's support and enthusiasm picked me up more than once, and I feel privileged to be one of her authors. I am also grateful to Margaret Pinette for seeing the book through the production process.

I accrued many personal debts while in the field. I cannot thank enough the people who appear in this book under the names of Ravi, Mayandi, Neelam, Thiagu, Attai, Abi, Mohan, and Sunil. They shared their stories to me; more important, they touched me deeply. Thank you also to Jothi, Anand, Kasthuri, Srinidi, and Karthik for your loyalty and assistance. The Fulbright staff in Delhi provided invaluable assistance with the logistics of my stay. M. Kannan arranged my affiliation with the French Institute of Pondicherry, and I am grateful for his hospitality and all the lively conversations we had in his office. Ulrike Niklas was my guardian angel, taking me into her home and offering help with many of the details of organizing and carrying out field research.

If there is any sensitivity or empathy in this book, it comes from my late husband, Jim Clark, who passed away a month after I finished it. While the conditions under which it was written were marked by the terror and sadness of his progressing cancer, it is Jim's love of life and books that ultimately shaped its form and ideas. For his generosity of spirit, his great laugh, his belief in me, and so much more, I thank him from the bottom of my heart.

THE RIGHT SPOUSE

INTRODUCTION

Tamil Preferential Marriages

Tamil people are always happy to know that
the groom and bride are related.
—Srinidi, September 2008
Nowadays people marry money to money, BA to BA.
—Kartik, January 2009

For the better part of my fieldwork I lived in a suburb of Madurai, a temple town in the South Indian state of Tamil Nadu, in a cement house with a gated yard and a veranda on the second floor. The veranda looked over a flat terrain of brush and trash where a neighbor had patched together a cow pen with tin, plastic, and canvas. The back door of the house opened onto a railway track and a rocky mountain, abruptly, like a movie set: end of town. The sound of water running over last night's pans entered my sleep every morning. Lying on the mattress on the floor of my blue-painted room, I waited for the milk boy to open the gate and put his *sompu* on the front stairs. Then I was up, standing at the window to peer out at the neighbor's cow stationed under its lurching shelter. How many times did I see this cow lift a banana peel out of the gutter and devour it, with its eyes half closed? By the time the flower man called out "*pūhe! pūhe!*" as he toured the neighborhood with his new supply of fresh jasmine, I was ready for my breakfast of sweet coffee and "milky" biscuits.

The first mornings in that house I could not tell that I was on the outskirts of a busy temple town. The sounds I heard took me back to the village in the northern part of Tamil Nadu where I had lived in 1990–1991: peddlers making their daily rounds, frenzied dogs howling and barking, brass and stainless steel pots being scrubbed on the concrete floor of a neighbor's courtyard. Nor was there much sign that I lived very close to villages, so close indeed that I could walk to the nearest one. From a topographic perspective, you could say that I lived in a strip of land that fell between the rural and the urban.

It was not easy to tell where the city ended and the village started. It was obvious that the folks over there toiled in the fields, following the rhythms of an age-old agrarian way of life, while the folks over here worked in government offices and businesses of all sorts. But on both sides you could see the same processes of change at work, including the destruction of the environment under the press of urbanization, the generalization of schooling, less segregation of the sexes, the commodification of social relations, the formation of classes and the growing gap between them, and the disjuncture between the abilities and expectations of the uneducated and those who had gone to school. Whether rural or urban, society was undergoing profound processes of restructuring and detraditionalization.

My location was ideal for my original ethnographic purpose, which was to study the transformation of marriage practices in Tamil society. Change I did find, as people on both sides of the rural urban continuum were less prone to contract the old preferential marriages of South Indian kinship organization. People still married relatives but less and less the "right" kind, and they increasingly wedded outside the kin group altogether. Although rural society is slower to embrace this change, marriage to cousins, maternal uncles, and nieces was disappearing as a characteristic of Tamil kinship in both town and village and with it a whole language of rules, obligations, and entitlements as well.

Although I went to the field to study matrimonial change, the old preferential marriages are the main focus of this book. In part this is because I spent much of my ethnographic time figuring out how they were contracted and why and what it was like to marry a cousin, an uncle, a niece. Moreover, the culture of "rights" in which they were firmly embedded intrigued me, raising questions such as: What is it like to live in a society in which you have rights, even first rights, to marry someone? What does that kind of entitlement do to people's overall sense of agency? of identity? of authority? of pleasure? What does *equality* mean, what can it mean, in such a context? What are the moral and emotional consequences when matrimonial rights are denied because the rules are not kept or because the rules of life are changing?

This book attempts to answer these questions by offering a cultural and experiential framework for understanding the old pattern of preferential marriages to cousins, uncles, and nieces: "cultural" because it focuses on the meanings I collected in the field; "experiential" because it deploys a case-study approach emphasizing the individual feelings and personal experiences of my Tamil consultants. Because these marriages have been either misunderstood (or not described at all), this book at its broadest level is an attempt to reinterpret them before they disappear from Tamil Nadu.

The Anthropology of Dravidian Kinship

The marriages described in these pages are peculiar to South India and Sri Lanka. North Indians also marry within a carefully delineated status group, the caste, but except for Muslims they prohibit marriage to anyone known to be a blood relative. As for South Asian Muslims living outside South India or Sri Lanka, their endogamous practices typically lack the characteristic features of South Indian, or what scholars call "Dravidian," kinship.[1]

"Dravidian kinship" was once on par with the potlatch and totemism as one of the great phenomena of anthropological interest. Because the study of kinship is no longer at the core of anthropology,[2] the extensive body of scholarship addressing kinship and its variants, which goes back to Lewis Henry Morgan, W. H. R. Rivers, Claude Lévi-Strauss, and Louis Dumont, has become a closed corpus—rather stultifying and of interest only to the very few in modern anthropology who have an inclination for formal and algebraic models of social life (in particular, Thomas Trautmann, Anthony Good, and Margaret Trawick). While this book argues that our discipline's early obsession with Dravidian kinship was misguided from the start, it invites readers to rethink the anthropological demotion of kinship studies (also see McKinnon and Cannel 2012; Sahlins 2013). It also attempts to make South Indian kinship visible again and retheorize its place in modernity.

It was Francis Whyte Ellis (1777–1819), a British civil servant in the Madras presidency and a scholar of Tamil and Sanskrit, who first recognized the unity and non-Sanskritic origin of the South Indian languages (Trautmann 2006). His "Dravidian Proof" later incited Bishop Robert Caldwell (1814–1881), an evangelist missionary based in Tinnevelly district of Tamil Nadu, to adopt the term *Dravidian* to separate languages prevalent in South India (Tamil, Telugu, Malayalam, Kannada, Tulu, and so on) from the Indo-Aryan languages (Hindi, in particular) spoken in North India (1856). Caldwell's comparative study of languages in turn led his contemporary, the American anthropologist Lewis Henry Morgan (1818–1881), to compare the Ojibwa and Iroquois kinship terms he had recorded in North America with the kinship terms missionaries sent him from South India. Morgan discerned that, like these Native American terminologies, Dravidian languages grouped into classes relatives (for example, father and father's brother[s]) who were genealogically distinct from one another.[3]

Morgan's contemporaries and successors eventually discarded the grand evolutionary story he derived from his data (Parkin and Stone 2004: 9), but in spite of criticisms (McLennan 1865; Kroeber 1909; Malinowski 1930) the notion that kinship terminologies encode critical information regarding past and present marriage arrangements and natural facts of procreation profoundly shaped the anthropology of kinship, in general, and of South Indian kinship, in particular. Again and again scholars emphatically made the case that South Indian kinship "classificatory" terminologies reflected marriage preferences, particularly the custom that the anthropologist Edward B. Tylor (1832–1917) first labeled "cross-cousin marriage" (1889: 263). As W. H. R. Rivers (1864–1922) explained, there was an obvious correlation between the Tamil practice of calling the mother's brother "father-in-law" and the father's sister "mother-in-law" and the viewing of children of kin traced to parents through opposite-sex or "cross" sibling links as potential spouses (1914: 47–48; see also 1907: 619–621; Emeneau 1941, 1953). That South India provided "a good example of a case in which we can confidently infer the . . . existence of the cross cousin marriage from the terminology of relationship" (Rivers 1914: 49) was not exactly what the French anthropologist Louis Dumont (1911–1998)—the next major surveyor of Dravidian kinship—set out to demonstrate. But as the title of his 1953 essay, "The Dravidian Kinship Terminology as an Expression of Marriage," suggests, Dumont too held fast to the Morganesque view that terminological systems contain principles that organize social relationships in human societies.[4] The difference is that for Dumont these relationships were theoretical constructs used to model social life rather than real or even directly observable.

South Indian languages, Dumont demonstrated, distinguish kin on the basis of four basic characteristics: generation, sex, age, and what he called "distinction of two kinds of relatives inside certain generations" (1953: 34; also see 1983: 229–237). English speakers are familiar with the first two, for we too differentiate grandparents from parents, children, and grandchildren, as well as mothers, aunts, sisters, and daughters from fathers, uncles, brothers, and sons. Unlike Tamils, however, we do not have separate words for elder and younger siblings, or for elder and younger aunts, uncles, and so on.

Nor do we make the fourth distinction which for Dumont was "the most important" as it embodied "a sociological theory of marriage" (1953: 12).

For Rivers the key distinction made by Dravidian terminology was between the marriageable cross cousins (children of kin traced to parents through opposite-sex or "cross" sibling links) and the cousins to whom marriage (and sexual relationship) is forbidden (children of kin traced to parents through same-sex or "parallel" sibling links). But for Dumont it lay somewhere else. "In the father's generation," he wrote, "there are two kinds, and two kinds only of male relatives . . . the father and the mother's brother respectively" (1953: 35), who are linked by a "principle of opposition" that neither "lie[s] in the relation with the Ego" (the child) nor in the relation with (the child's) mother (1953: 35). Here we may note Dumont's elimination of relationships (and emotions) between consanguineous relatives, in preference to the structural differentiation of two classes of kin, affines and consanguines. Even the relation between mother and child is conspicuously absent from his model because he postulated that the mother's brother is related to the child *not* through the mother (a genealogical relation) but through the father (a classificatory relation). As he saw it, in Dravidian kinship, "my mother's brother is essentially my father's affine" (1953: 37).

It is customary to link Dumont's analysis of Dravidian kinship to the alliance theory developed by Claude Lévi-Strauss, another French anthropologist, in *The Elementary Structures of Kinship* (1969 [1949]). There are grounds for this, as Dumont himself stressed, "the remarkable convergence between Lévi-Strauss' theory of marriage alliance and the emphasis put by [his own] Tamil informants on analogous themes" (1986: 4). The "convergence" in question, however, is uneven. As the noted sociologist Patricia Uberoi suggests, Dumont did not merely apply the structural approach to the South Indian data; he modified the structural vision of kinship in the process (2006: 161).

Dumont's method of analysis was structural in that it consisted in identifying sets of relations between abstract terms, kinship terms, so as to establish how their interaction—or rather opposition—determined the appearance and functioning of a phenomenon such as cross-cousin marriage. His conception of kinship was also structural in that, for him as for Lévi-Strauss, the true place where kinship originates is not in the nuclear family, nor in relations among individuals, but rather in the systematic relations of exchange that link social groups that stand in affinal relationships to one another (Gillison 1987:

167). Finally, both Lévi-Strauss and Dumont took their notion of exchange from Marcel Mauss (1990), but they focused on different elements of matrimonial reciprocity.

Kinship for Lévi-Strauss did not mean the functioning of descent groups or the organization of corporate lineages, as was the case for contemporary British social anthropologists such as Meyer Fortes and E. E. Evans-Pritchard. Kinship meant marriage, particularly the marriage rules that determine who is marriageable or not. These rules, Lévi-Strauss argued, vary in form and content, but in every human society certain categories of relations are regarded as too close for marriage, hence the universal "negative" or proscribing rules of marriage known to us as incest taboos. In so-called elementary societies "positive" rules "*prescribe* marriage with a certain type of relative" (1969: ix).

In claiming that men have a particular interest in rules of exogamy, particularly in the prescriptions that require them to marry a cross cousin, Lévi-Strauss stressed the calculative reason inherent in marriage exchanges. By "giving up" their sisters and daughters as potential marriage partners, men obtain other women in return. Meanwhile, the long-term consequences of particular kinds of marriage matter even more than the initial exchange, and there are three ways that stressing cross-cousin marriage shapes future exchange possibilities, as he cleverly demonstrated. Cross-cousin marriage permits three prescriptive or preferential modalities: (1) marriage (from a man's point of view) to the patrilateral female cousin, the father's sister's daughter; (2) marriage (again from a man's point of view) to the matrilateral female cousin, the mother's brother's daughter; and (3) bilateral marriage to either the patrilateral or matrilateral cousin. For Lévi-Strauss, the first two variants of cross-cousin marriage allowed "generalized" exchange between multiple groups and had the potential to integrate indefinite numbers of groups. As for bilateral cross-cousin marriage, its distinctive mode of exchange, and sociological reality, was "restricted" and much less integrative. In particular, he concluded, only matrilateral cross-cousin marriage was compatible with "long cycles" of exchange and durable sociological integration.[5]

In keeping with Morgan and Rivers's earlier analysis of Dravidian kinship, Dumont gave priority not to the logic of marriage rules but to kinship terminology. Moreover, he stressed the "vertical dimension" (1953: 38) of the relationship between "consanguines" and "affines" rather than its socially integrative power (or its lack thereof) as Lévi-Strauss did. To him, affinal roles and concomitant ceremonial obligations were inherited from parent (father in particular) to child (son) without being transformed into blood relations. And it was the function of the cross-cousin marriage and concomitant gift-giving relationships—Dumont took this much from Marcel Mauss—to perpetuate the alliance relationship that he found in the nomenclature and reaffirm it generation after generation. But, as against Mauss's rich view of animated exchanges, Dumont's vision of social life was devoid of any spiritual or political element. In his model, giving and thus relatedness was a matter of automatic differentiation between *specific* social categories. It did not pose any kind of existential problems, but did at least impose the stringent requirement to reciprocate, as it did in Mauss's famous essay on gift giving.

The Ethnography of Dravidian Kinship

Although I will soon show that there is more to Dumont's analysis than what I just made it out to be, in a nutshell, his alliance theory, more precisely his account of the inheritance of affinal alliance, came to define Dravidian kinship up until the early 1990s. This view prevailed despite the fact that newer ethnography challenged his theoretical model on many fronts.

Dumont himself worked from the basic premise that a phenomenon like marriage is best explicated by a structural model that (amazingly, we might add) remains independent from the real, and thus from actual, marriage patterns. In this respect, his perspective differed from that of Morgan, for whom kinship terminology reflected "real" social arrangements, particularly marriage rules. Hence Dumont's method could claim to be immune to empirical testing and refutation. As Alan Barnard and Anthony Good point out, for Dumont "there is in fact *no* necessary correspondence between the structure of a society's relationship terminology, and the structure of the alliance relationships among its social groupings" (1984: 12, emphasis theirs). The particular structure that was the focus of Dumont's interest, Dravidian terminology, was to be understood as implicating the entire culture, the manifestation of a collective consciousness informing the institutions (in particular marriage and ceremonial gift giving) of the society at large. But it did not determine concrete expressions of a social order or empirically given kinship conventions. As the French anthropologist stated: "Kinship terminologies have not as their function to register groups" (1964: 78).

A brilliant ethnographer, Dumont (1986) was well aware that around the time of his fieldwork in 1949–1950 various matrimonial rules prevailed in the Ramnad, Madurai, and Tinnevelly districts of Tamil Nadu. Among the Pramalai Kaḷḷars (one of the most numerous endogamous subcastes of the Kaḷḷars) living on the outskirts to the west of the town of Madurai, for example, "the sister's son should marry the brother's daughter" (1986: 206). It was the reverse among the Maṟavars irregularly spread out between the vicinity of Ramnad and the western boundary of the Tinnevelly district: They had a preference for the patrilateral cousin (1983: 58). As for the Naṅgudi Veḷḷāḷar located in the Tinnevelly district, they too favored the father's sister's daughter (1983: 55).[6] Dumont introduced such demographic and socioeconomic variables as migration, land tenure, ceremonies and prestations, rules of succession, and residence of a group to account for these different unilateral norms. But the "attitudes and institutions" that correlated with either the patrilateral or matrilateral application of cross-cousin marriage did not challenge his formal model of the logical or terminological structure of Dravidian kinship. The anthropologist Nur Yalman (1967), who more or less directly applied Dumont's analysis to Sinhalese kinship, went further when he stated:

> Marriage rules as we find them in South India and Ceylon are not related to any economic or group features of special communities . . . the principles are a language of organization and exist in themselves . . . it is the categories themselves, inherent in language, that determine marriage rules, and not exogamous lineages or the organization of kin that determines the terminology of kinship. (1967: 9)

Neither Dumont nor Yalman discarded ethnography as a basis of anthropological knowledge, but they kept the social facts they observed in the field—for example, the preference to marry on one side rather than another—separate from or, as in the case of Yalman, subordinate to the relationships (in particular, the opposition of father to mother's brother) they inferred from their structural analysis of Dravidian kinship terminology.

The British anthropologist Anthony Good (1981) was perhaps the first to empirically test how the linguistic categories of Tamil kinship terminology and local marriage rules or preferences interacted at the level of practice.[7] His data showed that, among the Koṇṭaiyaṅkōṭṭai Maṟavars of Tamil Nadu, "there is . . . no evidence of any behavioral bias toward the genealogical relative specified by the . . . rules" (1981: 119). That is, although this particular caste group favored marriage to the father's sister's daughter, its members married their mother's brother's daughter just as frequently.[8] Good interpreted his data to mean "that the symmetric prescription [encoded in their bilateral terminology] plays a greater part in regulating behavior than the asymmetric preference" (1981: 125). Yet he went on to show that other local subcastes (*ācāri* or carpenters) either observed the asymmetric rule to maximum extent permitted by the exigencies of demography or flouted it completely. Hence Good concluded that there was no "congruence" or "consistency" (1981: 109) among the model, the norms, and practice. As he put it: "One can never predict the situation at one level from the observations at either or both other levels" (1981: 127).

Before the reader infers that in Dravidian kinship anything goes, let me point out that, for Good, action is conceived as either execution or lack of execution of the models elaborated by his predecessors. These models, we recall, were developed without any input on the part of the Tamils—without their own explanations for asymmetric marriage, for example, or their understandings of kinship relations. It is therefore not surprising that ethnographic observation led Good to find no convergence between what his informants did and anthropological representations of Dravidian kinship. Why should Tamil castes conform to models that were constructed from a distant, detached position of theoretical reflection, like Rivers's or Dumont's?

And yet Good's empirical and ethnographic methodology was to deliver a major blow to Dumont's alliance theory. In 1980 he stated loud and clear what others had already said for some time: namely, that among many South Indian castes a man's most "preferential" marriage partner was actually not his "cross cousin" but his elder sister's daughter.[9] That uncle–niece marriage was not merely an upper-caste phenomenon, as Dumont believed, was later borne out by Katherine Hann's (1985) tabulation of the incidence of close-relation marriage, as reported for various South Indian communities in the four southern states (Andhra Pradesh, Karnataka, Kerala, and Tamil Nadu). Her results showed that "about 10 per cent of the marriages are between an uncle and his niece" (1985: 62). A decade later Good himself updated Hann's chart and again affirmed that "in several cases [marriage of mother's younger brother and elder sister's daughter] is the commonest form of close inter-marriage, while in most others it is comparable in frequency to marriage with either cross cousin" (1996: 6). He rightly emphasized that the statistics on uncle–niece marriage were "striking, because if relative age rules are taken into account it is to be expected that fewer people will have marriageable relatives of this type than have first cross-cousins" (1996: 6).

The high incidence of uncle–niece marriage led Good to state boldly, "There is *no* such thing as the Dravidian kinship system" (1996: 1, his emphasis). But the British anthropologist somehow shied away from making the obvious point that if there is no Dravidian kinship, the structuralist theory of Dravidian kinship cannot hold. Indeed, uncle–niece marriage challenges two of Dumont's key points. For one thing, when a Tamil man marries his own sister's daughter, genealogical relations (niece, sister) merge with affinal relations (wife, mother-in-law) so that there cannot be any sharp or stable "opposition between kin and affine," the opposition that Dumont argued was characteristic of Dravidian kinship in general (1983: 103). Moreover, the relations of exchange here clearly originate from within a very tight group of consanguines; so tight, in fact, that the category "exchange" cannot function in the broad sense of "alliance" as defined by this or any other French structuralist. It becomes clear thus that uncle–niece marriage forces us to rethink the nature of the social relationships involved in Tamil marriage patterns and to revise their anthropological description and theory—just as this particular marriage is on the verge of disappearing forever.

The Field of My Fieldwork

Although I ended up living about one kilometer away from Pramalai Kaḷḷar country, where Dumont conducted his first ethnographic research in India (1949–1950), I cannot say that I went to the field with the intention of revisiting his theory. Madurai was not even my first ethnographic destination. Because the Fulbright Program had arranged an affiliation with the French Institute in Pondicherry, at first I settled in a village located in the Union Territory of Pondicherry, an area known for its sugar factories, cotton yarns, textile mills, and tourist industry. The village was not a bad place to examine kinship change through the productive lens of age and generation, which was my original focus of ethnographic inquiry. It is true that, when I arrived there in 2008, about 32 percent of the households I surveyed included marriages to close kin,[10] a statistic that shows that even in the more industrialized section of Tamil society Dravidian kinship obligations continue to exert latent influence over marriage, but, as the stories recounted in Chapters 7 and 8 suggest, twenty-first-century youth in South India are forging more independent lives.

It was a combination of advice and luck that sent me five weeks later to Madurai, the so-called heartland of Tamil culture. The scholar Ulrike Niklas recommended that I work with Tēvar castes[11] that are known to be exemplary practitioners of close-kin marriage, and to this end she kindly made available the house she then was renting in Nāgamalai, "the snake hill," a rocky fold reaching a height of 300 meters, a line of boulders, which borders Kaḷḷar country. With this move, the focus of my fieldwork shifted to the idioms of "rules" (*murai*) and "rights" (*urimai*) which, I argue in this book, formulate a sociopolitical theory that, although peculiar to the Kaḷḷars, raises issues pertaining to the sharing, or not sharing, of identity, equality, and closeness that underlie non-Kaḷḷars' (and non-Tēvars') matrimonial practices as well.

The Kaḷḷars, Dumont was right to say on the dedication page of his ethnography, are "sociological geniuses" (1986). They also seem to delight in tutoring anthropologists. Specifically, as Indira Arumugam has also observed, "They take pleasure in talking and thinking about kinship" (2011: 175). But it was often difficult for me to follow their kinship analyses. This was all the more so because, as I document in these pages, anthropological models of cross-cousin marriage do not begin to approximate the many complicated ways in which Kaḷḷars (and the Tēvars in general) intermarry. I needed to visualize the descriptions of their rampant kinship connections and to this end drew anthropological diagrams, which most people could not grasp because, although familiar with the concept of "tree charts," they were not used to *seeing* kinship phenomena (Bouquet 1996). When people offered to draw complicated genealogies, their "charts" sprouted without clear descent or marriage connections, and although I was actively interested in recording such "native" representations I constantly had to revise my decoding system as each individual adopted his or her own idiosyncratic system of genealogical representation.

Before I knew it, I was meeting with some of the most helpful informants—mostly Kaḷḷars men of different backgrounds and ages—on a regular basis in my rented house so as to retrace the kinship scenarios I did not understand. Because the subject of marriage is abstract, impersonal, and objective only for anthropologists, and personal (even intensely personal) for everyone else, it was not unusual for conversations to be interrupted by cases in point. I report these examples not because I strive for an ethnography awash in talk but because I want the reader to hear my south Indian Tamil acquaintances speak for themselves. I am neither a biographer nor a psychologist but an anthropologist, interested in cultural meanings, group dynamics, emergent phenomena, and social patterns. But it is only when we get to meet our "informants" in depth and get to know what their stories are that we can appreciate that what an individual person thinks or feels plays as much as an important role in shaping life than any social norm or cultural concept.

The Kaḷḷars expressively forbid the uncle–niece marriage—a fact that partly explains why Dumont neglected it in his dense monograph on the social and religious life of this subcaste (1986) and his overall analysis of Dravidian kinship (1983). Not that Kaḷḷar men never marry their elder sisters' daughters—this book shows that some in fact do so—but it was among other castes and in low-income neighborhoods in Madurai itself that I mostly recorded this particular marriage. This was partly due to the fact that once in Madurai I became reacquainted with people I had known since 1989, which was when I spent nine months studying Tamil at the American Institute of Indian Studies located in this city. This reacquaintance process led my former associates to disclose their own personal experiences with the uncle–niece marriage, or marriage with kin in general, and their stories in turn extended my ethnographic practice into the subjective dimension of these kinship practices.

While in Madurai I also sought the company of youth who, like the young women and men I had previously met in the Union Territory of Pondicherry, prove to be more than examples of larger social processes of, say, social change or social conflict. Their experiences, in fact, taught me that, for Tamil youth operating within certain kinds of assumptions about themselves and their world, the relationship between "traditional" and "modern" marriage practices is not necessarily one of substitution or superimposition.

This book thus neither has a tight residential nor a social ethnographic focus. It relies on information I collected in a village near the town of Pondicherry, in Kaḷḷar country, during the morning in seminar-like meetings I held outside the city of Madurai and in low-income households in Madurai itself. My key consultants included young men and women residing in the north and the south of Tamil Nadu, members of the Tēvar castes (especially the Kaḷḷar caste), working-class families and old acquaintances from Madurai hailing from various communities. In my conversations with all these people, I found little support for the academic explanations of South Indian kinship and marriage reviewed in the last section. The Kaḷḷars did not say they marry cross cousins to create an alliance between consanguines and affines. What they did say, by contrast, was that the "right way to marry" was part of an honorific and emotional process: People said they felt loved and respected when they could exercise their traditional matrimonial rights and angry when they could not. My consultants did admit to an opposition between their father's and mother's brothers, but their idea of affinity was mediated by the relationship to their mother, who was intrinsic to their existence. In fact, it was because the mother's brother was related to the mother that he had the paramount "right" to marry his elder sister's daughter. Indeed, they said so many things that contradicted the structural interpretation of the old marriages that at this most general level this book is an invitation to rethink the practices that used to fall under the rubric of Dravidian kinship and their continuing relevance into the present.

The "Right" Marriages

My first argument in this book is that the priority given to the system of categories generated by the terminology has prevented scholars from discerning the critical meanings of social distinction underpinning Tamil kinship. Such meanings begin to surface once we realize that, although at the semantic level the two sides of cross kin (the mother's brother and the father's sister) are equivalent, and although bilateral cross-cousin marriage is ubiquitous in Tamil Nadu, all castes clearly prefer, and sometimes even prescribe, marrying the cousin on *either* the mother's brother's side *or* the father's sister's side. This is not a new observation. As already mentioned, Dumont noted that, among the Kaḷḷars, "The sister's son should marry the brother's daughter" (1986: 206). Likewise Brenda Beck recorded that, in the Koṅku region, the mother's brother's daughter preference is dominant (1972: 238). By contrast, Robert Deliège recorded that the Dalits (Paṟaiyar) of the Ramnad district practice marriage to a patrilateral cross cousin (1987)—or the father's sister's daughter.

In Tamil the preference or obligation to marry a cousin on one "side" (*pakkam*) rather than the other is framed as *muṟai*, a word that has strong connotations of normative suitability. If a young man is from a caste that favors marriage with the mother's brother's daughter, this girl is *muṟai* to him. He can marry the girl on the other "side," as the Tamil put it, but this father's sister's daughter is "not right"—*muṟai illai*. Hence *muṟai* introduces an idea of kinship that is selective and even exclusive.

What is more is the fact that the unilateral rule or preference discriminates among the "right" children themselves. Among the Kaḷḷars, for instance, all maternal uncles' daughters are "right" girls and all paternal aunts' sons are "right" boys. But, as I will expand in Chapter 2, only the children of the first-born uncles and first-born aunts have the *urimai* or "right" to marry "the right way." Hence *mu<u>r</u>ai* establishes distinctions not only between a husband and a wife (as one "side" inevitably prevails) but also between siblings of the same sex (as some are born before the others).

It is possible that Dumont did not adopt Lévi-Strauss's ideas regarding the forms of "generalized" and "restricted" exchanges produced by unilateral matrimonial rules because he was well aware that exchange in India, and in South India in particular, expresses "difference in social status" (1983: 43). After all, it was Dumont who put forward the theory that the "value" of purity and its counterpart, that of pollution, regulated caste rank along the poles of inferiority and superiority, preventing the pure Brahmins at the top to transact and accept boiled food from other castes, especially the impure Untouchables (who did not then call themselves Dalits) at the bottom. In fact, in a complex essay called "Hierarchy and Marriage Alliance in South Indian kinship" (1957, 1983) Dumont began relating his ethnography of Kaḷḷar marriage practices (1986) to his overall anthropology of caste society (1980). Noting that sons of "senior" wives did not intermarry with those of "junior" wives or of illegitimate unions (1983: 44), he explained that a notion of "pure descent" barred the former from misalliance with the latter. Hence, Dumont concluded, "There is no absolute difference between what happens inside and outside a caste group" (1983: 37). Dravidian kinship endogamy was of the same order as caste endogamy: It expressed a human logic that was deeply hierarchical. At this juncture, his interpretation of Dravidian kinship becomes very relevant to my argument in this book.

Perhaps because the key essay in which he developed these thoughts was a difficult read, or perhaps because Dumont himself did not pursue his hunch that marriage among the Kaḷḷar provides the context for displaying and establishing an order of precedence, scholars usually do not associate South Indian marriage and kinship with caste hierarchy. If anything, in fact, they resort to the principle of parity to characterize marriage and intracaste relations in South India so that the issues of unequal suitability and privilege raised in this book have taken a counterintuitive turn in anthropological discussions of South Indian kinship.

The egalitarian interpretation of South Indian kinship developed in the 1950s and 1960s, when anthropologists began making the case (albeit not always successfully) that the Sanskritic notion of marriage as the "gift of a virgin" (*kaṉṉikā-tāṉam*), a gift that comes with material presents and jewels to express her father's inferiority to the family that accepts the bride as wife and daughter (Gough 1956), was not a Dravidian conception. Far from turning daughters into "gifts" or commodities, it was shown, South Indian kinship structures allowed women superior freedom and access to material resources than in the North, where close-kin marriage was strictly prohibited (Karve 1953; Gough 1956; Dyson and Moore 1983; Kapadia 1985; Agarwal 1994). This was borne out by the fact that whatever the newly married Tamil daughter received from her parents at marriage was not "dowry" in the usual sense of this word because the gifts of money, gold, land, and household items remained for her exclusive possession, enjoyment, and dominion, even going to her own daughter(s) after her death (Agarwal 1994). This Dravidian difference was also indicated by the name of these Tamil wedding gifts: *cītaṉam* (a Tamil corruption of the Sanskrit compound *strī-dhana*, which means "woman's wealth"). Hence, marriage gifts and payments in the South did not create inequality of status between bride givers and bride takers as they did in the Sanskritized, northern part of India.[12] Such reciprocal exchanges sharply contrasted with the hypergamous practices of the North, where wife givers could not be wife takers, and vice versa, and where women were treated as "tribute" (Kolenda 1984). In short, unlike the North, marriage in South India was associated with egalitarianism between wife takers and wife givers, and that difference, as I will expand later in a later chapter, worked in favor of the "Dravidian" woman (Conklin 1973: 55).

Although this book enters the debate regarding kinship, equality, and hierarchy from the twin perspective that the Sanskrit concept of the "gift of a virgin" is not operative in Tamil marriage rules and that the "right" marriages do indeed sanction a sharing of identity, equality, and closeness between the brother and the sister who arrange them, it also suggests that the comparative analysis of North and South India marriage has obfuscated a critical aspect of Tamil endogamy. While the families who do intermarry see themselves as being on par, some are "righter" or more preferential—that is, more equal—than others. In this way endogamy establishes not merely sameness but also distinction, distance, and separation between kin.

Chapter 1 suggests that the Pramalai Kaḷḷar society was not exactly the best exemplar of the "gift-giving" economy imagined by French structuralists. It is true that marriage in this subcaste constitutes a network of alliances, or more simply of relationships, representing a heritage of commitments and debts of honor as well as a capital of rights and duties that can be called on not merely in extraordinary situations but in daily routine. It is also true that the Pramalai Kaḷḷars are wholly committed to an economy of ceremonial giving. But this first chapter suggests that Kaḷḷar practical economy is grounded in agonistic and aggressive practices that are anything but reciprocal in spirit (see also Arumugam 2011). It also puts forward the notion that Kaḷḷar ceremonial exchanges function to establish distinctions of rank, especially honors, which themselves are constitutive of superior status and authoritative rights. While Chapter 2 argues that the concern for social equality is very much at the heart of the Kaḷḷar "prescriptive law of marriage" (*kaliyāṇam muṟai*), it also chronicles the conflicts over matrimonial first honors and authoritative rights that make "force" (*vaṉmuṟai*) and "law" (*muṟai*) not opposed principles of social life but coexistent levels of a single reality. Although my discussion is anchored in Kaḷḷar ethnography, my argument that matrimonial rights are a source of constant conflict and violence that can damage kinship ideals and relationships extends to Tamil society in general.

The two life stories recounted in Chapter 3 illustrate how the normative discourse of Tamil matrimonial rules interact with the inner landscape of individual emotions and desires. These stories show how a language of rights and privileges creates such entitlements and expectations that when a "right" marriage does not take place the missed opportunity can deeply, and negatively, affect one's sense of self.

The Most Privileged Marriage

My second argument in this book is that we need to decenter the brother–sister relation from South Indian kinship. I will show that mothers and daughters, and same-sex kin in general, can be just as deeply involved and invested in endogamous matrimonial arrangements as the brothers and sisters who form the classical "atom" of Dravidian kinship. This argument leads me to take issue with a study of Tamil marriage that came out some forty years after that of Dumont.

For reasons that I will not spell out here, in the 1980s the anthropological study of kinship lost its momentum and appeal. Kinship gave way to the study of gender, with contributions from feminist anthropologists still interested in birth, marriage, and domestic life but from a rather different theoretical perspective (Collier and Yanagisako 1987). Likewise, the anthropology of kinship in India eventually shifted its analytical focus away from social institutions and their civilizational and textual sources to specific problems of the social construction of gender, personhood, and procreation (Östör et al. 1983; Busby 1995; 2000; Raheja and Gold 1994; Böck and Rao 2000). At the same time scholars began to look at marriage no longer from "the center," but both from "the margins"—as Lindsey Harlan and Paul Courtright (1995) put it—as well as from the "inside" perspective of the actor's experience. This notion of kinship as a locus of interiority is precisely what Margaret Trawick's ethnographic study of Tamil kinship (1990) puzzles over. I now turn to this fascinating study, which also has the merit of zeroing on emotion and fantasy as compared to the usual "dry" structuralist topics: gifts, marriage payments, economic cooperation, and reciprocity (particularly male reciprocity).

Trawick argues that emotions are crucial to understanding the "lived reality" of South Indian kinship, basing her claims on her intimate association with a South Indian landowning extended family of twenty members in a village outside Chennai, as well as on interviews with over 150 people from various castes near the town of Madurai. Of particular interest is her insight that the Tamil feeling called *aṉpu*, which she translates as "love," camouflages tensions within the four principal dyadic relationships of the nuclear family (mother–daughter, father–son, husband–wife and brother–sister). Suggesting that post-Freudian perspectives are suited to account for the Tamil affective investments in the family, she adopts a Lacanian language of insatiable desire to propose that fathers want continuity via their sons, but sons long for independence. Meanwhile, mothers devalue daughters, while daughters seek to retain a close bond with their mother.

To Trawick the intense attachment between brother and sister is the key to the Tamil preferential marriage with cross cousins.[13] Forbidden to act on their childhood sexual feelings—particularly the mutual transference of their "intense erotic love" (1990: 172) for the mother—Trawick suggests that brothers and sisters seek to realize their union in the next generation. As she writes:

> Never being fulfilled, the brother and sister's desire for each other will never be spent. It will remain chaste and eternal, but pervaded by pain. Each will feel sacrificed—the one a martyred protector, the other a martyred innocent. In quest of a cultural ideal . . . each will seek to recover the other. But only in death, out of time and beyond the code, will they find this recovery possible. (1990: 172; also see 170–178; 187–204)

Trawick's argument, then, is that "the continuation of a particular institution such as cross-cousin marriage may be posited, not upon its fulfillment of some function or set of functions, but upon the fact that it creates longings that can *never* be fulfilled" (1990: 152; her emphasis).

Despite her quite different analytic approach to kinship and interpretation of Tamil cross-cousin marriage, Trawick actually follows in Dumont's footsteps. She too recognizes the importance of kinship terminologies in principle, and she too excludes marriages that do not appear to have their source in such classifications, in particular the marriage to the elder sister's daughter. The problem is that this particular and most preferred marriage invalidates Trawick's post-Freudian vision of South Indian kinship. Quite simply, the sister is too old for the specific kinds of incestuous dynamics she invokes. Usually (but not always), by the time her brother is on his "first erotic partnership . . . with a sibling" (1990: 170), his *akkā* (elder sister) is already married and out of the house.

More damaging to Trawick's overall argument is that in my field experience the critical pair in arranging a marriage to an elder sister's daughter is not the brother–sister pair but the mother–daughter pair: The mother marries her son to her daughter's daughter, hence the groom is the bride's maternal uncle. This is not the only case of a filial bond turning affinal, and I must mention a marriage that, though admittedly rare (especially nowadays), is perfectly "correct" (*muṟai*) from a Tamil normative perspective. In some castes (Maṟavar, for example), a daughter can propose that her widowed (or, in the past, polygynous) father marry her daughter. In this way she becomes her father's mother-in-law. This is not exactly a new observation. As early as 1934, the South Indian anthropologist A. Aiyyappan noted instances of grandfather–granddaughter marriage (1934:282).[14]

While I show that the brother–sister bond remains a distinct and privileged one, as Trawick rightly emphasizes (1990), in my argument the "love" that implicates the ideal of marriage to elder sister's daughter is not interpreted within a psychoanalytic frame. Ultimately, I aim to question the associations that have set endogamous marriages alongside (or even within) the Oedipal complex, with its secularism and European-derived metapsychology, and to relocate close kin marriage in Tamil notions of devotion and sacrifice, particularly male sacrifice. Hence Chapter 4 shows that in the exegeses I recorded there is a constant theme: The younger brother, who is in the junior position vis-à-vis the woman who becomes his mother-in-law, namely his elder sister, takes less. He engages in a sacrificial process that asserts an idea of kinship quite different from that emerging from the "right" marriages. This is the idea that kinship ought to privilege the partaking of possessions, the sharing of sufferings and joys, what Marshall Sahlins in his recent attempt to define the pan-human essence of kinship calls "mutuality of being" (2013: 2). Indeed, in the Tamil world this kinship orientation and its emotional language—one of love, nurture, compassion, and empathy—is preferred over all others. Hence it trumps the norms of "rule" and precedence expressed in the unilateral cross-cousin or "right" marriages. And yet, in the mother's brother's paramount and exclusive "right" to his elder sister's daughter, he comes first before any other man, including the right boys, and we see again how Tamil endogamy has a way of simultaneously abolishing and reifying distinctions of rank. The difference here is that the sphere of social activity predominantly associated with men—coming first in society—is generated from the sphere of activity predominantly associated with the women who arrange this marriage and rank (mothers and elder sisters) above men (younger brothers). Chapter 5 shows that, for all their definite rules about the "right" way to marry, the Tamils engage in what we may call processes of structural superimposition, layering affinal bonds with consanguineal ties in such a way that the problem for them becomes one of sorting out and even undoing the ramifying connections that bind kinfolk to one another. The ambiguities that such rampant connections at times afford with regard to kinship roles generate conflict and shame and, I also suggest, a love that is neither particularly conjugal nor gentle. This book reveals that the emotions at the core of what scholars used to call "Dravidian kinship" are inherently inordinate, even pregnant with violence.

Ethnography, Kinship, and Change

My third and last concern in this book is to grapple with the decline of the Tamil "right" and preferred marriages. When anthropologists look at kinship as a changing field of social practice, they tend to invoke a causally significant, broader context. Two classic studies, for instance, link large-scale historical and institutional changes to the transformation of marriage and family. First, Jack Goody (1983) showed that from the early fourth century onward the Christian Church's interest in channeling wealth away from the family and into its treasury led marriage and family life in Western European society to undergo a radical reformulation. Quite simply, his argument goes, the Church imposed restrictions on "marrying-in," or endogamous marriages; on concubinage; and on adoption, to make it difficult for lay families to transmit property securely to their heirs. Property that did not go to heirs could go to the Church.[15]

Closer to my own field site, a study by C. J. Fuller (1976) documented the changes in the kinship and marriage patterns among the Nayars of Southwest India (Kerala) over a hundred years. At the close of the nineteenth century, it was usual for the Nayar residential and property-owning group to be a large, joint family. Men visited their wives at night, rather than living with them. However, by the time Fuller arrived in the field in the 1970s, the nuclear family and individually owned property were the new norms. Because Nayar husbands now had to provide for their own sons, economic considerations became a factor in the choice of a marriage partner, and the old claims of status diminished.

My book differs from the two studies just mentioned in that it does not purport to make an "objective evaluation" of the decline of Tamil preferential marriages. Rather than abstracting this historical trend as a fact, unfolding over there in South India, I follow the Weberian tradition of examining change from the viewpoint of actors within the social system (Weber 1949). My principal interest in the breakdown of what used to be called the "Dravidian kinship system" derives from the perspective that historical reality is already meaningful to its participants from a theoretically infinite multiplicity of standpoints, prior to any attempt to construct it as an object of analysis. Hence, my main concern in the last two chapters of this book is not so much to impute causal factors that could explain the waning of cross-cousin and uncle–niece marriages (although I do some of that, too) as to explore young people's understandings and experiences of this historical process.

To document and understand the conceptual world in which people live—before and after they become anthropological subjects—is easier said than done. The ethnographic endeavor, it is now commonplace but still critical to say, is fraught with epistemological problems of context, meaning, and subjectivity, the most critical being that its "data" spring from a highly subjective and contestable realm, including both the informant's and the ethnographer's experiences and their personal interaction. But these problems of inconclusive or at best incomplete results seem to me preferable to the alternative: the current tendency to bypass ethnography and its distinctive data-collection processes altogether. Such a tendency is detectable in anthropological studies of so-called modernity, many of which circumvent the business of closely attending to the particularities of other people's lives and focus instead on the expert discourses of transnational neoliberal markets and explore the second-order products of globalized forms of consumption, recreation, and entertainment. I do not contest that the human world of the early twenty-first century, as anthropologists suggest, is "cosmopolitan" (Appadurai and Breckenridge 1987: 2) or that the world of meaningful goods and human communities is in constant motion. But somehow the mind balks at the strong claim that "circulation" and "flows" are central to, constitutive of, all contemporary expressions of the social imagination, or that the traffic in culture makes for free-floating transformations of local worlds, that "just happen" from the outside as responses to or emulations of neoliberalism and modernity.

Chapters 6 and 7 document that two decades of neoliberalism in India and evolving state policy have contributed to the transformation of Tamil kinship. India in general, and South India in particular, is entering uncharted territory in demographic history. Birthrates have dropped to about two children per couple, and the age of marriage has considerably risen. Many more Tamil youth, including girls, pursue some form of education and are taught that the children of consanguineous relationships are at a greater risk of certain genetic disorders. New forms of salaried employment have contributed to the inflation of marriage payments, and so on. But rather than conceptualizing the breakdown of preferential marriages in a developmental and objective mode and leaving the reader with a compact, well-arranged list of determining factors or "emerging" conditions, such as changes in the life course, the spread of schooling, an increasingly monetized and consumerist economy, and the like, these two chapters focus on the stories of three young people. In forefronting the varieties, complexities, and counterlinearities of this breakdown, they illustrate how circumstantial predicaments, subjective experience, and time-honored assumptions must be as much part of its analysis as the context of historical change in which it occurs. While the three case studies offered in these two chapters document that the old, honorific marriages are no longer preferential or even optional, the Conclusion contends that some of their social and gender meanings extend into the present.

1

THE KAḶḶARS AND DUMONT'S THEORY OF ALLIANCE

The Tamils are born sociologists and the culture is beautiful.
—Louis Dumont (in Jean-Claude Galey 1982: 21)

La réciprocité impredictable, voilà le terrain privilégié des rapports de dons.
—Pouillon 1996: 159

I first went to the heart of Pramalai Kaḷḷar[1] country to check on a story I read in the Sunday section of the Tamil newspaper called *Daily Thanthi*. That morning, as I was making my way through the printed news, the usual ministerial exaggerations, the babbling of opposition leaders, a couple of murders, matrimonial ads, and so on, I came across the story of the "Beautiful Tēvar," who allegedly once lived in the village of Corikkāmpaṭṭi, located just a few kilometers away from my rented house. I already knew how it ended: This Kaḷḷar hero enters a bull-baiting contest (*jallikaṭṭu*) to win back the girl who "rightly" belongs to him. He fights courageously until a bull gores him to death, pulling his entrails out. But there were enough differences between the version featured in the weekend supplement of the *Daily Thanthi* and the one recorded by Ulrike Niklas (2000) in the same village (see next chapter) that I decided to pursue.

It is not that difficult to show up in a Tamil village with an ethnographic agenda. In my experience, at least Tamil rural folks do not seem to mind a foreigner and her assistant (in this case a young man from the area) dropping by out of nowhere to ask questions about this or that aspect of their lives. In fact, over the twenty years I have conducted ethnographic research in Tamil Nadu I have almost always encountered an extraordinary goodwill that never fails to astonish me. In this case, however, the reception in this village was beyond my expectations.

As soon as we reached the main tea stall, four or five men waved me in their direction. It did not take me very long to realize that they were not drinking tea. They were drunk, very drunk in fact, but not so stupefied that they could not figure out why I had come. Every Tamil New Year (usually mid-January on the Western calendar) foreign tourists come to Kaḷḷar country to take pictures of the popular bull-taming contest held in the nearby village of Alaṅkānallūr. Every so often anthropologists like myself turn up, confident that our semicommunicative competence in Tamil will get us closer to the "meaning" of Kaḷḷar cultural activities. And so as soon as I uttered the Tamil greeting "vaṇakkam," these men already knew who I was and why I had come, and they invited me to sit nearby on a stone slab.

After they recounted, I should say leaped through, the version of the story that I (and they) had read that morning, after they reenacted the ways in which the Beautiful Tēvar tries to bring the bull down, pressing on its neck so as to reach over its hump, we sat together in silence. Here we were at the familiar anthropological crossroad where culture is trafficked and peddled. There was no nervousness in the air, definitively none of that awkwardness that sometimes one encounters with earnest and helpful Tamil hosts. But then again these men did not make a big show of hospitality, asking me neither to sit in the shade, nor drink a soda, and so on. There were no complications whatsoever.

It took just a few minutes for one of them, a very thin fellow with deep-sunk pouches under his eyes, to ask permission to refocus my inquiry. "You ask about what you know," he said with an impish grin on his face, "but may I tell you what you don't?" "Well, of course," was my immediate reaction; "By all means, tell me what I should know," is what I very much wanted to say. In my experience a request like this does not come by often enough. The business of having an interlocutor volunteer information outside the ethnographic box is a dream come true.

A sort of glow came over my new friend, who despite the constant burst of inebriated-sounding commands—"Tell her this!" "Tell her that!"—managed to stay focused on what he wanted to impart to me, namely the time-honored brutal but moral dynamics of his society. His mode of instruction consisted of probing me with rhetorical questions. In the old days, he asked, there was no police or court, so how did the Kaḷḷars handle crime back then? How did they dispense justice when killed or wronged? "They took revenge," the man answered with a raucous laughter and launched into a drawn-out but apparently true story about two farmers who pick up a fight while working in the field. One slashes the other with a sickle and, when caught by the villagers, he violently throws his newborn baby on the ground, shouting: "A life for a life!" When the villagers deny him the opportunity to turn his crime into a sacrifice, his Dalit (untouchable) servant kills his own child, crying out: "Two lives for one then!" It was then that my narrator got to the moral of his tale. The Kaḷḷars cannot choose their own punishment. They cannot say, as he mimicked with a disparaging and exaggerated tone of supplication, "No sir, you can't penalize me; I did it myself!" "No sir, don't take my son's life, take mine instead!" Only the victims' families can decree the sentence and exact revenge however they want, as evidenced by the fact that in the story the villagers hackle the killer with the sharp, sweeping strokes of their sickles right on the main square (*mantai*) where the cows graze.

The men took delight in my horrified reaction, which I cultivated because I knew that was what they wanted. And because I was such an appreciative audience, they called up more examples of their society's passion for revenge. "What about the police and the state?" I finally asked, "Don't they deter you from exercising violence?" The men answered in unison, "No one can control us; we're masters of our lives." A skinny fellow with missing teeth added, "No one can change us. We the Kaḷḷars are brutal. If someone attacks us, we retaliate, and we never forget a slight; we are great keepers of grudge. Whether we are rich or poor, revenge is our trademark."

On the ride back to my home on the outskirts of Madurai that late afternoon I kept thinking about Louis Dumont, who resided among the Pramalai Kaḷḷars for eight months during the two years he spent in Tamil Nadu in 1949 and 1950 (1986: 4). The question in my mind was not so much, How did the French anthropologist manage to live with these tough people (although that too)? It was, How could Dumont have failed to incorporate the Kaḷḷar agonistic and aggressive worldview into his theory of alliance? This omission is all the more conspicuous in that Dumont was well aware of "the importance of rivalries among these people" (1986: 159) and "the frequency of conflict in Kallar life" (1986: 310). Yet his treatment of what he considered "the most important aspect" of Kaḷḷar marriage ceremonies, namely gift giving (1986: 239), and for that matter his entire analysis of their marriage practices, skirts the moral, social, and political issues that, as I show in this chapter and the next, are fully operationalized in Kaḷḷar matrimonial exchanges and Tamil intermarriage at large.

The Watchmen of Yesterday and Today

The Kaḷḷars Dumont met in the early 1950s had a complex history, which the Kaḷḷars of today (as my opening vignette suggests) use for the construction of their identities (see also Headley 2011). The trouble with this history is that both the Kaḷḷars and the Europeans have manipulated it for practical and ideological purposes. In the nineteenth century there was nothing the Kaḷḷars could do that was not perceived as hostile to the British and non-Kaḷḷars. The very name of this subcaste evoked suspicion, as *kaḷḷar* means "thieves." The British were keen on documenting that when these ex-martial castes[2] settled into new villages, they took up duties as village watchmen (*kāvalkarars*) but only to steal cattle from the very castes they were supposed to protect from theft. The belief that the Kaḷḷars forced farmers into paying for the return of raided livestock (Thurston and Rangachari 1987, Volume 3: 69) and practiced reprisals on anyone who tried to do without their protecting services eventually led the colonial administration to place them under the jurisdiction of the "Criminal Tribes and Castes Act" of 1911. From 1918 to 1947 the Kaḷḷars were subjected to intensive police surveillance, techniques of intimidation, and judicial discipline.[3]

For postcolonial scholars it has been hard to resist sympathy for a people targeted by the British Empire. Stuart Blackburn (1978), for example, has argued that the predatory Kaḷḷar watchman of the late nineteenth century was a perverse product of colonial administrative imagination and policy (Blackburn 1978).[4] More recently, the Kaḷḷars underwent an apotheosis in Anand Pandian's book (2009) that depicts them not merely as scapegoats of the Madras presidency but as unambiguously moral subjects and champions of virtue.[5]

My own sense is that Indira Arumugam, a young anthropologist (and a Kaḷḷar herself) is onto something when she writes that "subalternity is an inadequate framework for analyzing complex Kaḷḷar histories" (2011: 12). She argues that over the last half-century the Kaḷḷars of Thanjavur have acceded to the status of a dominant caste by means of intimidation and coercion (2011: 12). Her fieldwork experience accords to mine: The Kaḷḷars of Madurai have accrued power by almost any kind of force, or threat of violence, property damage, or harm to reputation. They still specialize in the role of dangerous watchmen but nowadays mostly in the city, bullying storekeepers into accepting Kaḷḷar protection for a hefty price or else vandalizing their merchandise.

In addition, the Kaḷḷars use violence to secure exclusive commercial control of profitable businesses. Here are three examples of their monopoly.

Some twenty years ago, villages located on the Vaigai's banks would lease the many access roads to the river on a yearly basis. This was done by means of auction, and the bidder who obtained the rental contract was permitted to levy the sand miners (*maṇal kuttakai ēlam*). Because river sand is an essential ingredient in the construction industry and because Madurai was then fast expanding, the business became very profitable. I was told that on a given day 100 bullock carts could come by, and, at 10 rupees a cart, the leaseholder's daily revenues could fetch 1,000 rupees, which was then, as it is still, a huge amount of money.

This was when, I was also told, the Pramalai Kaḷḷars took over the "sand-mining business," as it became known then. But instead of paying the middlemen or leaseholders for the right of access to the river, they "secretly" began buying coconut groves along the riverbank at double or even triple the cost of the prevailing land value. This gave the Kaḷḷars direct access to the river, where at dawn when the sun is not yet up they would mine up and down its bed and along its banks where the prized, fine sand needs to be filtered. Sometimes no sale took place; the Kaḷḷars entered direct partnerships with the owners of coconut groves, especially during monsoon time when the river floods and regurgitates more sand.

The unchecked expansion of these new sand merchants began causing environmental problems. The decimation of coconut groves along the Vaigai incurred soil erosion and desertification. As the river's sand level went down, the ground water level also fell, and some village wells completely dried up. These natural problems led to conflicts and litigation. Farmers dependent on the river or wells for the irrigation of their crops filed suits in court. Their legal action, however, did not stop the Kaḷḷars from mining the sand, sometimes with the complicity of the police, because the regulation of plundering is a Kaḷḷar speciality. Consider the following article from the online edition of one of India's national newspapers, *The Hindu*:

> Monday, Sept. 27, 2004
> **Sand mafia eating away Vaigai's northern bank**
> By Our Staff Reporter
> MADURAI, SEPT. 26. For more than a year now, V. Jeyaraman, a retired person, has been fighting hard to save his coconut grove along the Vaigai riverbank from the hands of sand mafia. With both the revenue and police

officials not showing any interest to put an end to the illegal activity, Mr. Jeyaraman is now contemplating to seek the Madurai Bench of the Madras High Court's intervention.

Two groups of sand miners operating from Viraghanoor and Puliyankulam are simultaneously eating away the western and eastern corners of the over three-acre "2-C" *patta* land, on the northern bank of the Vaigai. The sand mafia, which reduced the embankment for more than 200 feet, has already felled a handful of coconut trees. As a result, the riverbed has been widened by more than 80 feet in certain pockets after the miners dug the patta land for nearly 20 feet depth. ("2-C" *patta* land is Government "*poromboke*" land authorized by the Revenue department for individuals to take up farming on payment of an annual fee.)

"The unabated mining is posing danger to the Right Main canal maintained by the Public Works department. In the long run it will also affect the Viraghanoor regulator," an official said.

Mr. Jeyaraman first drew the attention of the district administration to the issue in May last year. In his complaint, he complained that the miners had threatened the watchman of the coconut grove with "dire consequences." Whenever he objected, the watchman was chased away by the mob, pelting stones at him.

Despite the complaint, the revenue officials did not take effective steps to check the illegal activity.

The Silaiman police refused to register the complaint, even as the miners had "trespassed, indulged in theft (of sand), damaged the trees, threatened the watchman, and pelted stones." "The police instead asked us to approach the Revenue officials," he said.

After the Village Administrative Officer dug a pit on the approach road, along the Right Main Canal, which connects the Madurai–Ramanathapuram road to the riverbed, the miners were now forcefully taking their trucks through the *patta* land.

Even after a second complaint lodged with the District Collector in November last year, the unlawful activity has been going on.

"I have no other alternative except to move the High Court to save the coconut trees that have been brought up by two decades of hard work," Mr. Jeyaraman said.

Since the publication of this article, the Tamil government has taken stringent measures to prevent the mining of river sand. Nowadays the Public Works Department (rather than the village presidents) leases the right of way to the river and only at permitted places. Apparently this development has induced some Kaḷḷars to bribe or intimidate the officials in charge of dispensing such rental contracts. I was told, however, that the Kaḷḷars who do acquire these leases do their own policing so as to purge the lucrative mining industry from "thieves."

A more modest example of Pramalai Kaḷḷar style of entrepreneurship involves the transportation of agricultural products (unripe plantains, sack of paddies, plantain leaves bundles, coconuts, firewood, cow dung for manure) to urban markets. For this service farmers pay "rent," for example, at the time of my fieldwork, 20 rupees per plantain tree, 20 rupees per sack of paddy, 12 rupees per bundle of plantain leaves, and so on. The money adds up quickly. One driver's account book showed that on October 2, 2007, he made a profit of 600 rupees, earning 1,700 rupees in transportation or "rent" fees but spending 1,100 rupees on the job: 700 rupees on diesel plus 400 rupees on the driver and the carrier's wages.

This business is open to all those who own a van or a rickshaw. But the Pramalai Kaḷḷars monopolize it. The word is that they bully farmers and carriers to work with them exclusively and retaliate against those who do not (by spoiling their goods, for example).

Finally, the Pramalai Kaḷḷars are also known for being, as Dumont already noted more than fifty years ago, "real usurers" (1986: 129). They lend money to people who for the most part live a hand-to-mouth existence, having no choice but to borrow when they meet some sudden and unavoidable expenses such as a funeral or a hospital bill. Usually a Kaḷḷar loan (*tavaṇai*) is paid on a daily basis in equal installments for 100 days, but the interest rate is high, somewhere between 13 and 15 percent. Let us say that a man borrows 100 rupees, the Kaḷḷar moneylender gives him 85 rupees, withholding 15 as interest, and expects a rupee a day for one hundred days. If a creditor cannot repay on a given day, he can make it up the next day. If he defaults for a week, the moneylender comes to his house and makes a scene. If he defaults for longer than a week, the interest rate goes up. As a lawyer told me in English, "If you borrow money from the Kaḷḷars, it won't be very easy to pay back. If you can't pay back, they'll keep on charging more interest." "It is not just difficult," this man emphasized, "but *very* difficult." When the Kaḷḷars do not get their money back, he added, they intimidate clients forcibly, taking away their possessions (things such as TVs, VCRs, and so on). "The extortions of these usurers," he said, word for word, "are well known."

My fieldwork thus leads me to be sympathetic to Arumugam's argument that "for Kaḷḷars, violence is a mode of agency and . . . has been a basis for accruing power (2011: 12). About their economic ascent there is little doubt, as nowadays the Pramalai Kaḷḷars control much of the economy of the town of Madurai, a startling development when we recall that, according to colonial and ethnographic records for the first half of the twentieth century, these people were either on the run, in jail, or destitute.

Of course, not all Kaḷḷars participate in the "economic" activities just described, and we simply cannot say that they are achieving their political projects by the sole means of theft, coercion, and usury. There is another explanation for the Pramalai Kaḷḷars' expansion and ascent: their mode of ceremonial gift giving, which Dumont regarded as "the most important aspect" of their marriage ceremonies (1986: 239).

The Ethnography of Kaḷḷar Ceremonial Gifting in the Past and the Present

By the time Dumont arrived in Kaḷḷar country, he noted, marriage was "more economical" (1986: 239) than in the past when it "involved considerable expense" (239). According to the French anthropologist, the Pramalai Kaḷḷars had "undertaken a reform" (238) and "recently introduced" a "simplified form of marriage" (244) that took place at the temple (*koyil kalyanam*) instead of home (*vittu kalyanam*), and this new ceremonial venue was less costly. "For example," Dumont wrote, "an informant was married [at the temple] . . . for Rs 25 during the [second] war, while his brother was celebrated [at home] in 1939 with the traditional pomp and cost Rs 1,500" (239).

The first thing to note is that 1,500 rupees in 1939 would have been an exorbitant sum of money, as indicated by Dumont's comment that when he was in the field the weekly wages of a male unskilled laborer were 7 rupees (1986: 126). It seems odd that Dumont does not raise the question of how the poor and destitute Kaḷḷars of his ethnography came up with such large amounts of cash. It would have been also good to learn something about the causes of the economic and religious (as the move to the temple suggests) "reform." But whatever was behind the reduction of ceremonial expenditure, Dumont's documentation of gift giving at Kaḷḷar marriages points to the fact that marriage in South India presupposes and reifies relations of exchange.

The first gift, he noted, is *paricam*, a gift of money of at least "8 pieces of gold" from the groom's father to the bride's father who "is supposed to spend at least twice the amount of it for making jewels for his daughter" (1986: 252). According to Dumont, the *paricam* sets the pattern best described in the Kaḷḷar formulation: "Gifts sent to the bride's house return increased twofold or threefold" (1983: 80).

The data Dumont collected suggest, however, that the bride's parents are not quite the givers he makes them out to be. For Dumont discerns a second or "internal" (1986: 252) category of gift giving at Kaḷḷar marriages, a collection of money taken both in the bride's house and in the groom's house among the relatives assembled. This *moy*, a word that conveys the sociality of this taking of donations because it means "crowd" and "assembly" (1986: 256n23), Dumont observes, "amounts to a partial compensation for the family which has given the feast" (257). Here too economization has affected what Dumont also calls this "system of credit or insurance" (127) on grounds that the assistance received has to be returned. "Traditionally," he records, "[the amount collected] was from Rs 500 to Rs 1,000; in an average example of a simple modern marriage it is Rs 150" (257). Again Dumont offers no explanation for the drastic devaluation of these collections; nor does he comment on the mother's brother contribution of "Rs 60 or 100," which I calculated, is twelve to twenty times larger than that of the "other participants [who] give Rs 5 each, for example, in no fixed order" (257). In fact, the mother's brother's donation would appear to equate the value of *paricam*, the "deposit," handed by the groom's father, which by Dumont's reckoning amounts to half the amount spent by the bride's father for her jewels. Because the *moy* is framed as public compensation for the family's marriage's expenditures, it is reasonable to assume that the maternal uncle reimburses his brother-in-law, the bride's father, for his half of her jewels. By the look of things, the man finances his niece's marriage.

Now we jump to my own ethnographic data on *moy*, which exhibit deep continuities with Dumont's documentation. In my fieldwork experience, however, the term *moy* was interchangeable with the verbal compound *ceymuṟaihal*, which means "to do" (*cey*) "what is right" (*muṟai*) or rather "the right things," because *muṟai* here is given in the plural form (*muṟaihal*). In *ceymuṟaihal*, as in the *moy* collection described by Dumont, relatives and acquaintances give with the expectation that their remittance will be returned when their turn comes to hold a particular life-cycle ceremony. To this end, families record each donation in a copybook, just as Dumont noted more than sixty years ago. However, there is one critical exception: The girl's maternal uncle not only hands out many times over what others give—a fact that is consistent with Dumont's records—but his "right deed" is never repaid, as also evidenced by the fact that the family does not enter any amount for it in the notebook. Rather than a rupee figure they leave a blank space after his name. The mother's brother's contribution, then, is not merely one-sided; it is unspecified, even obliterated.

Before I attempt to shed some light on these facts, let me point out that, as far as I know, most castes in Madurai "do the right things," and this for good reasons. "*Ceymuraihal*," I was told, "is an ingenious system," "a loan of money free of interest" (*vaṭṭiyilla kaṭaṉ*), and a way of spreading over time the cost a ceremony. But for the Kaḷḷars, *ceymuraihal* works more as a capitalist lending venture than as a traditional ritual cooperative. At the time of my fieldwork, the depreciation process noted by Dumont was well over, and the sums of cash circulating at Kaḷḷar ceremonies were astronomical. Moreover, only a fraction of the cash was used to cover ritual expenses; most of the "good things" were invested in real estate, businesses of the sort previously described, or in bribes, the latter to ensure, for example, that a husband would get a desirable position at a government bus company, an electricity board, or the like. Thus one Kaḷḷar man told me that in 1998 he and his wife were able to raise 39,000 rupees at their daughter's marriage. They spent 10,000 rupees on the wedding, putting the rest (29,000 rupees) toward a 40,000 rupee piece of land. At the time of my fieldwork, ten years later, the land was worth 150,000 rupees. This man told me that were he to marry his daughter when we met (in 2008) he would be sure to raise 700,000 rupees in ceremonial contributions.

The Kaḷḷar system is so "ingenious" that families do not so much "use" the cash as raise it because the Kaḷḷars do not wait for the natural sequence of life-cycle ceremonies to "do good things"; they jump-start them, inviting, for example, relatives and friends to a "house function" (*vīṭṭu vicēṣam*) or to a second enactment of a child's "ear-piercing" ceremony, this time with fancier studs than the last one, and so on.

In any case, by the time the ritual starts, the family (or couple[6]) has already negotiated the money they need for their specific venture. A few weeks or months before the event, they approach their relatives with precise figures in mind. At the ear-piercing ceremony of her child, a woman, for example, may ask her parents and married brother(s) to "do the right things" in the amount of two to three *lakhs* of rupees (200,0000 or 300,000 rupees), which at the time of my fieldwork was about twenty to thirty times more than the average (approximately 10,000 rupees) monthly income of a middle-class family. She requests large sums because she does not have to pay back her natal kin, but she makes sure that other relatives (her married sisters, for example) pledge money as well. The husband does the same, asking each of his sisters and brothers for this or that amount, which is always much less than what his wife asked of her brothers. If his siblings cannot give right away, he too requests a promissory note so that, before the ritual or function begins, the couple knows what to expect. They also invite friends, neighbors, and colleagues because naturally they want as much money as possible.

It is very likely that processes of neoliberalism and monetization have inflated ceremonial gifting among the Kaḷḷars. Indeed, a few Kaḷḷars suggested that much to me. "In the old days," a fifty-year-old man told me, "when we had a function, everyone came. Relatives helped us cook, ate, and left. Back then we gave 5 rupees, now we give in the thousands." He added, "Before, ritual used to be about giving and receiving respect (*mariyātai*); now it runs on money." But Dumont's ethnography suggests that already in the early 1950s "the amount of the [*moy*] collection" was "far from negligible" (1986: 257) and that, in at least one instance, "these people were more interested in cash" than in ceremonial baskets of plantains, rice, and vegetables (253). When we recall his comment that ten to fifteen years *before* he arrived in Kaḷḷar country, cash contributions were even much larger, it is difficult to avoid the impression that there is more to current Kaḷḷar ceremonial gift giving than the present or at least recent deregulation of trade in India.

The Obligation to Give and Take

By definition, to give is to hand over something to someone without expecting to receive anything in return. Yet Marcel Mauss, the well-known French sociologist with whom Dumont studied before World War II (Galey 1982), taught us a surprising lesson. Far from being a one-way transaction, a gift is always followed by a countergift (Mauss 1990). Hence a gift is the starter of a reciprocal relationship between two partners, a differed exchange. Mauss also revealed, somewhat counterintuitively we might say, that the return of gifts (be they material goods, politeness, feasts, services, dances, or whatever) is a strongly sanctioned requirement. It is this element of imperativeness that led the French sociologist to employ the word *prestation*, glossed in the Oxford English Dictionary as "the action of paying, in money or service, what is due by law or custom, or feudally; a payment or the performance of a service so imposed or exacted, also, the performance of something promised."

Mauss's influence on Dumont is evidenced by his focus on Kaḷḷar ceremonial gift giving at marriage. It is also at work in his understanding that both the "external" prestations between the groom's and bride's families and the "internal" collection of money on the wedding day indicate and construct social relations, an "alliance" in the former case and a system of "insurance" in the latter, characterized by solidarity. But in Dumont's ethnography, nothing in particular seems to compel Kaḷḷar reciprocity. Mauss (1990) speaks of a "religious" "force" (the *Hau*) in Maori cosmology and a code of honor in the "ostentatious" and "agonistic" exchanges of the Melanesians and potlatching Northwest Coast Indians. But let us face it: There is no spiritual or political angle to the exchanges described by Dumont. It is as if the Kaḷḷars give goods and money back and forth mechanically without compulsion, spirit, or any pressure, for that matter.

Yet according to my ethnography, and I believe that of Dumont as well, the Kaḷḷars always return more than they receive. This is evidenced by Dumont's observation that the bride's parents disburse twice as much as the groom's family—the family that makes the initial gift or "deposit." As he emphasizes: "People know perfectly well that in gift-giving, generosity rests in the final analysis on the woman's side" (1986: 254).[7] One expects the French anthropologist to ponder on this imbalance, but in Dumont's description the affinal relationship does not come up so much tilted or asymmetrical as structurally equivalent and "projective" (290). In essence, the flow of gifts differentiates two classes that are in identical positions in relation to each other; "wife givers" always give more than "wife takers" (see also Uberoi 2006: 163)—a representation that is consistent with Dumont's model of Dravidian kinship, particularly his distinction between kin and affine.

As for the Kaḷḷar collection of ceremonial money among relatives and acquaintances, it is deeply steeped in notions of defiance and provocation. The people I consulted were clear on that much: The character of the "good things" is aggressive and competitive. You contribute money so as to challenge recipients to put in more when your turn comes to hold a life-cycle ceremony, which is consistent with Dumont's observation that "increase is the law of the whole cycle" of Kaḷḷar gift giving (1983: 84).

Although profit definitively factors in, the purpose of inflated returns is not merely to gain additional goods and cash. According to my consultants, the goal, or the thrill we may say, of giving more is to put relatives and acquaintances in the difficult position of having to repay more. Beyond profit and loss it is status (one's own and that of others) that is at stake here. Quite simply, the pressure to uphold one's prestige *and* topple another man is the "force" (in Maussian language) that lies behind the constant and maddening attempt to up the ante.

I learned this over time, as when I asked, "What happens when people do not return more than they receive?" Inevitably I was told: "We lose face and our place in society." Because a life without prestige in Tamil Nadu is simply not worth living, families borrow or pawn whatever they have to reciprocate liberally. The stress and havoc caused by one's ever-increasing level of debit and liability is well captured in the following statement: "The "doing of right things," a consultant complained, "is a disease (*nōy*), a trap (*kaṇṇi*), you can never get out of it." Indeed, participation in these ceremonial plots puts a huge strain on families who *must* do anything to avoid defaulting altogether, for failure to pay back is the worst possible position to be in. As the lawyer already quoted in this chapter gave me a feel for this predicament: "If I, a Kaḷḷar man, bring 5,000 rupees to your ceremony, I expect you to do more for me when you come to mine. If you don't show up with anything, not even with what I loaned you, I'll send my washerman [a low-caste man] to your house the next day. That will be a tremendous blow to your ego, a terrible humiliation, a huge *māṉam* ['prestige'] problem." His point was clear: "If you default on me, I put you down," which in Tamil Nadu is tantamount of saying, "I kill you socially and psychologically."

And the matter will not end here because, as the opening vignette to this chapter suggests, the Kaḷḷars go to many extremes to retaliate against those who shortchange them one way or another. This may include, as Dumont also noted, "acts of self-mutilation or self-destruction" that are meant to "hurt the adversary—as . . . when a Kallar persists in a ruinous and hopeless lawsuit in order to ruin an enemy" (1986: 312).[8] Recently Indira Arumugam reported that "mutually ruinous tactics" (2011: 136) are de rigueur among the Kaḷḷars of Vaduvur, adding: "Recourse to the law and the police is a calculated tactic to impose protracted punishment. One may lose some but the objective is to ensure one's enemy loses even more" (2011: 136). I too have recorded such behaviors among the Pramalai Kaḷḷars of Madurai, as when one man told me that he asked his wife to bang her head on the wall until it bled so that he could bring a formal charge of assault against an enemy.

What I am saying here is that reciprocity and therefore relatedness among the Kaḷḷars is definitively not as free, easygoing, supportive or even sustainable as what Dumont made it out to be. More problematic is the fact that the French sociological construction of a gift economy (as first theorized by Marcel Mauss) does not begin to describe Kaḷḷar ceremonial exchanges, which consist in handing out not personal property but borrowed cash. A Kaḷḷar man brought out the unequivocally uncharitable, and capitalist-like, imagination at work here when he explained the mechanism of the ceremonial collection of money in these terms: "In order to cover up a hole (*kuṇṭu*) I take from another pit (*kuḻi*)." His statement clarified the "devious logic" (*kaḷḷa-naṭattai*), as he put it, of an economy that basically runs on both inflation and credit.

Finally, Dumont downplayed the role and contribution of the person who is a big—perhaps the biggest—player at these exchanges, namely the mother's brother. Recall that in his account this man reimburses just about all the money expended by the bride's parents on her jewels by contributing amounts of cash that are twelve to twenty times larger than those given by the other participants. This avuncular generosity is all the more striking when we realize that the maternal uncle does not enter in any kind of bilateral reciprocity with the bride's father. He is apart, a one-sided giver, and one cannot say that he gives with the expectation to receive more. One does *not* give back to the mother's brother; one does not even record his generous contribution. His unilateral and untraceable mode of exchange is actually encoded in the Kaḷḷar matrimonial rule that in the abstract at least favors no direct reciprocity between givers and takers. As Claude Lévi-Strauss (1969) has formally demonstrated, matrilateral cross-cousin marriage requires a minimum of three groups involved in unilateral transfer of women and accompanying material gifts in marriage. To go back to the Kaḷḷar scenario: The maternal uncle ideally gives his daughter(s)—at least one, as I will expand on in the next chapter—to his sister's son, but his sister gives her own daughter(s)—at least one—to the son(s) of her husband's sister, who in turn gives her own daughter to her husband's sister's son, and so on. The same unilateral logic applies to the maternal uncle's "duty" (*kaṭamai*), as the Tamils put it, to "do the right thing" at the marriage of his sister's daughter(s). His prestation comes back not from the side that takes the girl (her father's sister) but from that of his wife's brother who (ideally) provides a bride for his (first) son.

There is thus something inherently different about the mother's brother. The man who gives a daughter to his sister and her husband is not sure to receive a bride from his wife's brother. The (same) man who pays for half of his sister's daughter's wedding jewels cannot be certain that his wife's brother will "reimburse" him when he marries off his own daughter. The Kaḷḷars are happy to explain these risks to the anthropologist, all the while emphasizing that the mother's brother is nonetheless not taken for granted. As Dumont himself observed, at the *moy*, the bride's mother's brother "arrives at the very beginning of the ceremony," "eats separately," "is first on the list" of givers and of the distribution of betel (1986: 256–257). To scholars of South Indian society, such precedence in all things would undoubtedly be indicative of great respect and even superiority and, indeed, as I will expand on in Chapter 4, the mother's brother is the most honorific relation in Kaḷḷar (and in Tamil) kinship.

In the end we understand that Dumont had some twisting to do to make his Tamil subcaste fit his structural model of Dravidian kinship. Here I am not simply referring to his erasure of the Kaḷḷars' turbulent history and their (temporary) attempts to "reform" or rather scale down their ceremonial contributions in the 1940s (1986: 239). I have in mind his attempt to flatten this subcaste into categories of givers and takers who exchange for no other reason than perpetuate their (or his?) kinship structure. That Dumont did not see the political or competitive dynamics in the Kaḷḷar inflationary logic of gift giving is consistent with his most fundamental assumptions concerning the separation of power and status in India (1980). But that Dumont did not make much of the mother's brother distinctive role and status is puzzling. Could it be perhaps that a closer analysis of the man's unilateral contribution and high standing would have led him to revise his structural analysis of Dravidian kinship? I do not know the answer to this question, but in neglecting the structures of prestige impinging on Kaḷḷar ceremonial gift giving, Dumont cast the wrong impression on affinal relationships in South India, and, as I now turn my attention, on Tamil preferential marriage.

2

DOING THE RIGHT THING

> It is only when we turn to kinship that we can discern indigenous notions of individual rights. . . . Such automatic rights come with corresponding duties—recognition, respect and therefore non-infringement of each other's rights . . . While such rights and duties are the jural and moral constitutions of kinship as citizenship, they are not structurally deterministic. These latent claims and obligations must be activated through choice and action by individuals. They must be operationalised into citizenship through consenting to be subject to them and participation in the political process or not as the case may be.
>
> —Arumugam 2011:7–8

When anthropologists describe Tamil kinship they usually focus on the terms that express the much-reified opposition between nonmarriageable or "parallel" kin and marriageable or "cross" kin. Their discussions inevitably contrast the mode of exchange peculiar to the first category—the brothers or patrilineal kin (*aṇṇaṉ/tampi/paṅkāḷi*) who inherit and "share" property—to that of the second, the brothers-in-law (*maccāṉ/macciṉaṉ/campanti*) who exchange wives, gifts, prestations, help, and so on. Later in this book I will show that membership in these two kinship categories is much too fluid and fuzzy for this distinction to be useful. In this chapter I want to suggest that the obsession with dividing Tamil relatives into "parallel" and "cross" kin has hindered the recognition of other and more productive terms; terms that clearly show that entitlement rather than exchange is the value that is crucial to the organization of Tamil kinship relations and action and specifically Tamil close-kin marriages. The two Tamil kinship terms *contam* ("mine") and *muṟai* ("rule"),[1] in particular, express this value most succinctly and meaningfully, evoking an emotionally powerful language of "rights" (*urimai*), which, I also suggest, serves as a systematic basis for articulating ongoing kinship competition and violence. Although my discussion is anchored in Kaḷḷar ethnography, it applies to Tamil matrimonial practice in general.

Kinship Means "Mine"

In day-to-day life, the Tamil term for kin, *contam*, denotes a general and unbounded class of kin, both marriageable and nonmarriageable, who stand opposed to *a<u>nn</u>iyam*. *A<u>nn</u>iyam* means "other," and the contrast with *contam* indicates that the Tamils do not conceive "strangers" in the same way as themselves. It is important to note that in the context of marriage these two categories are not as all inclusive as they would seem. Marriageable kin exclude the grandmother, the father and his brothers and their children, the mother and her sisters and their children, the sister, the brother, the son and daughter, and the grandson. Marriageable strangers extend only so far, in theory at least excluding people outside's one's caste, because even today Indians usually insist on caste endogamy. Caste (*jāti*) is so much associated with concepts of natural distinction and of fundamental difference (Mines 2009: 76) that marrying outside of one's *jāti* evokes notions of specieslike incompatibility and unsuitability, as is nicely captured by this statement: "We don't give the elephant to the cow. We give the bull to the cow so that they can reproduce." This provides one more clue that the Tamils marry on the basis of likeness.

Contam and *a<u>nn</u>iyam* are relative categories: They vary according to context and the level of kinship considered. The Tamil families I befriended would assure me that I was like *contam* to them. Conversely, they would not hesitate to refer to this or that relative as "*a<u>nn</u>iyam*," by which they meant, "He or she isn't one of us; we don't want to marry him or her." To be *contam* or *a<u>nn</u>iyam*, thus, is a matter of degree, not of absolute distinction.

Karin Kapadia writes that in the Tamil village of Aruloor (in Tiruchchirappalli), "The term [*contam*] had an extremely positive connotation" and its "profound emotive depth . . . was closely connected with economics" (1995: 40). To have kin in Tamil Nadu can work to one's advantage; but *contam* is first and foremost associated with notions of rights, entitlements, and privileges. Witness the Tamil Lexicon's entry for it: "one's own peculiar right, exclusive property, that which belongs to oneself" (1924–1936: 1651). Thus Arumugam is onto something when she writes: "It is only when we turn to kinship that we can discern indigenous notions of individual rights" (2011: 7). But in my field experience it is not merely members of the patrilineage who are "individuated in terms of . . . inalienable rights" (Arumugam 2011: 7). Each and every Tamil kinship relation comes with rights that are quasi-legal. That the category *urimai* is pervasive across the entire field of Tamil kinship, including relations with same-sex siblings, parents, and children, became evident when I asked mostly mature women to define this word. "I've *urimai* in my husband," they would say, or, "I've *urimai* to ask anything from my mother or father. I've *urimai* to their property." One of these respondents volunteered that "after moving in with her in-laws, a newly married girl has *urimai* to proclaim: 'This is my house.'"

Notice that the Tamil gloss of kinship makes reference neither to relations of biological or genetic connection nor to genealogical ties arising from procreation. It does not even mention consubstantiality. *Contam* may be mutually related because they share blood or suckle the same milk. But such notions do not come out in conversation. What is said instead is that what my kin have is mine. I can help myself to their possessions. I don't even have to ask because my claim goes without saying. The reverse is also true, and what I have is theirs—as I learned when I was told that a young girl I knew got pregnant out of wedlock. She could not abort "because she's carrying *contam*," meaning the father was related to her and so he (and his family) had a claim (*urimai*) on the baby.

In theory, then, the world of *contam* exists outside a gift-giving (or market) economy. Tamil kin do not exactly give or receive; they help themselves to whatever each and all of their roles (as mother, sister, wife, daughter, and so on) entitle them. When applied to the pragmatics of day-to-day life, this means that with *contam* one is at home, somewhat free from the elaborate codes of conduct regarding appropriate media and appropriate contexts of gift-giving activities and commensality (Appadurai 1981, 1985). Because these codes, as scholars of Indian society have amply documented (Dumont 1986: 155–159,417; Appadurai and Breckenridge 1976; Dirks 1987; Fuller 1992: 79–81; Mines 2005: 81), serve to index relationships of social difference, as well as establish social "distinction" (*mariyātai*) or "precedence" (*mutalmei*), it is logical to assume that the absence, or at least the reduced presence, of formal codes of transaction among kin expresses relationships of identity or similarity. Indeed, it is because *contam* share the same life (locality, residence, food, memories, suffering, and so on), feel responsibility for, and feel the effects of each other's acts that they have the license to appropriate each other's possessions. As one middle-aged woman casually put it to me in English: "I own my kin and whatever they have." We are very close here to Marshall Sahlins's recent attempt to gloss a wide range of ethnographic descriptions of kinship in terms of "mutuality of being" (2013: 2–3).

We should not underestimate the sheer sense of relief the Tamils feel when they are exempted from the intricate and competitive formalities of giving and taking. It is not merely that these formalities carry such critical messages of status that they are sure to cause deep anxieties: Are we showing proper respect? Have we offended anyone? Are they correctly appraising the value of our presents? Are we receiving as much as they would receive in the same circumstances? And so on. It is also the case that in giving and taking there is not much room for spontaneity, for ease—especially, for making claims that are not already prefigured in the transaction.

That the Tamils would rather not be put into a situation in which they have to give to and take from people not like them, in other words from *a̲n̲n̲iyam*, is a major reason why families preferred, and still prefer, intermarrying. With *contam*, that is, with one's own, one does not have to worry about being placed in the types of awkward and socially risky, or even humiliating, situations that are only too common in the public sphere of exchange where one has no right of ownership. More importantly, with *contam* one has leverage and power. As a Dalit (Pa̲raiyar) man explained to the anthropologist Robert Deliège:

> Suppose my daughter is married to my sister's son and I pay a visit to her. I reach their house but there is nobody home; the door is locked. But since it is my own sister's house, I can go in, take some food and feel at home. On the other hand, if my daughter is married to a stranger, in the same situation, I have to wait outside their house for their return. I cannot go in, otherwise my daughter would be insulted by her in-laws. They would say that her father only came here to steal food, that he wants to spoil them, that he does not respect them etc. For this reason, it is better to marry close-relatives. (1987: 225–226)

With *contam* there is also less pressure to give large marriage payments: "You give what you can," I was told. Again and again my consultants maintained, "*Contam* are not as demanding. At marriage, they take less than *a̲n̲n̲iyam*." This corroborates the anthropologist David Rudner's finding that the marriage of a Chettiar man's daughter to his sister's son was "less expansive because . . . [t]hey accepted whatever I wanted to give" (1994: 172; see also Jones Allison 1980: 126). Likewise, Linda May reports this statement made by a Nātār woman, "Among ourselves we don't ask [dowry]. Whatever they want to give is all right" (1986: 161). In practice, she adds, relatives do receive dowry and expect dowry (1986: 161). But the point also made by my own consultants is that, with *contam*, one does not have to negotiate as much because one is more or less on an equal footing and therefore under less pressure to prove one's social rank or raise it by the measure of how much cash and gold one gives or receives at marriage. I write "more or less" because, as I show in the next section, when it comes to some marriages at least not all relatives are on par: Some have more rights than others.

The Rule of Distinction: *Muṟai*

As opposed to *contam*, which, as I just said, refers to one's property and by extension to one's set of relatives in a general way, the word *muṟai* has classificatory meanings, designating the specific terms used to distinguish kinship relations from one another (also see Dumont 1986: 301). As an informant explained: "We have to differentiate (*piri*) kinship relations (*uṟavu*). This process is called '*muṟai*.'" Most consultants would simply state, "There are lots of *muṟai*s" and list examples: "*Ammā* ("mother") is *muṟai*. *Appa* ("father") is *muṟai*," and so on.

Muṟai also means "order," "approved course of conduct," thereby suggesting that Tamil classifications, be they categorical or social, are endowed with normative, even jural, significance. The positive evaluation of the art of making distinctions, as a part of everyday social life, is evidenced in Margaret Trawick's description of her relation with the "high-caste, highly educated, landowning man" (1990: 12) who taught her the subtleties of Tamil literature and religion. He referred to her "as a *muṟaiyillāta poruḷ*, a 'lawless thing,' whose life had no order and followed no rule" (1990: 17).

In the old Caṅkam corpus of Tamil literature, *muṟai* was associated with notions of "action" (*viṉai*), "result" (*paḷam*), and "fate" (*ūḻ*) (Encyclopedia of Tamil Literature 1990: 61). In modern parlance, *muṟai* remains linked to action that causes effects, as evidenced by the combination of this term with the participle of the verb *to do* (*cey*): *ceytal*. The expression *muṟai ceytal* means "doing the right thing." In this very conception of rightness we see again the moral meanings associated with the activity of making social distinctions: Classifications produce good results.

"Doing the right thing" (*muṟai ceytal*) is different from the compulsory ceremonial contributions discussed in the last chapter. *Ceymuṟaihal*, the reader will recall, refers to obligatory monetary prestations by relatives, neighbors, and friends at life-cycle ceremonies (also see Rudner 1994:

177–179). The process called "*mu̱rai ceytal,*" by contrast, allocates not so much material things, although that, too, as social distinctions and authoritative rights. Occasions for publicly differentiating someone from all others in the same class, a form of honor, are frequent in Tamil Nadu. But as far as I know, "doing the right thing" in this more moralized and classificatory sense only takes place in three auspicious contexts: agricultural harvests, women's puberty rituals, and marriages.

Doing the Right Thing at Harvest

It is well known that in the old political economy of rural South Asia the wealthy agricultural patron was linked to his servants (laborers, tenants, and performers of such practical or ritual services as washing clothes, drumming at funerals, and so on) in a relatively closed, nonmonetary, reciprocal system. Nowadays, the common use of cash has altered this former agrarian economy or rights and reciprocities, but something of its fundamental character is still inscribed in the Tamil landowner's obligation to ceremonially distribute fixed shares in the produce of the land (food-grain, especially) right after the harvest is in and the grain is threshed and winnowed.[2]

The one time I observed this rite in Kaḷḷar country, the landlord began doing the right thing by offering the "first"[3] measure (*marakkāl*) of grains to his family deity. The "second" *marakkāl* went to the man whose specialty it is to open and close the sluices controlling the flow of water (rain or river) in irrigation canals. The "third" went to the ironsmith, the "fourth" to the carpenter, the "fifth" to the potter, the "sixth" to the washer man, the "seventh" to the barber, and the last or "eighth" measure went to the Dalit (formerly "untouchable") gravedigger. After the ceremony, each of the women who cleaned the yard received three fistsful of whatever they swept up, so their share was a mixture of grain and dust and sand. But that portion too fell under the category of *mu̱rai*.

The inescapably sequential dimension of this distribution gives meaning to another gloss for *mu̱rai*: "turn by which work is done," "regularity," "repetition" (Fabricius Dictionary 1972: 815). It also establishes a conceptual frame of serial (first, second, third, and so on), and therefore hierarchical, relations among the workers that are based, I was told, on the moral distinctions associated with their distinctive forms of labor. The life-giving, auspicious irrigator comes first, and the inauspicious funerary specialist last. But each worker is singled out and made the subject of a special turn, which confers on him (or her) a renewed social and ritual status and a degree of importance or precedence relative to others. The temporal context—a seasonal harvest—naturalizes this distribution of honors, overlaying it with positive meanings. The message, it seems to me, is that a social order based on different and ranked specializations produces crops and therefore life and social continuity, hence the landlord's absolute "obligation" *(kaṭamai)* to ceremonially re-create this order.

Doing the Right Thing at a Woman's Puberty Ceremony

The critical role played by a Tamil man at his sister's daughter's puberty ceremony (*caṭaṅku*)[4] also epitomizes the ritual process known as "doing the right thing." On the day of the *caṭaṅku*, which takes place not after the girl first menstruates but a few years later when her parents are ready for her to be married, her mother's brother[5] has the duty of bringing "*cīr*," which includes her first sari, gold jewels, flowers, and cosmetics. These gifts and their very appellation—*cīr* means "prosperity" and "beauty"—suggest that this man's main obligation is to bear the expenses of beautifying his sister's daughter.[6] Indeed, when the young woman comes out of the house wearing *cīr* to stand under a lavishly decorated thatch awning built for the occasion, everyone exclaims: "She is beautiful!"

The concern for the young woman's looks is related to the *caṭaṅku*'s main purpose, which I was told is to "advertise her readiness to marry." Kapadia, who recorded puberty rituals in the Tiruchi district of Tamil Nadu, elicited the same interpretation. According to her informants, *caṭaṅku* "is an advertisement [*viḷambaram*] that announces: 'Here is a girl ripe for marriage! Come and ask for her!'" (1995: 107). Such a notice is sure to generate public interest. When I first recorded a *caṭaṅku* some twenty years ago in a village located in the northern part of Tamil Nadu, nearly 200 people watched the proceedings. In 2008, at a *caṭaṅku* performed in a Madurai suburb, I counted approximately 350 spectators.

The maternal uncle's contribution at a *caṭaṅku* has much in common with the landlord's ceremonial distribution of the grains after the harvest. Both men preside over an auspicious process of maturity or ripeness that is associated with sustenance and reproduction: Crops nourish people, and a mature woman is ready to marry and most likely give birth. Both also publically distinguish the persons who are essential to this process: The landowner honors his workers' respective specializations, and the maternal uncle his sister's daughter's sexual maturity and beauty. To give such respect is a duty (*kaṭamai*) and a "must" (*muṟai*). Even if there is a quarrel between the landlord and a worker or between a brother and his sister, the "right thing" must be done. Finally, we note that the seasonal or cyclical context also introduces a notion of timeless but regular rotation to this obligatory action. The same notion resurfaces in the third (and for the purpose of this book, the principal) context for doing the right thing: marriage (*kalyāṇam muṟai*); but first, a few preliminary words.

Doing the Right Thing at Marriage

I have already stated that the priority given to the system of categories generated by the so-called Dravidian kinship terminology has led to the basic, but in my opinion erroneous, impression that the Tamils systematically and indiscriminately marry cross cousins. This is "erroneous" because two basic facts contradict it. First, although at the semantic level the two sides of cross kin (mother's brother and father's sister) are equivalent, and although all castes practice bilateral cross-cousin marriage, many castes have a marriage rule (*kalyāṇam muṟai)*—or at least a preference—for marrying on one "side" (*pakkam*), as the Tamils put it, rather than the other. Among many families, a boy's "right girl" (*muṟai poṇṇu*) is *either* his mother's brother's daughter *or* his father's sister's daughter. For a girl, the "right boy" (*muṟai paiyaṉ*) is *either* her mother's brother's son *or* her father's sister's son. Thus, in general, one and only one set of so-called cross cousins (either on the mother's or the father's side) is right or preferential, or at least more so than the other.

Secondly, the marriage rule or preference does not apply to all boys and girls. Let me make this more concrete by taking the case of the Kaḷḷars. First let me say that for this caste the *muṟai poṇṇu* can be only the maternal uncle's daughter (Dumont 1986: 206) and that "*muṟai*" does not mean "preferential" as in "it is best to marry her." It means "obligatory," as in "you have to marry her" (or someone in the same kinship class). This is evidenced by the fact that, among the Kaḷḷars, the "right" boy or girl is often called "*karai paiyaṉ*" or "*karai poṇṇu*." To us the word *karai*, which means "bank" as in "the bank of the river," may evoke images of habitat, territory, geography, as well as flora (as yellow irises growing among poison ivy) and fauna (as when cormorants sun themselves on a half submerged log, or in images of shooting sparrows on the banks of the Rhine). But for the Kaḷḷars, a bank holds back water—the same word is used for the edge of a pond or an artificial tank—so that by metaphorical extension the right spouse is likewise "stored up." A Kaḷḷar woman expanded on this notion of containment when she said, "The *karai* girl should not cross over to the other side. She's shut in a place (*aṭaṅku*) like water in a bank."

This image of storing or saving a girl (or a boy) for a particular patrilocal unit (which is another meaning of *karai*[7]) is not the only one. The Kaḷḷars also call the "right girl" the "hereditary girl," *cutantira poṇṇu*, from *cutantaram*, which means "perquisite compensation, hereditary right or privilege." Hence Dumont was not wrong to argue that Dravidian affinal roles and ceremonial obligations, such as gift-giving relationships, are passed down from parent (father in particular) to child (son). In Kaḷḷar country you can inherit a spouse, the way you might inherit a job. But there is a critical proviso: Not everyone inherits a spouse; only an elite group among kin does so. Let me make this more concrete by taking the hypothetical case of four married siblings born in the following order: brother, sister, brother, sister. As I proceed, the reader should keep in mind that we must look at Tamil marriages from the point of view of the senior generation.

The first brother does the "right thing" with the first sister by marrying his (preferably) first daughter to her (preferably) first son. The second brother does the same thing with the second sister. Now, let us consider the case of three elder brothers and their younger sister. Here only the first brother is required to do *muṟai* with the sister. If he does not have a daughter, the second brother must offer to do it for him (and so on). But if the elder brother does *muṟai* with the sister, his younger brothers are free to marry their children however they wish.[8]

The social order evoked here is consistent with that represented at the ceremonial distribution of shares in the harvest and the puberty ritual. In all three cases we discern a sequential process that distinguishes those who have precedence (in time or position) as well as those (castes, young women, siblings) who are next in line (for producing the harvest, marrying, and intermarrying). In all three cases "doing the right thing" is about honoring the values of priority and succession and their transmission. In the third case—the very subject of this book—the right thing to do for the firstborn (or their heirs) is to intermarry so that right marriages provide the context for displaying and maintaining distinctions of rank among Tamil kin (*contam*). It should be stressed that the preferential matrimonial status of the firstborn children is a cosmic-ritual status and not status honor in the Weberian sense, an individual quality of prestige, for example, that accrues to or is achieved by the individual. It also should be noted that this status has a natural, even biological, quality to it, so that it appears integral to the field of kinship—a field that is otherwise conceived as egalitarian—and essential to the worlds of human existence and social relationships.

Taking Turns, Taking Sides

In the Introduction I pointed out that it is Louis Dumont more than any other anthropologist of whom I am aware who first discerned that a principle of hierarchy organizes South Indian close-kin marriage. Among the Pramalai Kaḷḷars, he noted, the children of a senior wife do not intermarry with the children of a junior wife. For Dumont the explanation for this case of kinship endogamy was the same as for caste endogamy. The highest ones (Brahmins and first wives' children) are the purest, who remain differentiated and opposed to the lowest and the most polluted ones (Untouchables and last wives' children). It is somewhat puzzling that Dumont applied a Brahmanical value such as purity to a caste that, from his own account, "has a tendency to segregate itself geographically, and . . . has shown itself relatively impervious to Brahmanic customs and ideas for at least a century" (1986: 10). But we must recall that in his analysis the purity–pollution opposition unifies the whole of Hindu society, especially the relation of parts or castes such as the Kaḷḷars to it (1980).

I reevoke Dumont's insight for its relevance to my discussion and also to clarify my own argument regarding the "principle of hierarchy" in Tamil preferential marriage. In the three aforementioned contexts for "doing the right thing," the persons who are the recipients of precedence or distinction stand not for purity but for auspicious and life-giving meanings: (1) workers who contribute to the production of crops, with the irrigator first in line; (2) women who are ready to marry and reproduce; and (3) firstborn children whose very existence, I was told, makes them living signs of fertility and continuity. Hence my suggestion that the encompassing principle of the social order represented in these three contexts is engaged with basic understandings and experiences of life-giving processes. Quite simply, the categories of people who are identified with the sources of life (harvest, puberty, birth) are distinguished and ranked first in the Tamil world of my ethnography.

My fieldwork experiences also lead me to take issue with Dumont's conception of hierarchy as a determining cosmology incapable of being something else. The social distinctions I studied may have a natural anchor, but their very ideological basis in biological processes allows for more democratic possibilities than does Dumont's strict opposition between the caste world of India and the conceptual realities of European and North American ideologies founded in egalitarianism and the valuation of the individual.

This began to emerge when I asked the Kaḷḷars why they—more so than any other caste around Madurai—insisted on making the "right" marriages not merely preferential but prescriptive. The Kaḷḷars I consulted took me aback when they answered that the absolute obligation to enforce the marriage rule (*muṟai*) ensures that everyone has the chance (or the misfortune) to do "the right thing." They explained that unpredictable factors, such as fertility or infertility, infant mortality, proportion of cross siblings, and so on, make it at times possible—indeed obligatory—for junior or unmatched cross siblings to do the right thing. A firstborn sister is infertile, thus the second sister must give a son to their elder brother's daughter; the first two sons have only boys, in which case the last son must marry his daughter to their sister's son; and so on. The randomness of life guarantees that at any time anyone might be called on to do *muṟai* (which, we recall, also means: "rotation," "turn by which work is done").

Thus we come to understand that, in theory at least, the Kaḷḷar marriage rule serves two diametrically opposed social functions. It can create social distinctions and sustain relations characterized by difference, distance, and precedence, or it can protect society from the depredations of inequality, preventing the concentration of wealth and power. For the Kaḷḷar men I interviewed—and the reader must recall that these conversations took place in a seminar-like setting that encouraged philosophical engagement—it is the second function that prevails. "The matrimonial law (*kalyāṇam muṟai*)," a man told me, "is not an accident but something our ancestors deliberately devised. Without it, the rich would join the rich, the poor would join the poor, and the Kaḷḷar community would be divided. The law is there to keep the unity (*oṟṟumai*) and similarity (*oppu*) among us." It follows that, in the "right" world, wealthy brothers cannot restrict their exchanges (material and otherwise) to wealthy sisters; they have to do "the right thing" with poorer sisters, and vice versa. In this way matrimonial rights circulate, obliging families of different status and income to reciprocate or rather help themselves to whatever each has.

We must not lose sight, however, of the compulsory nature of the Kaḷḷar marriage rule. If a person's "turn" comes up, he or she has no choice but to do the right thing. "Even if the right girl is poor or handicapped," Kaḷḷar informants told me, "you've got to marry her," adding that, in the past, "If she were older, you still had to marry her."[9] Such an element of coercion might be expected from a society that, as suggested by the opening vignette of the last chapter, is committed to a vision of justice that denies individual moral initiatives. But we must keep in mind that very few Kaḷḷar men (or conversely very few Kaḷḷar women) are actually under the obligation to marry rightly.

To make this clear, let us return to our hypothetical case of four married siblings born in the following order: brother, sister, brother, sister. If we suppose that each has a progeny of three children on average (a conservative figure given that twenty to thirty years ago fertility rates were well above today's average), we notice that only four of the twelve children ought to marry according to the unilateral rule. Hence the question: How will the other eight marry?

Because marriage to *contam* confers prerogatives that are very much appreciated (the right to relatives' possession, in particular) families will prefer a suitable kin to a stranger. But the question that inevitably arises is: On which side (*pakkam*) will parents find a spouse for their child, the wife's *or* the husband's? The question does not come up in the *muṟai* marriages just discussed because there the marriage law or preference already assigns differential rank between two sets of kin, one of which is styled "right" and the other not. But outside the law there is no stipulation that one side ought to prevail over the other, no agreement that father and his sisters, for example, should come before mother and her brothers. Hence the questions: "on which 'side,'" or "in which 'line'" (*vaḻi*) should our child marry? "Do I honor my sibling or do I let my spouse honor his or hers?" "Who will come first?"

From the point of view of the people involved, the answer is predictable. As the woman who cooked in our house put it to me: "The mother always chooses her relatives and the father his." That each parent tries to prevail is suggested in her next comment: "The mother asks to marry her daughter on her side, only to hear her husband reply, 'What's wrong with my sister's boy? My side is better for our girl.'" This woman's statement echoes Robert Deliège's observation that, among Dalits (Paṟaiyar):

> Quarrels . . . arise frequently between spouses in order to decide on whose side a daughter or son should be married. The mother will insist on marrying them on her brother's side, the father on his sister's side. This provokes situations, which are sometimes difficult since by choosing one side, there is a serious risk that the other party will be put out. (1997: 181)

It is not merely husbands and wives who fight to keep children on their respective "side." Siblings of different birth order also compete among themselves. Even when they hold clear-cut matrimonial rights, they vie to secure marital agreements with one more (or the same) sister or brother. Notice what is happening here: In addition to the cosmic law *(muṟai)* previously mentioned, mundane power sanctions the hierarchical relationships between senior and junior siblings and between spouses or parents. In the conclusion to this chapter I will show how in practice the distinction law/power is not sustainable; for now I want to stress that the struggles I am referring to here are not trivial. To begin to convey something of their intensity and what is at stake in them, I now turn to my record of a ram-fight, which I believe brings to dramatic realization a dimension of the Tamil experience of winning and losing normally obscured from view.

A Tamil Ram Fight

My arrival on the scene of a Tamil ram fight (*kiṭāmuṭṭu*) was anticlimactic, nothing like Clifford Geertz's dramatic encounter with a Balinese cockfight and a police raid (1973). By the time I showed up, halfway through a beautiful Saturday morning in January 2008, the police were already leaving. Because India's Animal Welfare Board and the courts have banned ram fights in Tamil Nadu, the police's job is to stop the many undercover or "private" fights regularly taking place in villages around Madurai, not to give them legitimacy as they did here. But then again, this particular public ram fight was somewhat legal: Its organizers had received a long-awaited, one-time clearance from a son of the Tamil chief minister who lives in Madurai.

The event was well organized. It began on time. The "announcer" on the loudspeaker did a good job introducing the rams' owners and the animals themselves (they had names), acknowledging the sponsors, instructing everyone to abide by the referee's decision, and thanking everyone for being there, including me, the foreigner. The spectators behaved themselves, and no violent incidents marred the proceedings. No one can say how stupid I was to be there alone, among approximately 5,000 men, many of whom were inebriated.

When I watch a sporting event I am so absent, so out of touch, that I am not even marking time. Although I do not "get" sports, it did not take me very long to grasp the gist of the proceedings, which consisted in encouraging ("enraging" is how the Animal Welfare Board might put it[10]) two rams, male sheep, of approximately the same age to butt into each other within the confines of a ground about the size of a small local soccer pitch. On that particular day, perhaps as many as fifty pairs of rams took turns sparring, while the men (the "announcer" and spectators alike) kept score, collectively counting the number of times the animals collided. The sounds of their recitation of "1," "2," "3" and so on, of their whistling ("men shrill because they are happy"), and of the clashing horns were all I could hear. There was no blood, little violence, and as far as I could tell the animals were not injured, even when a ram used enough force to knock its opponent down.

Some animals were more aggressive and confrontational than others. Those who were not disposed to fight were quickly thrown out. Only five or six pairs, I reckon, fought until the men called out "75," the number that effectively marks a tie. The "brave" rams that made it to this number were held in high honor, and the "event manager" rewarded their owners with an offering of a towel (an honorary gift). But most of the time the contest was declared over when a ram walked away, resisting its handler's entreaties and pressure to charge again.

Partly because Clifford Geertz's interpretative methodology opposes any sensory, intuitive grasp of another culture, I stand by his "guiding principle" that "societies, like lives, contain their own interpretations. One has only to learn how to gain access to them" (1973: 453). But in this case, I did not need to engage in "thick description" to know what the Tamil ram fight was "saying." Sprinkled with pink-, red-, and yellow-colored powders and shaved at the shoulders so that they gained a mane and looked like miniature bison, the rams were theatrical symbols of two kinds of masculinity: brave and combative or weak and diffident. That much was clear. And the performance that separated the macho rams from the cowards offered a glimpse of what men admired and valued most: bullying an adversary into defeat. The owners of the victorious rams were rewarded with the Tamil equivalent of a trophy, namely a big brass vessel. The basic message the ram fight imparted was that the powerful man who fights with all his might is worthy of honors; the weak man who retreats is disgraced.

The themes this animal competition brought forth also underlie the dramas of polarity and rivalry alluded to above. Recall how the right marriages set apart the brothers and sisters who marry their children together, granting them the privilege of treating themselves and their respective possessions as "mine." Such entitlement is a real reprieve in a society in which higher rank and lower rank define the boundaries and means of existence (harvest, women's puberty, marriage), as well as relationships among people outside the kin group. This is why husbands and wives and siblings with no particular matrimonial right fight like the rams in the man-made ring. They too want to marry the right way, which is neither beneath nor above; in the latter case they would feel inferior to sons- or daughters-in-law's families (*campanti*). There is honor in their bullying a matrimonial rival, be it a spouse or a sibling, into retreat, but more in victory.

The Legitimacy of Violence

In Tamil Nadu it is psychologically and socially very painful to lose any kind of contest. But the worst thing is to have one's rights and due rewards taken away by someone else. This especially applies to the kind of quasi-legal matrimonial rights (*muṟai*) discussed throughout this chapter.

Because these rights are embedded in an ethics of parity ("what you have is mine"), their violation is tantamount to a rejection of equality. In 1972, Brenda Beck also noted that, when a marriage agreement is broken,

> It will invariably be interpreted as expressing a feeling of superiority on the part of one sibling relative to the other, and as arising from a situation that is considered not to have existed when they were children, but rather to have developed as a result of economic disparity in later life. (1972: 252)

Her further observation, that such a refusal of what is right is likely to generate "extreme bitterness and ill will . . . between brother and sister" (1972: 252), is also consistent with my field experience. I was told that when one side tries to get out of a "right" marriage, the folks on the other side feel deeply injured and seriously snubbed.

It is therefore tricky to get out of a marriage that is backed by the customary law of marriage rights and duties. But because both sides are seldom equally enthusiastic about the match, it does happen. Linda May is correct to state that the family who want out of an obligation "cannot bluntly refuse" (1986: 241). Instead, they "propose a delay" (1986: 245), giving the excuse that their child wants to finish college before marrying, or that they cannot afford wedding expenses at the moment, or that a death has just happened (1986: 241–249). If such a ploy does not work, they may offer a substitute (a younger sibling or a classificatory equal) for the "right" child, or pay a "penalty" (*tanṭam*), a legal term the use of which suggests that breaking the marriage law is tantamount to a crime.[11] But money cannot always undo the moral damage caused by a refusal to honor a matrimonial right. The party whose expectations have been thwarted may resort to violence, as Dumont also noted among the Kaḷḷars, or "set fire to the house of the person who has perhaps preferred a profitable marriage to the one prescribed by custom" (1986: 209).[12]

Here we need to appreciate that the Tamil word for violence, *vāṉmuṟai*, is a compound of the word *muṟai*. This compound, which literally translates as "extreme" (*vāṉ*) "action" (*muṟai*), suggests that at times force is needed to enforce the social rules (*muṟai*). That much is corroborated in reports that in the past a spurned Kaḷḷar man could win his right girl by lifting the heaviest rock, or throwing it the longest distance, or by taming bulls during the *callikaṭṭu* season (January). A Kaḷḷar story suggests that the exercise of force can also serve as a legitimate means of punishing families who do not honor kinship rights.

I am referring here to the story of the "Beautiful Tēvar," which the drunken villagers of Corikkāmpaṭṭi so dramatically recounted for my benefit (see the introduction to the last chapter). In their version, a sister refuses to marry her daughter Oyyammāḷ to her brother's son, "Beautiful Tēvar." The brother, the father of the spurned boy, takes the "extreme action" of killing his sister, and this despite the fact that the marriage here is not exactly "right" (the Kaḷḷar rule is for a boy to marry on his mother's side).[13]

In the version recorded by Ulrike Niklas in 2000, the rest of the story goes as I paraphrase below:

> In order to console his daughter [of her mother's murder], her widowed father gives her seven bull calves, which Oyyammāḷ brings up and trains for a bull baiting festival. One day Oyyammāḷ announces she will marry the one who will subdue her seven bulls in her village's bull-taming contest. "Beautiful

> Tēvar" (the boy she was supposed to marry) comes forth and triumphs over the first six bulls. The hero also subdues the seventh bull but during that last fight he is mortally wounded. He marries Oyyammal only to die after the wedding. (2000: 14)

Niklas's transcript reads as a story of power and retribution. The hero's "extreme action" here is to marry his girl before dying so that she becomes a widow, a very undesirable fate for an Indian woman. In the version I recorded in the village of Corikkāmpaṭṭi, the hero exacts a harsher sentence, arranging for his loyal untouchable servant to marry Oyyammāḷ before succumbing to his wounds. Now she and her family become outcasts.

Nowadays the law has become the weapon of choice against those who do not honor kinship rights. One would expect that, when conflicts arise over matrimonial rights, families living in rural areas would turn to the *panchayat*, which remains an ordinary forum for the settlement of a wide range of disputes among dominant castes in Tamil villages. But arbitration—what the customary law of the *panchayat* delivers—is, more often than not, not what is wanted. Instead, families turn to the modern judicial system inspired by the British model, precisely so as to escape resolution altogether. They want the satisfaction of knowing that the suit will drag on in the overloaded Tamil courts, thereby incriminating their "defendants" for years. The methods of, and contexts for, inflicting "extreme action" have changed, but the cultural intent has remained constant. The goal, as the following case study also suggests, is to do violence.

Virumandi and His Sisters

A small Kaḷḷar farmer with a passion for rams, which he raised on the side so as to augment his earnings, Virumandi was what the Tamils call a "spoilt boy" (*cella piḷḷai*)—an epithet used for men like him who are the only sons in a family of many daughters. When I met him, however, Virumandi did not think of himself as particularly lucky. Having no right girl (his maternal uncle had died before bearing a child), he had married an "outside" woman whom neither his mother nor his four sisters liked. "Before my marriage I enjoyed my life," he related, "but since it has been a struggle every day." The conflicts with his siblings were such that his unkempt and extremely thin wife had twice attempted to commit suicide.

Being the only son, Virumandi expected "to do the right thing" with his eldest sister. Everyone, in fact, trusted his first daughter to marry his eldest sister's first son, but the young man instead eloped with another girl. Angry, Virumandi married his daughter "on the other side," that is on his wife's side, without even consulting his sisters. It was Virumandi who taught me that, "out of affection, we Kaḷḷar men marry in our sisters' houses. And out of anger we don't."

His sisters were appalled, especially the eldest, who felt that she had been deprived of her *urimai* to arrange her brother's daughter's marriage. She kept her feelings to herself, but Virumandi knew she was angry. When, some time later, his third sister proposed to marry her daughter to his son, who was then fifteen, my Kaḷḷar friend was not excited. "This sister is allied with the first," he said in lieu of an explanation.

Because this proposal was not legally binding, he was under no obligation to accept. But the Tamils, Linda May is correct to state, "go to enormous lengths . . . to avoid saying 'no'" (1986: 228). A direct refusal to a marriage request, especially, is most inappropriate because, as we have already seen, it can be interpreted as a sign of arrogance. So, instead of flatly turning his third sister down, Virumandi ducked and dodged. "Right now, I have no money for a marriage," he pleaded, "I'll give you an answer in the month of Tai." Having no intention of getting back to his sister, he nonetheless played up to her, as if he could be persuaded to accept her request.

Two months later I was visiting Virumandi's house when the police arrived, followed by curious neighbors. From the threshold an officer read out the complaint against Virumandi lodged by his three sisters: He was not feeding their parents. "This isn't true," protested Virumandi, "I give them ten sacks of paddy and 10,000 rupees a year." The policeman shut him up, summoning him to report to the station the next day.

When I returned a few days later, Virumandi was facing a lawsuit for something he understood very well. He was confronted not merely by kin in the search for a compromise or reparation, but by an intimate enemy bent on bullying him. From his perspective, his sisters were now locked into a legal process meant to crush him for his refusal to marry their children to each other. As he put it, "I was ready to give my girl to them but not my son. Now my siblings have turned my parents against me and brought a case against me. It may take us twenty-five years to resolve this deeply adversarial situation.

Every day I get up in fear of what these people will say or do to me. I just want to live in peace."

It is through such cases of conflict that we can most clearly observe that the persons who hold matrimonial rights see their privilege as completely authoritative—*mu̱rai*, as the Tamils say. Their sense of matrimonial entitlement is such that it is difficult for me to corroborate the French interpretation of preferential cross-cousin marriages. Rather than exchange, the Tamil right marriages are conceived as control, even ownership, of the bride and groom—in fact, as the precise opposite of exchange. As one of my informants put it, "[Matrimonial] *urimai* is a special kind of power: the power to claim you as my spouse and my in-laws. I don't have to ask. I can just help myself. You're already mine. I was born to have you. It's in my DNA, my natural right." The theory at work here is that, in effect, my sibling is not *giving* me his or her child, that son or daughter is *already mine*. Even if, as was the case for Virumandi's sister, my son elopes with another girl, I still have the right to arrange a marriage for his "right" girl. Such a basic and hardly negotiable prerogative, we have seen in this chapter, makes for relationships that are not merely taken for granted but potentially violent. "Extreme force," I will now show, is not the only reaction to the loss of one's matrimonial right.

3

THE REMAINDERS OF RIGHT MARRIAGES

Behind every man's demise there's a woman.
—Mayandi, interviewed in Madurai

That evening, the South Zone Progressive Artists Association
and the Tamil Nadu Cinema Technicians Union
co-hosted a reception for the Czech visitors . . .
"Very good film, very good film!" said the Czech leader.
Ram Singh accepted the compliment wholeheartedly.
"Only the tragic element was a bit overstressed," the Czech added . . .
"Life is but a tragedy," Ram Singh said.
"We were invaded by the Nazis, Millions of people were massacred.
Still there seems to be more tragedy in your stories than in ours."
Thiraviam stood there obviously distressed, cursing
himself for starting the conversation.
The Czech had the last word. "I have seen three Indian
films. Your heroes seem overly effeminate. The actor in
your film, in particular, weeps for everything."
—In Star-Crossed by Ashokamitran (2007: 76) (in Tamil 1969)

I obtained much of the "data" I have presented so far with the standard methodological tool kit available to ethnographers: interviews, surveys, the extended case method, recording conversations in both formal and informal settings, observing routine activities, and so on. But as indicated in the Introduction, my work in Tamil Nadu also included a regular morning seminar with people who enjoyed theorizing about Tamil kinship.

For the first few months I assumed that two men who showed up on a regular basis, taking the time (on occasion a very long time) to walk me through the complexities of marriage with *contam*, did so out of a sense of urgency or pride. Certainly both men, who hailed from the Tēvar caste (one from the Kaḷḷar subcaste, the other from the Maṟavar), deplored the impending loss of collective knowledge about "right marriages," and they agreed that only the Tēvars married "correctly." The other castes had "no rule" (*muṟai illai*) and therefore were less "civilized"; for, as we have seen, in the conception of marriage rules also lie ethical representations of society and justice. But one never knows for sure what leads people to "inform" an anthropologist about custom, as we used to say, or to "consult" in our work, as we now more often put it. Pride? Nostalgia? Money? Boredom? In the case of these two men it was more personal than that.

We are familiar with the notion that all writing is autobiographical to a certain extent. Some writers are actually very clear about the fact that their work is closely related to their own lives. The same thing can be said of ethnography. More often than not, anthropologists choose a project because it resonates with their lives, if only in a largely covert way (as is my own case). But the people who assist us also bring a strong autobiographical component to the work, as well as desires, anxieties, and intentions of their own. At the very least they have some story that pertains to the ethnographic topic. In the case of the two men I profile in this chapter, their personal story was, for each, a sad one—both had been denied their "right" to experience the very meanings and feelings they were helping me to understand.

To understand why these men did not marry the "right" way, we have to shift the ethnographic focus from the realm of normative rules to how they play out in actual lives. Instead of viewing preferential marriage, including Kaḷḷar preferential marriage, as a function and expression of ideal principles and formal rules, we need to see it in terms of its practice. This move takes us to Pierre Bourdieu's theory of social action, especially his notion that "social agents, in archaic societies as well as in ours, are not automata regulated like clocks, in accordance with laws which they do not understand" (1990: 9). Rather, they act according to the particulars and the demands of the various situations in which they find themselves.[1]

Bourdieu's attempt to theorize marriage not from the point of view of the "rules" but from the perspective of the actor and his or her "strategies" is critical to an understanding of the unions described in this book in general and in this chapter in particular. Strategies, in Bourdieu's sense, result from a sense of the "game" that is being played, and aim to reach the best deal possible (1977: 58). In fact, my consultants spoke of marriage in these very terms of "play" or "sport" (*viḷaiyāṭṭu*). But for them the marriage "game" was dangerous, even deadly. Bourdieu's theorization of practice (with its reference to, or rather divergence from, rules) needs to be refined to incorporate this sense of risk and threat.[2] In fact, the picture of "play" projected by my consultants was not merely darker than that suggested by the French sociologist but at odds with his way of theorizing the actor as an agential subject. To be sure, Tamil matrimonial rules do not determine marriage practices, but a few players—players much more powerful than others—do control the arrangement of marriages. Although chance, and bad luck in particular, is also a factor in matrimonial outcomes, the game is one of power—not merely of agency and ingenuity.

The two men who taught me what it is like to play and lose these Tamil games did not immediately volunteer their personal experiences. They inevitably drew examples from their family histories in our discussions, but at first their references were to the point, instructive, not particularly revealing of subjective thoughts or feelings. Because we were in a seminar-like situation I did not probe; when I teach in the United States I do not investigate my students' lives (though perhaps in this case it was because here I was the student). In hindsight I can see that from the beginning both men were hinting that Tamils marry the "right" way not merely out of the imperative to play by the marriage rules. They *also* come to expect, feel entitled to, perhaps even desire the "right" union. But it was only much later on, when Mayandi and Neelam opened up, revealing stories about themselves, that I came to understand how much Tamil preferential marriages set the frame, or context and constraint, for personal expectations and "right" dispositions. What Mayandi and Neelam taught me is that when the "right" marriage does not take place, lives can be spent in regret over the missed opportunity.

Mayandi

The first man who spoke to me about all this was a fifty-year-old Pramalai Kaḷḷar. With a spot of red *kumkum* between his eyebrows, a fantastic laugh that moved around and around like a wheel, a hoarse voice, and a regular cough that opened his gap-toothed mouth, Mayandi demolished the stereotypes that colonial and postcolonial scholars alike have perpetuated of his subcaste. Not that he denied that his people were "rough and tough" (*karaṭu muraṭu*) (also see Pandian 2009: 36). Quite to the contrary, Mayandi embraced such epithets, sporting them as badges of honor. But he anchored them in a strongly assertive rhetoric of male honor, focused by power, strength, autonomy, and (above all) law (*muṟai*) and rights (*urimai*). Moreover, much like the Bedouin men in the Western Desert of Egypt profiled in Lila Abu-Lughod's ethnography (1986), he spoke another language as well, which has no place in his caste's honor code: a private, oblique poetry of personal feelings centering around grievance, dependence, weakness, and loss.

Mayandi lived in a village that was once labeled "criminal" by the British. Of the 15,000 or so people living there now, only old women with parched skin and lobes stretched out by heavy gold pendants evoked images of that long-ago, almost mythic time; they served as living and fragile monuments of the Kaḷḷar past—not that the village was emptied of "historical" content. But the historical seemed replete with present significance as the daily routine of residents such as Mayandi spanned multiple political economies.

The year I met Mayandi, he woke up every morning at six to water his one acre of paddy-cultivated land. His yearly agricultural net returns (from selling forty bags of field rice in each of two harvests, at 400 rupees a bag) only amounted to 16,000 rupees (roughly $400) because, as he often lamented, half of his total gross went to purchase seeds, fertilizers, insecticides, and other such essentials. His income was far less than the 5,000 rupees a month his family needed to live on, and so his wife worked at a local brick factory whenever her health permitted it, stacking and moving burned bricks from the kilns into trucks for 80 rupees a day. Mayandi himself had other jobs, watering groves of coconut trees or repairing motor irrigation pumps here and there, for which he was paid in leaves and fruits that he sold at a local market. Usually, after his early morning work in the fields, he would come home, take his children to school and, after his first meal of the day, either return to his paddy cultivation or labor for other farmers.

Sometimes he came to work with us instead, and whenever he showed up at my rented house, the general atmosphere was lively and we (the cook, her daughter, my assistant, and whoever else was there) knew we were in for some laughter, because Mayandi loved to joke. "If you laugh," he would say, "you cure your troubles." His sense of humor verged on the scatological and nearly amounted to bad taste, but he giggled so much that it was impossible not to laugh with him. He recounted, for example, how back in the days of the British a white man once used a five-rupee note as toilet paper. The punch line did not make fun of this chap or white guys in general, but of the poor Kaḷḷar fellow who waited to pocket the filthy bill. Mayandi loved making fun of himself and his community.

His sense of humor brought a special touch to my research, highlighting, or caricaturing even, the cruelties of Tamil matrimonial requirements. Mayandi would mimic, for instance, the way young Tamil women might joke about a "right" boy who is not so right looking: "Eh, Runny Nose has come to see you," he pretended to warn an imaginary girl friend, "Egg Shell Eyes is at your door," "Small Ears Boy is on his way." From Mayandi I learned that, far from being a way to sweeten the marriage law, or of providing comic relief in the face of its unbending requirements, humor stubbornly highlighted its cruelties, because the source of humor here is not joy and fun. The truth is that the groom cannot possibly be "right." The truth is that a girl is trapped by an obligation to marry a runny nose, a pair of protruding eyes, or small ears. The truth is that what is prescribed so formally cannot be the object of desire. This is no joke.

Mayandi had married his elder sister's daughter "to further the relationship," as he told me, which is one explanation for marrying a niece in Tamil Nadu. But much later on, out of the blue (or so it seemed) I learned that his explanation completely obscured the uniqueness of this particular marriage. As it turned out, Mayandi's marriage had been arranged as a last resort.

From an early age, Mayandi had been destined to marry his maternal uncle's only daughter, as is the rule among the Kaḷḷars. For reasons he recounted in detail, however, this marriage did not take place, and Mayandi, who loved his "right" girl, was crushed. For the next twenty years he refused to marry, and only when his elder sister's daughter came of age did he relent, finally yielding to his *akkā*'s request to "join."

The circumstances that prevented him from "doing the right thing" remind us that the Kaḷḷars, or some at least, do live violent lives. When Mayandi came of an age to marry, his maternal uncle was charged with murder after a fatal altercation with his father's elder brother's wife. After the woman's family destroyed the man's house and fields in retaliation, his own homeless and needy wife and daughter moved in with relatives in Madurai, where they earned a little money by selling home-cooked snacks. The point for Mayandi was that while his maternal uncle was in jail, his "right" girl vanished in the city.

My Kaḷḷar friend managed to locate her, living in a small alley of the temple town. He began visiting her new house regularly, each time sporting the one and only new shirt he owned and bringing a small bundle of jasmine flowers. I am not sure Mayandi actually ever saw his girl, for in all of his reminiscences she remained out of sight. But the two found ways to communicate. Once on the way to see her he accidently smeared his new sandals with cow dung. While he was talking to her mother, she went out through the back door, picked up his sandals from the front threshold, and washed them off. Her devotion touched Mayandi so much that to this day he does not wear sandals. On another occasion, she talked to Mayandi from behind a closed door. "I'm alone," he recalled her lamenting, "I don't have a brother."

Mayandi's widowed mother repeatedly proposed marriage only to hear the girl's mother reply, "My husband will soon be out of jail; let's wait for his release." Eventually the two women (Mayandi's mother and her brother's wife) got into a fight. They had a "prestige problem," Mayandi said, using an expression commonly used by the Tamils when they want to convey that someone feels insulted because someone else is not respecting the formal rules of respect that obtain between their particular categories of relation. In this case, the two women were not merely related as sisters-in-law, a difficult relation as it is. Mayandi's mother's brother's wife was also Mayandi's father's "right girl."[3] In any case, this woman decided to marry her daughter to her brother's son (thereby reversing the Kaḷḷar matrimonial rule). Mayandi's family made a scene; they had the *urimai*, but, as my Kaḷḷar friend said, "My mother didn't really want me to marry that girl."

Mayandi still remembered the day his *poṇṇu* got engaged. It was January 26, 1980. "In the morning," he recalled, "I heard a song on the radio that was meant for men like me who fail in love." Without prompting, he sang *Pallakku Vaanga Ponen* into my tape recorder—a song first performed by MGR (a movie actor who also served as the chief minister of Tamil Nadu for three successive terms) in the 1964 film *Panakkara Kudumbam*:

> I went to buy a palanquin for the procession. I came back alone in the middle of the day.
> I went to buy jasmine for my bride. The flowers had to be thrown on the sand.
> I went to build the marriage stage. There was no auspiciousness.
> I went to meet the bride. There was no red powder.
> I lived in love. There was no semblance of reality.
> I lived in love. There was no possibility.
> The wedding was not in our hands. What a shame!

Back on that January day in 1980, Mayandi sang that song to himself a few times. Then he went to lie down on a tiny bridge, over which the road to his village passed, and cried. Having crossed this bridge a few times myself, I can vouch that it does not make a safe bed, being no more than four feet long and two feet wide, over a canal ten feet deep, but Mayandi still delights in lying there at night.

Later, when he could neither sleep nor eat, he began writing down lyrics. "Sadness is the source of poetry," he said as he handed me the thick notebook in which he wrote his lyrics. A simple line caught my eyes: "Sorrow is heaven." He explained: "I couldn't talk to anyone about my pain. People would have spoilt my name, so I shut up and kept my sorrow all to myself." What I understood Mayandi to be saying was that paradoxically it was in silence that he found his personal voice as a poet. Unable to talk, he began anthologizing his love, and over time his infatuation for the girl, his desire for her and to be with her, became indistinguishable from his passion for poetry.

For the next twenty years Mayandi refused to marry. Because his younger brother had no children, the family pressured him to wed his elder sister's daughter, which he finally did in 2000. He was then fifty and she thirty-five. "Because my wife is fifteen years my junior," he laughed, "I call her a 'martyr.'" They have a boy aged fifteen and a girl aged eleven. "I'd like to have more children," Mayandi volunteered, "but I can't afford to bring them up."

As for his "right girl," he has not seen her since 1980. Although her husband's village is located only four kilometers away from where Mayandi lives, he has never visited. "I don't want to see her as someone else's wife," he said in lieu of explanation, "it's not our culture." One month before I left the field, the woman's mother died, and Mayandi (in capacity of affine) was expected at her funeral. His mother protested: "She was my brother's wife, and I'm not going. Why should you go?"

Neelam

I have known the man whom I call Neelam since the late 1980s. Back then I had no idea that he had been involved in a crime in his teens and served time in a home for juvenile delinquents. I did not even know he was in a bad marriage, for whenever I visited his house his wife, who was short and rather round, and their two children greeted me cheerfully. When I saw him again in 2007 Neelam had not changed very much physically. To be sure, he had puffed up a little and his hair was turning gray, but there were no visible signs of the losses he had recently endured. People warned me that since the death of both his wife and his son he was drinking. But our reacquaintance generated a current of warm feeling—perhaps a feeling of gratitude for the chance to meet again; beyond this, amazement for that opportunity. I hired him on the spot, hoping that work would distract him from his sorrow.

Neelam is a member of the powerful and numerous Maṟavar caste, which is scattered over the southern districts of Tamil Nadu. The British often compared the Maṟavars to the Kaḷḷars, with whom they are indeed connected.[4] Both castes are descendants of warriors, both castes gave the British much trouble in the early phase of the colonial period, and both are named after dubious occupations. Kaḷḷar, the reader will recall, means "thieves"; as for Maṟavar, Edgar Thurston long ago surmised, their "name may be connected with the word *maṟam*, which means killing, ferocity, bravery and the like, [and] clearly [relates] to their unpleasant profession, that of robbing and slaying their neighbours" (Thurston and Rangachari 1987, Vol V: 23). Unlike the Kaḷḷars, however, the Maṟavars never became "notified" as a "criminal caste," and by the late nineteenth century Thurston noted that they "are now much the same as other *ryots* (cultivators), though perhaps somewhat more bold and lawless" (Thurston and Rangachari 1987, Vol. V: 23). Fifty years later, Dumont observed that the Maṟavars were mostly "agriculturalists" (1983: 40) and that "certain families [at least in Tinnevelly and Madurai] have become wealthy" (1983: 58).

The Maṟavars, however, have their own distinctive kinship organization (Thurston and Rangachari 1987, Vol. V: 32–47; Dumont 1983: 54–64). I should write "kinship systems" in the plural, for there are seven major subdivisions among the Maṟavars, and each has its own variety of kinship. Yet, all the Maṟavar groups share a preference for what anthropologists call patrilateral "cross-cousin" marriage, though it ranges from outright obligation in some localities to indifference in others (Dumont 1983: 58). This means that when the marriage rule (*muṟai*) is enforced, as is still the case in many subcastes, a young man's "right" girl is not his maternal uncle's daughter (as is the case among the Kaḷḷars) but his father's sister daughter. Dumont noted that "all [Maṟavar] groups also condemn the uncle–niece marriage" (1983: 54). But according to Neelam this was not true of his subcaste, and, in fact, he himself regarded his own elder sister's daughter, as the woman he had the right to marry, although, for reasons he recounted, she never became his wife.

Neelam was born on May 1 in either 1955 or 1957. He is not sure because, as he explained, "Back then they didn't keep records; there were too many children." His date of birth, however, is not how he began the story he wanted me to hear. Of his serious intent there is no doubt, as he bathed, shaved, and dressed for the occasion and was more solemn than usual. As he spoke, he kept checking the green light on the digital recorder lying on the table before us. He insisted on telling his story, even when I protested in the end that the process was too painful for both him and me.

What Neelam first said was that he was a junior brother, and his tale of his upbringing, in a village located about 100 kilometers away from Madurai, can be heard as proof that in a society that ascribes social rank at birth you cannot do very much to change your status. You may have the right mind and body; you may be talented; but if you are born after the others you have fewer rights and privileges. What follows here is my slightly edited and abridged transcript of his biography. While he narrated himself, I was not an intrusive listener, breaking in to ask for explanations, and yet I was not absent either:

> My grandfather had two wives. My father was the firstborn child; he had twelve brothers and five wives. His first three wives left and remarried. Why did they leave? My father was a bad man, a womanizer. Other than that he was a good fellow. Because he was the eldest, people respected him. But again and again he had affairs. The fourth wife didn't like it either. After she gave birth to three children, she committed suicide [she jumped into a well and drowned]. For many years afterward my father didn't remarry. He didn't need to; he had lovers [*vaippāṭṭi*] in every village.
>
> It was only after his daughter [from the fourth wife] bore her first child that my father married my mother. She was between twelve and fifteen and he fifty. I'm the firstborn of this [fifth] wife. There were five children; three died. Now we're five [here Neelam includes the fourth wife's three children, two of whom are still alive].
>
> In my village we could study up to fifth standard. After that we had to walk to a school located about five kilometers away. Around the time I reached ninth standard, it didn't rain for two to three years, and we went hungry. We couldn't do anything. It was very difficult to go by foot to school without food. This was true for everybody. Those days there were no [free] meals at school. We ate only once a day, at night, just a small amount of porridge made from millet or barley. Every morning we woke up hungry, but there was no food. On the way to school, we'd steal vegetables from nearby agricultural fields. We ate raw onions and garlic that burned our stomachs; that's how famished we were. We plucked raw bananas, and the sap blistered our lips. We broke raw papayas with a stone, and the unripe flesh inside caused the inside of our mouths to swell. It was only years later, when I came to Madurai, that I saw what a ripe papaya looks like. Back then we were too hungry to wait for the

fruit to turn yellow. When we couldn't steal, we ate the root of a plant that looks like aloe vera. It's too bitter to eat raw; you have to cook it with water and tamarind. Even boiled, it irritated our stomachs, but we ate it all the same. On Saturday and Sunday we'd collect firewood and sell it in a village located six or seven kilometers away. We didn't get money for it, we got rice paddy; we had no use for money.

Because he was the village leader [*nāṭṭaṇmaikkārar*], my father didn't work in the fields. He was a big man, so he didn't work. He sent his wife and children to labor in the fields instead. No sooner did we reach the age of fifteen than he sent us to slave for others. I intensely hated my father. I was his last wife's son and got no respect. I was humiliated by the fact that my father had remarried. I very much resented my position (as son of the last wife). That's why I hated him. I didn't quarrel with him, but I hated him. In the village people didn't make distinctions between us (the children of the fourth and fifth wives). We were close, and the relationship with my brothers and sisters was very thick. But my father's siblings [twelve altogether] treated my elder brother [the fourth wife's first son] better than me. They'd talk to him a long time, only to ignore me. They'd pour him a full tumbler of coffee, but half that much for me. They had a lot of affection for him, none for me. It was hard; it was difficult for me.

At some point in time the drought was so bad that we went to live in the village of my mother's mother's younger sister, where we all worked hard as coolies in the fields. When the rain came back, we returned to my father's village. Life was hard; a little millet at night is all we'd get to eat.

Then something happened that was to change my life. I must have been around sixteen or seventeen. One day, around noon, two strangers from a [nearby] town came to rest in the shade of the village temple where I used to hang out. They were waiting for the bus that wasn't scheduled for another two or three hours. They were nice to look at. All I had was one shirt and one waistcloth, which I'd wash everyday and put back on still wet. So when I saw these two men dressed in white dhotis and white shirts, my first thought was, "They look like superior people [*uyar makkaḷ*]." And when they talked to me I felt great. I felt superior; I felt like an important person. I was happy. They asked me "Where can we get some water?" and I, like an idiot, took them to my *māmā*'s [maternal uncle's] house.

These men were thieves. But back then we didn't know they had come to rob us; we didn't know anything about them. After they freshened up, they asked my *māmā*, "Why are you living like this, in such poverty?" We didn't know what to say and looked away at the only things we had, a few earthen pots lined up on the floor. "We have printed counterfeit currency," they added, "if we give you that money, you too could have a comfortable life. You too could take an oil bath; you too could wear a nice shirt." I thought, "Yes, perhaps I could have these things too." I wanted to. So I asked, "When can we meet again?" They told us to visit them the next day.

The morning after, my *māmā* [who was about ten years older than Neelam] and I went to town to meet them. These two men were about to trick us, but when I saw them I felt happy. All I could think was, "Such great people are waiting for us." They treated us to *idlis* and *dosas* and made us a business proposition. "Give us a little money," they offered, "and we'll double it." I didn't feel it was wrong to associate with them. I was happy. I'd get to dress well. That's all I could think about. We were to have the money ready a week later.

I still remembered the day they showed up in a taxi. We had asked them to come at night when everybody sleeps because we didn't want anyone to know we were about to get rich. They waited for us outside the village by the cremation grounds. My *māmā* gave them 1,000 rupees, and they were to return 2,000 rupees. They didn't. Instead they fabricated kinship ties with us. "Do you know such and such person in such and such village?" When we said we did, they inevitably added, "In this case we're related." They called my *māmā* "*māmā*," and so I became their "*tampi*" ["younger brother"]. Giving them money was the right thing to do, they assured us. We were *contam* [kin]!

They couldn't pay us the 2,000 rupees because, they explained, the ink wasn't dried on the counterfeit bills. Instead they asked for 4,000 rupees, promising to return 10,000. Another day they treated us to *parottas* [flat bread] and arrack [distilled alcohol]. I was excited; I loved the good life they gave us. One afternoon they took us to the cinema. When the film was over, they told my *māmā*: "The money isn't ready. Go home, we'll keep the boy with us, he'll bring you the money tomorrow." I welcomed the arrangement. I had nothing else to do then except sleep in the village temple.

These men were bad yet somehow I got entangled with them and became their con man [*aṭikaḷ*]. But back then I didn't understand the situation I was getting into.

Had it not rained the day I was supposed to go home, the story would end here. I'd have escaped the situation, but water [the rain] came down hard. My two new friends hired a taxi. "It's pouring," they said, "We'll drop you at the bus stand." This ride was my bad luck [*keṭṭa nēram*]. They took me to one of their agents, along the way stealing 300 rupees from an acquaintance. By the time we reached our final destination, a village off the main road, it was dark, and we were high on ganga and alcohol. The men tried to persuade their agent that the car was full of counterfeit money. The man, a tough and rowdy Naicker, ran to steal the cash. The driver tried to pull away but lost control of the steering wheel, and the car went rolling down the hill. Before hitting a tree, it knocked down the Naicker who feel on the ground. When the driver backed up, he ran over him. The Naicker died on the spot. I shouted: "*Ayyō*! You've killed him!" and fainted.

The driver was caught, and he identified us. I was arrested and sent to Ottachanam jail, not far from where the accident took place [between Palani and Dindigul]. The police beat me. I was only sixteen and locked up with traders of illicit liquor who kept saying that I'd die in jail. I was so scared. But luckily the subinspector was a Maṟavar like me. He listened to my story, and because there was a backload of cases in this jail he transferred me to Madurai where a month later I was sentenced to seven years for the "accident." Because I was young, I was sent to a juvenile institution. And because of my good behavior I served only two years and nine months.

At first the jail in Pudukottai reminded me of a school, for the boys there were my age. But this was no regular school. Each inmate had a duty, a chore, and a leader. My job was to clean the ward, and my leader was a short tough boy from Madras who swore all the time. His cussing was very offensive to a simple boy like me. I had never heard this kind of language before. I fought with him until I understood the boy spoke like this to everyone. It was just his Madras slang.

One of the vocational teachers, a tailor from a place not too far from my village, took me on as an apprentice. He wanted me to have a job in life. I wanted to join the jail band, but he argued, "What's the use of learning this music? It won't help you later." I learned his trade and became a supervisor in his shop. I received good conduct certificates and obtained a sentence reduction.

I was about twenty when I was released. I wanted to go back to my village, but my elder brother didn't want me to. He was afraid I'd return to my old ways, so he leased some land in one of our sisters' villages where I was to grow vegetables. On my way to buy pesticide or sell produce from the leased land, I'd visit him, for back then my brother worked as a guard in the Madurai agricultural office. One day his boss asked me to watch the house he was building, and when the construction was over he found me a job as watchman of a new apartment complex. I learned to wear a shirt and pants and shoes. I became a city boy.

Now I was around twenty-five, and my relatives began to speak of marriage. Ten years before they had decided that I'd marry my elder sister's daughter [*akkā poṇṇu*]. That was my right [*urimai*]. The girl liked me, and I liked her. But my sister refused to arrange the marriage. Why? Because I had gone to jail. That's what she said, but she had never wanted this marriage in the first place. I was the last wife's son. It is a "minus point" to be the issue of the last wife; you're lower than them [the previous wife's children]. In order to marry this girl, I needed my older brother's support. But he wasn't about to help, for his wife wanted to marry her [the girl] to our father's younger brother's son. This wasn't a good idea; the boy didn't have a good job, but he was like a son to my elder brother's wife [this woman and Neelam's paternal uncle's wife were sisters, and a Tamil woman treats her sister's child like her own].

My brother let me down. Everybody let me down. They'd say, "Now that you live in Madurai, it won't be difficult to find you a bride. No one knows about your past there." But they weren't looking. They did nothing.

Around that time I became friends with a man who trained dogs at a police station near my workplace. One day he asked me to marry his sister's daughter, who lived in Kerala. I explained that it wasn't up to me to find my own bride. It was my parents' and elder siblings' duty to arrange my marriage. But my family wasn't looking, and my new friend insisted, so I went off to Kerala. A few days later he invited the girl and her mother to Madurai. It would have been very rude to ignore his call, so I asked my family to visit them with me. On the way back to our village I made it very clear that I wasn't interested. My parents agreed: The girl was too short. But my brother said he had given his word to the policeman. I had to marry her.

This was when my elder sister changed her mind; I could marry her daughter after all. But my brother insisted: "It's too late; the date of the ceremony has already been fixed." My sister got angry. Who were we to deprive her of her *urimai*? She had first "right" on me. How dare we insult her like this? She also threatened. If I were to marry this *an̲n̲iyam*, she'd neither attend the ceremony nor bring the *tāli* [a woman's marriage necklace—elder sisters usually do this]. But my brother ignored her, saying she had made nothing but trouble from the beginning.

He began giving the impression that I was marrying on my own. He became less involved in the preparations, keeping his distance from me. If he wasn't arranging my marriage, our sister couldn't be mad at him. He told me, "I'll pay for the ceremony, but I won't come." His words hurt me very much. They still hurt me today.

I got married in 1985 at the Madurai Māriammā temple. My sister didn't show up. My parents didn't show up. My brother came late, and the impression everyone got was that ours was a love marriage. After the ceremony my wife and I went to her house in Kerala for three days [as is customary]. We should have brought back three vessels filled with snacks (*cīr*). But where was I supposed to take *cīr*? Not to my parents' house, not to my brother's house. My new in-laws begged me: "For the sake of our honor, take something; take a small vessel of sweets and some small gifts!" Families who give nothing to the groom lose respect.

When we got back from Kerala, my family didn't receive us properly. They didn't even offer us food. My brother's wife slept the whole afternoon, and my sister and mother kept saying: "You've spoiled your life!" That's how they spoke to me on that day.

My wife and I didn't have a good marriage [*nalla uravu illai*]. Somehow we were married, but a couple only to the outside world. I had no love for her, not even a drop [*tuḷi*] of affection. We moved into the house next to my workplace in Madurai. I bought what we needed, vessels, beddings, and so on. But my heart wasn't in this marriage. We fought about everything, money in particular, and when we argued my wife would yell at high volume. I was afraid of these fights and after a while made a habit of taking off on my own. I was never home. Her family feared I'd divorce her, and that's exactly what my own father advised me to do. But I said, "We wouldn't like for our sister to divorce. My wife and I'll manage."

Our firstborn was a girl, the second a boy. But right after my boy's birth, my wife and I stopped talking to each other [meaning we stopped having sex]. I wouldn't eat with her. I wouldn't take food from her. For fourteen years we didn't speak at all. Only a couple of years before she died did we start talking again.

One night she woke up in the middle of the night only to fall in a comalike state. I didn't know she had been seriously sick for the past two years. I didn't know she was taking medications for kidney failure and heart problems. I didn't know she was dying. But my children knew. "Father," my boy said that night, "our mother has only six more months to live, that's what the doctor from the Meenatchi hospital said." But I shouted back, "*There's nothing wrong with her*! It's nothing [*cuma*]." I went right back to sleep. Later on a plaintive sound woke me up again. She was moaning in pain. When I turned on the light I saw my son by her side. "What do you think you're doing?" I yelled, "I've to get up early in the morning, but you two are playing and disturbing me." My son wept, "She isn't playing, she isn't faking; she's suffering." [Neelam cries]

That night I carried her downstairs. I hadn't touched her in fourteen years, and her body was a burden to me. "You're just pretending to be sick!" I threw at her on the way to the Meetnatchi Mission Hospital. When the doctor understood I was her husband, he raised his voice, "She has been in treatment for two years, but you never come. She said you were out working, but we thought she was divorced. Are you aware of her condition? How can you not know? She doesn't have much time to live; the least you can do is take care of her!"

Eventually they moved my wife to the General Hospital where she could get free dialysis, one day at a time. The doctor recommended a new kidney. I volunteered mine, but I had the wrong blood type. Her brother refused to give his. Finally a kidney was made available at the Madurai kidney center, but my wife's condition had deteriorated. She was in no condition for a transplant. Her heart failed. No injection worked. She had fever. Her body was pocked all over with needle marks. Because she no longer responded to any medication, the doctor asked me to take her home. She died as soon as we laid her down on the bed. The women in my family had the nerve to cry out, "We married him to this woman, and now he's alone!" They were feeling sorry for me rather than for her. As for the women in my wife's family, they made up dirges like: "If we had married her to someone else, she wouldn't have died." The whole thing was so very painful to me that I exploded, "I'm the one who's having this loss. It's not yours. Go home, you shouldn't be here!" After the funeral, I went home, but as I was climbing the stairs I fell and broke my leg. I had to lie down. For thirty-one days I was in a cast.

After my wife passed away, it was just my son and I in the house [Neelam's daughter was already married]. On weekends my boy would go to his [maternal] grandmother, who began putting the idea that I'd soon remarry into his head. This disturbed my son, who had seen his best friend mistreated by a stepmother. He became anxious and often cried. Things got better after my daughter gave birth and moved back with us for a few months [as is customary].

The morning after she returned to her in-laws I had to go to Pondicherry. When I arrived I called my son, who cried on the telephone because his sister had left with her newborn baby. I tried to console him, "Don't be sad, I'm on my way home." He replied, "By the time you get back, I won't be here anymore; I won't be alive."

I panicked and rushed back to Madurai. By the time I arrived, my boy was dead [tears came to Neelam's eyes; his lips twitched, but he added this:]

My son's death is a big loss for me, much bigger than that of my wife. I didn't feel anything when she died, only tormented by the people who were around me on that day. But my son's death was a terrible blow, I cried and still cry.

Rights, Rejections, and Regrets

Sometimes there are moments of grace in the field. You meet someone you do not know at all, or you speak with someone you knew at some point in the distant past, and you feel yourself passing through a magnetic field that sends you in a new direction. I felt such things, and more, as I listened to both Mayandi and Neelam talk about their lives. At so many moments of their narratives I had to fight back tears. Emotions were flowing and carrying me beyond the rigidity of my research agenda. Even today it is hard for me to describe the jolt that ran through me at the improbable realization that these two men embodied the culture I was researching, perhaps more so than the men who did marry "the right way."

The day Neelam finished his narration, I asked him to stay over. Why should he take two or three buses to get home when we had a room with a bed on the roof? After dinner I heard him go out. He must have drunk hard because the next morning I found him spread out on the floor in a deep sleep. I woke him up with a tumbler of coffee. What was the point of putting further questions to him? Such questions as: "Were you drunk when you broke your leg?" "What about your father?" "Why did you not mention his death?" I did not have the heart to ask him anything. All I could think was: What have I done? Instead of protecting Neelam, I had encouraged an emotional outpouring, a confession that might leave him devastated for days.

We took two days off and resumed our work on the few kinship charts I had collected in Kaḷḷar villages as if he had not spoken of his past. But a couple of weeks later, actually the very day before I left the field, Neelam offered these concluding remarks on his story:

> I married in 1985. It's a long time ago, but I haven't forgotten that no one helped me marry my elder sister's daughter then. I still feel that my family spoilt her life and mine. I should have eloped with her. I had the right to do so. Had we married, she'd still be alive today; instead she died before my wife did. Now my brother and his spouse tell me: "You should have come in person; we'd have arranged your marriage. We wouldn't have denied your *urimai*." And I reply, "If I were your brother [from the same mother], you'd have given to me. I wasn't born with you, so you didn't." Like this they blame me, and I blame them.

It is possible that the very topic of my research directed Neelam's evaluation of his life. After all, we talked about marriage with *contam* most of the time. But our conversations could not have generated what I think is the main thrust of his account, as well as the source of his major anguish in life: his "lower" birth rank. The belief that he would have been better off had he married his elder sister's daughter might have resulted from our work on "right" marriages. But the belief that his elder brother and sister-in-law rejected his matrimonial "rights" and rushed him in an improvised marriage because he came "after" them in life did not.

In Neelam's account we clearly see, then, the association of equality with endogamy. It is because *contam* are on par that they marry together, and when they are not they do not. We can appreciate why, as already noted in the last chapter, the Tamils feel very bitter when one of their kin rejects their matrimonial rights (also see May 1986: 228). Such rejection—the equivalent of a provocation—is sure to cause them to feel that "they don't think I'm good enough for them." But in this chapter we witnessed a different—but no less extreme, I believe—expression of the kinds of agonistic responses depicted in the last chapter, in the form not of destructive retaliation but of life-long feelings of self-depreciation and resentment.

On the surface, Mayandi's experience, as recounted in the first part of this chapter, seems to highlight how chance and circumstance (such as the timing of an uncle's incarceration) can also bar an otherwise appropriate marriage.

But it is not just bad luck that prevented Mayandi from marrying his "right" girl. From his perspective, his mother and paternal aunt were to blame. The same point of view is also present in Neelam's narrative, when he makes it clear that his elder brother's wife had her own plans for his girl. These two men share a standard joke that runs: "Behind every man's demise there's a woman." This saying intimates that even in a patrilineal and patrilocal society—such as that of the Kaḷḷars and Maṟavars—the enactment of marriage rights still largely depends on personal schemes, and on women's personal schemes in particular.

These personal accounts of marriages missed, thus, also suggest that whatever prevents a marriage (and here we can include such variable factors as a womanizing father, low birth rank, hunger, crime and its punishment, or feminine "strategy"), the marriage law or preference becomes a crucible that brings one to feel the "right" emotions—if not up to the satisfactory performance of the "right" marriage, then in the tragedy of the near miss. Both Mayandi's and Neelam's accounts underscore that, when men like them are stripped of their matrimonial privileges, they may become entangled in regret for lost entitlements and missed expectations. In the end, however, I must point out that the two men were not exactly in the same situation.

When I met Mayandi, he and his wife and their two children lived with Mayandi's younger brother, who was married to Mayandi's wife's sister. We note that this particular "joint" family consisted of two brothers married to two sisters who were related to their husbands as elder sister's daughters and the children of each couple. This made for a household thick with consanguinity, one in which people were as equal as one can be in Tamil Nadu; but they were not necessarily happier for that, as hinted by Mayandi's response to my comment that he was lucky to be surrounded by such close kin. "Yes," he said, "I live in a crowd (*kuṭṭam*), but I'm always alone." Not knowing what to say, I clumsily offered the thought that many people in my country felt the same way. Mayandi gently protested, "No, they don't feel the same way."

As for Neelam, he lived in his own house with his married daughter and her family, an unusual arrangement because usually a Tamil man resides with his married son, not his son-in-law. This made for a household in which exchanges of food, which in India almost always convey all-critical messages about rank (see Appadurai 1981), were tricky. Because a husband (and his family) usually get served before a woman's father, and because Neelam did not want to come second in his own household, he regularly left the house at mealtimes. He actually cooked and ate his own food so that he would not have to accept that of his son-in-law, which would have been another demonstration of inferiority. For these reasons, and because the son-in-law himself (and his parents) did not feel "free" in his house when he was there, Neelam spent much of his time back in his natal village.

Once he and I went there together. The old temples—seven in total, including the one where he had met the thieves in his youth—were all in bad repair. Two identical three-story buildings, completely new and painted in garish colors, lined the main street. But behind these new buildings were empty lots strewn with the rubble of abandoned courtyard houses and stores. What had perhaps been a lively warren of alleys and streets was now mostly vacant. Fewer than fifty people, all related to Neelam in one way or another, remained there; the rest had moved to towns and cities.

This village's ruins conjured a world before monogamous marriages, before family planning, before small families—a world that had exploded during Neelam's lifetime. One element of his account serves as a particular case in point. In Neelam's father's time, a man's remarriage created a social drama for the sons of successive wives, of different social status. Nowadays, the prospect of a man's remarriage creates a private trauma—as tragically suggested by Neelam's son's suicide. This is because the current trend for Tamil families is to become nuclear, individualistic, and conjugal, so that relationships between wife and husband, on the one hand, and between parent or stepparent and child, on the other, are more focused and intensely personal than in the past. It is when we contrast Neelam's unhappy distant marriage with the dutiful marriage contracted by Mayandi with his sister's daughter, the very marriage that Neelam wanted for himself, that we can begin to appreciate the magnitude of the changes in kinship practices they have witnessed and experienced in their lifetimes, inaugurating a world in which neither of their marriages could play out the same way.

4

THE YOUNGER BROTHER TAKES LESS

They married me off to my maternal *māmā*. I was madly in love with him long before my marriage, since I had been brought up expecting to marry him ever since I was a little girl. Now that I've left him, do you think I'll be able to love anyone else?
—Vaasanthi, *A Home in the Sky*, 2007: 183

The mother's brother [*tāymāmā*] is the first person to do anything for the child.
—Abi, interviewed in Pondicherry

The eternal conflict between spouses is abundantly reflected in Indian mythology, especially Tamil, which debates the issue of male versus female superiority back and forth endlessly on a cosmic level, in the form of battles and contests between deities or demons and their real or would-be mates.
—Margaret Trawick 1990: 180

Mother is the one person to whom you don't return gifts. You can thank her, but you don't have to pay her back.
—Neelam, interviewed in Madurai

It is not surprising that, not that long ago, Neelam longed to marry his elder sister's daughter and Mayandi married his. Up until recently uncle–niece marriage was "the commonest form of close inter-marriage" in Tamil Nadu, as Anthony Good has also observed (1996: 6; 1980). Such marriages were not merely more frequent; they were given priority over all other kinds of marriages. As David Annoussamy, a judge and professor of law in Pondicherry, recalls, "Uncle–niece marriage [used to be] not only normal, it [was] considered the ideal marriage, even *preferred* to cross-cousin marriage" (2003: 69, my translation and italics; see also McCormack 1958; Rao 1973; Jones Allison 1980: 125).

However, when Tamils speak of marriage with the elder sister's daughter, the normative and jural language that is de rigueur with marriage to the mother's brother's daughter or the father's sister's daughter does not come up. Rather than "rightness" (*muṟai*) in the sense of norm or rule, the emphasis is solely on "right" in the sense of privilege (*urimai*). Among most (but not all) castes, the mother's brother has the exclusive license to marry his niece, and he can claim this girl before any "right" man. The full extent of this advantage was vividly conveyed by one consultant: "The [younger] mother's brother has the freedom to come to his sister's house whenever he wishes, ransack the place, elope with her girl and joke about it, if it pleases him. The girl is his." We may note that the hierarchical principle of birth order governing the "right" marriages discussed in Chapter 2 is reversed here. It is because he comes *after* his sister that the maternal uncle has the license to marry his niece, and a Tamil man should not marry his younger sister's daughter.[1] It is therefore obvious that, in examining this form of marriage, we are entering the cosmology of matrimony from a different vantage: one in which a junior (and therefore inferior) status and relationship to a senior woman are the major matrimonial qualifications.

Two Views on Marriage with the Elder Sister's Daughter

As a point of departure I want to review two opposed scholarly conceptions of the Tamil marriage to the elder sister's daughter. The first, from Louis Dumont, maintains that it "is a type of marriage completely different from Kaḷḷar marriage" (1986: 204), which, the reader will recall, when "right" is a marriage to the mother's brother's daughter. The second perspective, advanced by Anthony Good (1980), squarely *equates* uncle–niece marriage with marriage to this very matrilateral cross cousin. I begin my discussion with materials that incline me to lean in favor of the former, structuralist stance, but I show toward the latter part of this chapter that formal typological modalities of this sort (patrilateral, matrilateral, avuncular) inhibit a more dynamic and experiential understanding of Tamil preferential marriages. For one thing, all these modalities are based in what we might simply call, for now, a common culture of kinship and fundamental notions of relatedness. Moreover, as I show in the next chapter, these modalities coexist with so many marriage choices that it is difficult if not futile to define Tamil preferential marriages in terms of fixed anthropological classifications, or even Tamil normative categories for that matter. Finally, because power, prestige and economic interests are at stake in Tamil "matrimonial games" (Bourdieu 1977: 58), the relationship between formal rules and social reality is quite complex.

Dumont does not elaborate on his position that marriage with the sister's daughter is opposed to marriage with the mother's brother's daughter. But because he shares Claude Lévi-Strauss's definition of kinship as originating not in the nuclear family, nor in relations among individuals, but in the relations of exchange that link social groups, one must assume that for him marriage with elder sister's daughter is "incapable" of realizing the kind of "overall [social] structure" said by Lévi-Strauss to result from matrilateral cross-cousin marriage (1969: 445). Dumont says as much when he writes, employing Lévi-Strauss's language, that "marriage to the niece is . . . a sort of restricted exchange," and one, he adds, that would make "the [Kaḷḷar] flow of prestations and the [Kaḷḷar] mother's brother's role . . . impossible" (1986: 204). Hence Dumont is not surprised to find that "the Kaḷḷar vigorously condemn sister's daughter marriage" (1986: 204).

For all their "condemnation" of the practice, the Kaḷḷars are not above marrying their elder sister's daughter. As we saw in the last chapter, both Mayandi and his younger brother married theirs. But Dumont is essentially correct: In theory, at least, the Kaḷḷars prohibit uncle–niece marriage on grounds, I was told, that it is bad luck for a man to appropriate the woman who is "right" for his son. Mayandi himself never brought up the issue of misfortune, but he did once acknowledge, with a joking tone of voice, that he had married his daughter-in-law, or rather the girl who should have married his son. I want to underscore that in respect of the proscription of uncle–niece marriage, the Kaḷḷars represent a unique case among Tamils, including the Tēvars.

The many castes that practice uncle–niece marriage praise it for the very reason that Lévi-Strauss and Dumont object to it—it restricts the circle of exchanges. I was also told that this marriage allows daughters to stay close by—a formulation often put to me as: "We don't want our girls to marry far." "We don't want to let go [*pōhaviṭa*] of our love [*pācam*] for them." Sometimes people expressed this wish—to preserve the relation (*contam*) with daughters—in economic terms. "We don't want to lose the money and jewels." This last comment has to be understood in light of the fact that when this marriage is repeated, jewels, gold, money, land—the usual valuables gifted to daughters at marriage—keep coming back at the very next generation (see

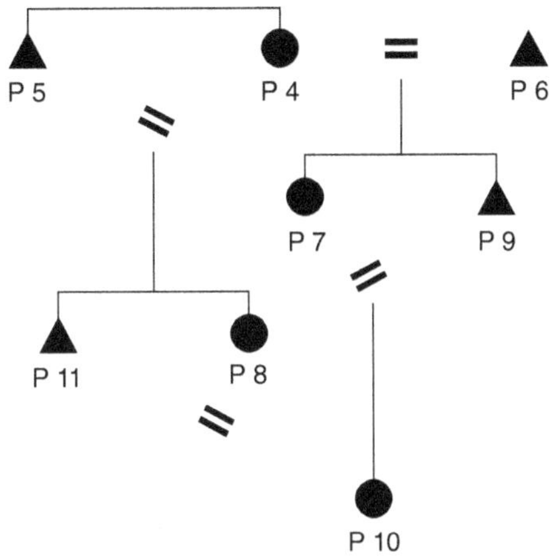

Figure 4.1.
For P11, his sister's (P8's) daughter P10 is also his mother's (p7's) brother's (p9's) daughter p10.

Figure 4.1). Everyone agreed that no one likes "to share or divide property (*cottu*) with outsiders."

I elicited other points of view, too. "We know the daughter-in-law; she obeys us and takes good care of us when we get old; an outsider has less affection." "An unrelated wife tries to divide her husband and his sister, but not a sister's daughter." I was also told that these marriages were more stable. Because the mother-in-law is the girl's grandmother, problems in the family do not escalate. The wife and husband cannot make that all-too-common accusation in Tamil Nadu, "You don't respect my parents." Finally, the couple is less likely to separate. As Neelam of the last chapter put it to me: "When they fight, the wife can't go back to her mother's house. What is the woman to do? Keep her daughter away from her brother?" He underscored that the fight would not last anyway: "If the husband raises his voice, his wife forgives him. She tells herself, 'He's my mother's brother; he has the right to grumble.'" "An outsider," Neelam reasoned, "wouldn't be that understanding; she'd complain and leave."

In sum, these marriages are best because they prevent the family and the couple from breaking up. Mothers and daughters (note that there are no fathers and sons in the exegeses reported so far), brothers and sisters, maternal uncles and nieces are to remain *cērntu*—from *cēr*: "be near," that is "together," "united"—forever. For the many castes that favor marriage with the elder sister's daughter, the "optimal" or "preferential" society is one in which there is no flow of signs, no institutionalized exchange of women between families, no general circulation of goods and therefore no transversal social networks. The social cosmology evoked here is one that lends itself in an especially powerful way to self-segregation, sameness, repetition—in short, to the complete negation of the regime of reciprocity celebrated by alliance theory.

Anthony Good's (1980) argument[2] *contra* Dumont is more formal than my own (at least thus far). For him, repetition of the uncle–niece marriage produces a situation in which the elder sister's daughter merges with the mother's brother's daughter (look again at Figure 4.1). For Good, this genealogical (but not terminological) conflation casts a negative light on the Lévi-Straussian argument that the uncle–niece marriage is essentially different from matrilateral cross-cousin marriage. Good's thinking goes something like this: If repetitive marriage with the elder's sister's daughter is like marrying the mother's brother's daughter, the key concept—"exchange"—that organizes the many differences between these two unions loses its analytic value. As Good writes: "I do not regard the notion of 'exchange' as particularly helpful in the context of [matrimonial] prescription" (1980: 490).

There is no denying that, at the level of the model, repetition of marriage to the sister's daughter makes this girl her mother's brother's daughter as well (because my mother's brother is also my elder sister's husband, his daughter is also hers). But my field experience is more like that of Kodanda Rao's in a Telugu fishing village, where he observed that "the two terms designating these two categories of relatives . . . are not merged together" (1973: 31). Moreover, the groom is said to marry his elder sister's daughter, not his mother's brother's daughter, so the former identity clearly prevails over the latter. Good himself notes: "Such marriages *are* regarded as being with eZDy [the elder sister's daughter]" (1980: 485, his italics). To me this suggests that, rather than a conflation of two kinship categories, we witness here the disappearance or occlusion of one of them. In effect, repetitive marriage with the elder sister's daughter dislodges the mother's brother's daughter, and if the latter girl "goes missing" (or at least, the category she might occupy does), then she cannot be wed.

What I am saying here is that repetition of uncle–niece marriage rules out the possibility of matrilateral cross-cousin marriage. It is precluded by the operation of what anthropologists call the "system," and one thus finds an explanation for the Kaḷḷars' "vigorous condemnation" of the first union (Dumont 1986: 204). They "condemn" it because they understand that an uncle–niece marriage threatens the existence of the mother's brother's daughter, who happens to constitute their idea of the "right" girl. The very notion of "vigorous condemnation" says it all. For here we must ask, What would be the point of condemning a marriage (to the elder sister's daughter) that formally results in the "right" marriage (to the mother's brother's daughter)? Such a denunciation of a "lawful" way of marrying would make no sense. It would be very confusing. The only logical explanation is that at the theoretical level the Tamils see the two marriages as fundamentally different and incompatible. They express this view on a practical level as well.

I sympathize with Good's objections to Lévi-Strauss's exchange-based theory of kinship. So far, in this book I have attempted to show that cultural notions of social precedence, legitimate right, and equality best capture the meaning and purpose of Tamil preferential marriage. Yet I have also shown how the Kaḷḷar exegesis of their "marriage rule" (*kaliyāṇam muṟai*) supports Lévi-Strauss's argument that "positive" marriage prescriptions require groups to trade. No matter how onerous it might be, a Kaḷḷar firstborn at times has no other choice but "to do the right thing" with the lastborn. Such an obligation ensures that firstborns do not keep on marrying firstborns and thus encourages what Lévi-Strauss calls "a better integration of the group" (1969: 448). In the more general Tamil theory of marriage with *condam*—which expresses a rejection of the formal rules of exchange with those who are "mine" and a refusal to marry those who are not equal—we also have seen, if only in the negative, a validation of Lévi-Strauss's idea that cross-cousin marriage works as an affirmation of reciprocity with otherness.

The comparisons I elicited also underwrite the French anthropologist's theory that each preferential marriage orientation comes with its own regime of reciprocity and a particular sociology and psychology. "If I want dowry," a young man told me, "I go to my father's side; if I don't mind forsaking it, I go to my mother's side." When asked to expand, he explained: "If I marry my father's sister's daughter, our family will get back the dowry given at my aunt's marriage. If I marry my mother's brother's daughter, I don't know what to expect." His reasoning has to be understood in light of the fact that in the second scenario spouses are not exchanged. In the pure form of matrilateral cross-cousin marriage, at least, wives takers, such as the mother's brother, are not wife takers. The mother's brother takes wives for his sons from his wife's brother, not from his sister, to whom he gives his own daughter. Such asymmetric and potentially chancy exchange (how does the mother's brother knows for sure that he will receive wives from his wife's brother?) contrasts with the patrilateral form of cross-cousin marriage, according to which wives do not "circulate," as anthropologists put it, and the relationships between givers and takers alternate every generation. The man who took my father's sister will give me his daughter; hence, as the youth quoted at the beginning of this paragraph indicated, the guarantee of receiving what was given in the previous generation. He was basically in agreement with Lévi-Strauss, who writes, "From an individual and psychological viewpoint . . . [matrilateral cross-cousin marriage] is a risky venture . . . The system of patrilateral marriage is a safer operation" (1969: 451).

Marriage to the elder sister's daughter entails a form of exchange that is even more "restricted" than the two just mentioned. Wives givers are the same as wife takers, and the exchange of women and gifts does not skip a generation. The man who took my sister gives me his daughter. From the sister's perspective, the exchange goes like this: I marry my daughter to my younger brother, and he marries his daughter to my son. It would seem that the more narrow a field of matrimonial reciprocity is, the more "direct" and "symmetrical" the exchange becomes, but, according to consultants, marriage to the elder sister's daughter involves a real imbalance.

I was told that the sister "doesn't have to spend much on this marriage." Again and again my consultants would say, "The younger brother is not as demanding. He takes less." Less than whom? Less than an outsider (*a<u>nn</u>iyam*)—who nowadays asks for a sizeable dowry—but also less than the "right" boy: either the mother's brother's son or the father's sister's son. As one man told me, "The brother isn't expecting grand things. He understands that his *akkā* [elder sister] can't afford to give more." The same notion came up when a Tamil woman hypothesized the following scenario. "Let's say," she said, "that I marry one daughter to a brother and one daughter to an outsider. From the time of marriage to the time of death I need to spend money on my two sons-in-law. At each family function I have to tender gifts, or they complain to their wives, and a dispute with my daughters isn't what I want." "The difference," the woman added, "is that I don't have to give as much to my brother; I give what I can. A brother always takes less than an outsider."

Not only does the sister give less, but she also takes more. She visits the couple whenever and for however long she wants, helping herself to whatever they own. This is not a likely scenario if the brother is married to an *a<u>nn</u>iyam*. Even with a "right" girl, the *akkā* is prone to curb her acquisitive tendencies. But with her daughter in charge of her brother's household, she feels free and at home. Better yet, if the young couple lives with the brother's parents and male married siblings in a joint family situation, this woman *is* at home, not in her capacity as estranged guest or in-law but as daughter.

Such representations strongly suggest that marriage to elder sister's daughter is a world and transaction of its own. On that much I agree with the French structuralists. But we must ask: What kind of world? What kind of transaction? For it is not enough to reduce, as Lévi-Strauss and Dumont do, this marriage to an example of failed "generalized" reciprocity, a kind of social aberration. Such a stance does not do justice to the facts just reviewed. Let me restate them.

A younger brother has first "right" to his elder sister's daughter. But if the girl is "his," his sister does not give and he does not receive. He simply helps himself to what is already due to him. Thus he is not beholden to anyone, his sister in particular. As for this sibling, she gives what does not cost her, so that her gesture is neither onerous nor gratifying. Let there be no mistake: There is power and appropriation in this relationship, even violence. But because the younger brother does not actually take and the elder sister does not actually give, the force at work escapes from the logic of compulsive reciprocity characteristic of the flow of ceremonial prestations between in-laws (Dumont 1983). This becomes obvious when we review Marshall Sahlins's classical definition of reciprocity as "a *between* relation, the action and reaction of two parties" (1972: 188). As Sahlins expands on the point, "Reciprocity stipulates two sides, two distinct socio-economic interests. Reciprocity can establish solidarity relations, insofar as the material flow suggests assistance or mutual benefit, yet the social fact of sides is inescapable" (1972: 188–189). But the *akkā-tampi* (elder sister/younger brother) do not exchange in the way defined by Sahlins. They take each other for granted: What is his is hers, and vice versa. Their relationship is anything but "two sided," anything but "affinal," as anthropologists might say of the relationship between in-laws. In the rest of this chapter I continue exploring the brother's marriage to his elder sister's daughter, as it unfolded in my fieldwork.

Feelings for Elder Sister's Daughter

When I was in the field I was not thinking about this type of marriage in the terms just discussed. I understood that blood relations were at its center, that its emotional life was focused on consanguinal plots—stories about a generous or stingy brother, for example, a demanding sister, a prolific mother, or some other aspect of the birth family. But because I grew up assuming that marriage is about the founding of a conjugal couple I was curious. What about the couple? Were they truly irrelevant? What about their feelings and personal dispositions? Were they sexually attracted to one another?

Edward Westermarck's old argument (1922) that two people living in close domestic proximity during the first few years of their lives will later be immune to close sexual attraction was not particularly good to think with. Many of the uncle–niece couples I worked with had met only a few times before marriage, often in the context of festivals, weddings, and puberty ceremonies that are already socially approved opportunities for encountering the other sex, a place to "discover" the feelings associated with the culturally privileged matrimonial bonds. It is true that some couples had grown up together—if not exactly in the same house, in the same neighborhood at least—and for them familiarity indeed was a problem. Men, in particular, grumbled that the trouble with marrying a niece is that "there isn't mystery," and a few admitted, "I had no interest in her. I knew everything about her." Women did not bring up their feelings, and out of an old-fashioned sense of discretion, perhaps, I did not ask.

But Tamil culture has ways to trump "nature" and any instinctive aversion to sexual relations. In time I observed that as they grow up together some related children are taught, even pressured, to frame their sexual "preferences" within the cultural framework of "right" or "privileged" marriage choices, and this from an early age. Questions such as "Who is your *māmā*?" "Who is your *poṇṇu*?" teach them that they are related not as brothers and sisters or other age-mates are, but as potential sexual and marital partners. "Children may not know what that relationship means," a woman told me, "they may not be thinking about it, but they know." As they get older, relatives may conjecture, in their presence, when and where their marriage will take place. Or they may tease the youngsters about their marriage, or leave them alone together in the house. In sum, these children are caught in an encompassing world of subtle and not-so-subtle allusions to their special relationship. Out of this discourse emotions and sexual dispositions are constructed, and the wedding itself furthers the couple's "interest" in each other, as also illustrated by the epigraph to this chapter from the Tamil novel *A Home in the Sky*.

With the aim of making this discussion less dry, I turn to an account of my friendship with Sundari, who lived two blocks from my rented home in Madurai. In addition to her own two sons, ages eighteen and thirteen, Sundari was raising Tangam, her daughter's daughter. At first, I thought that the girl, who was twelve, merely served as "extra help," and there is no doubt that Tangam did more than her share of chores around the house. But Sundari clarified that she planned on giving Tangam to her younger son, because her daughter, who lived in Kerala with her husband and two younger daughters, did not have the means to marry off three girls.

For the children themselves, marriage seemed to be the last thing on their minds. As far as I could tell, the boy was not interested in girls, and his main passion in life was to watch cricket on TV or play in a nearby vacant lot. As for Tangam, she followed her "mother's brother" everywhere, despite Sundari's admonitions that she was getting too old to hang out with boys. To my neighbor this behavior was evidence that Tangam was still a child.

During my fieldwork, Tangam reached puberty. A few months later the family celebrated with the required ceremony (though it was kept simple due to budgetary constraints). Her parents and two younger sisters came from Kerala with sweets and small gifts. Because Tangam's mother's brothers were too young to bring *cīr*, it was Sundari's own brother who bought the nice sari in which Tangam paraded around with a shy smile, along with the jewels rented for the day, new plastic sandals, and bright hair ties. It was the first time that she had worn a sari, and on that day she looked, as everyone exclaimed, "beautiful!"

The boy's role was to serve coffee to the guests who kept teasing him. "Look at her!" they would urge with a smile. "Why should I look at her?" he asked, inevitably, brushing them off with a shrug of his shoulders. "Because she is pretty," came the invariable reply. The boy peeped at Tangam a few times but clearly did not know what to say. At some point, Sundari's brother joked that now that Tangam was a woman she would start bossing the boy around. "When she tells you to go to the market, you must go!" he laughed, thereby hinting, among other things, that little Tangam would not run errands in the neighborhood anymore.

I cannot say whether this kind of "sexual" socialization works, and if so to what extent. But another neighbor, a retired science teacher who understood the nature of my research, hinted that Tamil culture had other ways to encourage "familiar" children to develop desire for each other. The fact that the family lived together in a small house meant that Tangam would be the boy's first sexual interest. "He'll have more access to this girl than any other," the old man said, "and the proximity will create opportunities for touching." Our conversation further clarified that the possession of matrimonial *urimai*, that powerful form of entitlement, can override the famous Westermarck effect. As my neighbor continued: "The boy will think, 'This girl is mine' and touch her." I understood him to say that in the Tamil world a sense of ownership invites sexual possession. When asked whether the family would let the boy "mix" (*kala*) with Tangam (a way Tamils sometimes refer to acts of intimacy), this man answered, "There isn't much the parents can do; he has *urimai* on this girl."

Some of the uncle–niece couples I met had married for "love," as they put it, using the English word. In this case, sentiment was mixed with sorrow and something like chivalry. A typical scenario would involve a young mother's brother attending the funeral of his niece's father (or paternal grandfather) only to think: "*Pāvam*! Poor girl. She's alone. She has no one to care for her. If I marry her, she won't suffer." The reader will recall that the same protective impulse led Mayandi, the Kaḷḷar man of the last chapter, to care for his own fatherless "right" girl.

This kind of impulse or desire to feel for others is rooted in the world of South Indian emotionalism, as beautifully described in David Shulman's interpretation of the twelfth-century story of the just king Maṉunīticoḻaṉ (1993). This is a story of extreme concern and empathy for the feelings of others; "extreme" because Maṉunīticoḻaṉ kills his son, who has accidently killed a young calf, so as to suffer "the same grief [its mother cow] feels" (1993: 13). I am not suggesting (at least not yet) that a mother's brother who pursues a distressed niece acts out the type of radical self-abnegation depicted in this story. But intense feelings of compassion, and pity—based in what Shulman calls a "Tamil psychology of interaction" (1993: 115)[3]—do factor into the mother's brother's love. Moreover, as is also suggested by the king's filicide, this kind of love is definitively not fatherly in nature. I cannot stress this enough: The maternal uncle is not a paternal figure. Not only is the age disparity between him and his niece not that much above the average for spouses (see also Good 1980: 491), but if he is much older or has helped raise her, my consultants stressed, the couple "cannot share"—for "fathers" and "daughters" cannot share.[4]

Let me state again my understanding of the maternal uncle's intimate relationship with his niece. If the couple is not acquainted, the relationship is conceived in straightforward terms and linked to the work of enculturation—the process through which individuals are socialized to adopt cultural roles as normal or even desirable. If the couple is too familiar for this process to take place "naturally" or "spontaneously," the relationship is fostered by more direct, even coerced, socialization, with adults actively preparing the children for their future marital roles. There is also a mentality of entitlement and a process of sublimation at work. The relationship may include the experience of real emotions, but, rather than being linked to the archaic feelings of childhood (as we Westerners might expect), these feelings derive from a kindly concern aroused by the misfortune or suffering of another and beyond that refer to sacrificial enactments (as I will discuss in the following pages). What the relationship cannot be is an analogue of a paternal bond. When the maternal uncle is too closely identified with a father, he cannot perform as husband. And yet, recall that, in the typical case just discussed, in which the mother's brother and sister's daughter encounter each other at the girl's father's funeral, the maternal uncle steps in with love when the father dies. We are left with the following paradox: The man replaces the missing father but offers something other than paternity. What could this be?

The Mother's Brother

We know the French structuralists' answer to this question. The avuncular figure is not, in sociological fact, a mother's brother—someone tied to the child through his or her mother—but a wife giver or a wife taker (see also Gillison 1987: 167). As Dumont put it in the context of Tamil society: The man is "an affine pure and simple" (1983: 77). The problem, as Thomas Trautmann points out, is that Dumont gives no evidence that the Tamils themselves conceptualize what we call in English "the mother's brother" as the father's brother-in-law (1981: 175). In fact, in my experience the Tamils seem to think of this man as indeed just what they say he is: the mother's brother. This is evidenced by the fact that the word *tāy* means "mother." The Kaḷḷar term *ammāṉ* is even more indicative of his relationship to mother because it is undoubtedly related to *ammā* ("mother"). Moreover, in a small survey I conducted, four out of ten respondents defined *tāymāmā* as "the one who was born with mother." Two answered, "*Tāymāmā* is another mother."

A strong indication that the mother's brother is coupled with mother is that both personify the emotion of love (*pācam*), as many women said in answer to a survey conducted by my young assistant Abi (whom I will introduce in Chapter 6):[5]

> *Ammā* has a lot of love for her daughter. The first love of her first love is for her daughter.—*Padmini, age 40*

> *Ammā* is like a God. She protects her child from the world until her death. She never loses her love.—*Sridevi, age 25*

> *Ammā* is the first eye to her children. Until she dies her love remains the same.—*Thangal, age 61*

> *Ammā* is everything to me. If I don't eat, my mother won't eat either. *Ammā* is the only one who can feel her daughter's feelings.—*Indira, age 28*

> Without *Ammā*, we wouldn't be in this world. We wouldn't exist.—*Minakshi, age 33*

> *Ammā* is the bridge of the family. She has the first place. Without mother, there's no family.—*Celvi, age 44*

> *Ammā* loves her children until she dies. Mother's affection [*pācam*] is the best in the world. Nothing compares to her love.—*Arulmori, age 55*

Of course, these are idealized statements made to "inform" the anthropologist of positive cultural stereotypes. They are not necessarily representative of personal experience. In fact, over the many years I have worked in Tamil Nadu, I have met women and men who did not think that their *own* mother was particularly wonderful. Neelam, whose story I discussed in the last chapter, for example, revealed that he had "little affection" for his mother, and the reader will see that the protagonist of the next chapter's case study lived in great fear of his own mother.

But, in general, "*Ammā* is a wonderful relation," as one of the surveyed women put it. I should say "*ammās*" because the mother's "big" and "little" sisters are mothers as well. These *periyammās* and *ciṉṉammās* love their sister's children the way they love their own. The same holds true for the mother's brother; he too has "immense affection [*pācam*] for his sister's children," as Karin Kapadia also notes (1995: 20). As Neelam explained about his relationship to his nephew in particular, he can feel his feelings and is always willing to help.

According to the women just quoted, what characterizes motherly "love" is that it transcends the field of mutual exchange. In anthropological terms we might say that it falls outside the Maussian sociology of reciprocity. "You don't return a gift to mother," they pointed out. It is much the same with the mother's brother: He is a one-sided giver, and a very generous one at that. Recall how, at the ceremonial collection of money among the Piramalai Kaḷḷars of Madurai (see Chapter 1), the bride's mother's brother makes a donation (the first to be recorded in the account book) that, no matter how substantial—and it is likely to be very substantial—remains unspecified and unreciprocated. The Kaḷḷar brother "doesn't have the right to ask for his money back."

What about the father? Does he not worry? Does he not give? He does, of course, but according to the respondents to the survey just mentioned he is not as "near" or "close" to his children as their mother's brother is. Besides, his function is different: The father is there to raise children, impart knowledge, and pass on a profession to them. As the women put it:

> *Appa* educates his children. Without *Appa*'s help we can't grow. Father is the provider of basic things.—*Padmini, age 40*
>
> *Appa* thinks of our future. He is the only person who thinks of the child's future. He provides for his children.—*Sridevi, age 25*
>
> *Appa* is a god until the children grow. He helps his child, then he is a friend.—*Thangal, age 61*
>
> *Appa* is a strict person. If we do something wrong, he beats us.—*Indira, age 28*
>
> *Appa* is strict. He's the only one who can fulfill our desires and buy us things like a bicycle, for example.—*Minakshi, age 33*

> *Appa* is a friend. He's strict.—*Celvi, age 44*

> *Appa* leads the family. He makes the family. He's like a captain. He leads us.—*Arulmori, age 55*

Appa's disciplinarian role is extended to all "big" (*periyappa*) or "little" (*citappa*) fathers, who see to it that any wayward son (be he his or theirs) is scolded and punished. Hence, when in trouble a boy does not go to his father(s). Instead he confides in his mother's brother, who has a way with him—"Talk to me, what are you worried about?"—and knows better than to report any personal disclosure to exacting *appa*(s).

For Neelam, the difference between the father's and mother's "sides" came down to this. The father and his siblings share "blood" (*rattam*), a substance he correlated with aggression. For their part, the mother and her siblings share "affection" (*pācam*). The first are prone to fight, the second to protect. Mayandi (also profiled in the last chapter) basically agreed with this, but his theory had a different twist. The folks on the father's side (especially the brothers and their children) share a residence and property as well as rights and duties in a cult. People on the mother's side (her brothers and sisters and their children) own nothing in common. Because they do not live together or socialize very often, the latter category of kin have love (*uṟavu*) for one another. On the few ritual occasions they do get together, they do not fight (as the "sharers" of property do on a regular basis) but "share" joys and sorrows instead.

Thus, from the perspective of a Tamil child the mother's brother is associated not with affinity but with kinship, particularly filiation, and is related not through the father but the mother. Born with her, he loves her sons and daughters in the way that she does. What more do these meanings bring to our understanding of the marriage to the elder sister's daughter?

A Marriage against Husbands and Fathers

To answer this question, we need to examine the role of the mothers most likely to arrange this kind of marriage, the groom's mother and the bride's mother—who also happen to be in the relationship of mother/daughter. The mother has the right[6] to marry her son to her daughter's daughter (hence the groom is the bride's maternal uncle) and vice versa. This fact leads me to suggest that the most critical bond of this most preferential marriage is not that between a man and his brother-in-law (as Dumont contends of Dravidian marriage on the whole) nor between a brother and his sister (as Margaret Trawick generalizes about Tamil kinship) but between a mother and a daughter.

If the elder woman's son marries the younger woman's daughter, these two women are de facto in-laws: They are related by marriage. But their mode of transaction is anything but affinal. For one thing, the daughter does not give the way she would to an in-law. When she offers fewer gifts and less money to the brother who becomes her son-in-law, she shortchanges her mother as well. Moreover, after the marriage the two women are likely (or eager) to live together with the couple—which is not at all what "regular" in-laws do. Of course, the groom's mother is already part of the household, for a Tamil woman is entitled to live with her married son. But the bride's mother visits for long periods of time and is likely to move in altogether because she likes being with her mother, younger brother, and daughter, "more so," I was often told, "than with her own husband and/or her own married son(s)." Needless to say, in the day-to-day functioning of the household the two "mothers" do not stand on ceremony with regard to each other. They certainly do not behave as if they were in-laws, and they help themselves to whatever they want without being specifically invited to do so. They act like the mothers and daughters that they are.

In such a family, all the usual boundaries between "in-laws" and "kin" are blurred: My son-in-law is my brother, my mother-in-law my sister, my daughter-in-law my granddaughter, and so on. Notice what is happening here: Consanguinal identities encompass affinal relations, as well as conjugal roles of "husband" and "wife." This last point is evidenced by the way in which the couple relates to one another: The wife is the sister's daughter (*akkā poṇṇu*), and the husband is the mother's brother (*tāymāmā*).

The mode of exchange in the household, then, is one that the old language of economic anthropology used to call "redistribution," or "pooling." As Marshall Sahlins explains this last category, "Pooling is socially a *within* relation, the collective action of a group . . . [it] stipulates a social center where goods meet and thence flow outwards, and a social boundary too, within which persons (or subgroups) are cooperatively related" (1972: 188–189). Pooling, I hasten to add, is also characteristic of the "average" Tamil patrilocal family, and indeed of any patrilineage (Arumugam 2011). But in the household I am describing here it is the women who mainly "share" because women occupy the "central position," as Brenda Beck noted of "the kin nucleus in Tamil folklore" (1974: 7; see also Fuller 1995). Moreover, whereas members of the patrilineage have to engage in give-and-take relationships with affines, members of this female-centered nucleus do not need to: They are both kin and affine.

We may now begin to see why the masculine and ever-enterprising Kaḷḷars would "condemn" a marriage that, according to my description, flattens male sexuality, restricts the field of social and economic exchange, and keeps men in a position subordinate to their mothers and elder sisters. The worldview encoded in this marriage is antithetical to the Kaḷḷar political economy of expansion and living on credit. Yet in that condemnation we see all the elements that the people who do practice this marriage like and seek in the union, or at least idealize for the benefit of the anthropologist. With this marriage "girls do not marry far." They stay at home or come back. The family does not have to divide property or even transact with outsiders. They remain "together."

On the face of it, the household described here would seem to vindicate the old argument that *Dravidian kinship* is advantageous for women. In the 1950s and 1960s, when scholars (women scholars, in particular) began to compare the variability of marriage and kinship institutions in India, they made the case that the South Indian woman was better off than the North Indian woman (Karve 1953; Kolenda 1987 [1967], 1993; Deliège 1997: 182, Kapadia 1995). According to Karve, who pioneered this comparative analysis of Indian kinship, this was because the South Indian girl

> . . . is not thrown among complete strangers on her marriage . . . The distinction between the father's house and the father-in law's house is not as sharp as in the North. The distinction between 'daughters' and 'brides or wives' is not as deep as in the North. A girl's behaviour in her husband's family is much freer. (1953: 251)[7]

However, it is difficult for me to make the case that "Dravidian" marriage, seen from within the couple, always works in favor of the South Indian woman. My impression, at least, is that relations of power and deference between husband and wife in a Tamil household do not automatically benefit a related wife (see also Conklin 1973: 62; Kapadia 1995: 54; Trawick 1990: 181; Narasimhan 2006). This impression is borne out by the many conversations I had with women who complained that husbands took related wives for granted. On the one hand, they would say that "it's easier to make demands on outsiders," because "they fear our family's reaction and don't dare to say 'no.'" On the other hand, for the same reason, an outsider thinks twice about beating his wife, and as one woman put it: "If my right boy strikes me, my parents don't care."

In the specific case of uncle–niece marriage, however, something else is at stake—and this does seem to provide women a certain room to maneuver, in the game of preferential marriages. This marriage does not so much fulfill or fail to fulfill a woman as it gives her (and her mother and grandmother) a chance to stay (or come) home. I began forming this impression when my lawyer friend from Madurai returned to the old contrast between "Dravidian" and "Aryan" marriage institutions. He said in English,

> In Brahmanical culture, mistreated or widowed women had to stay with their in-laws. They were cut off from their kin. In Dravidian culture women married their daughters to their brothers so that if they were in a bad marriage or widowed, they could live with the couple. It was a good setup. Women weren't dependent on husbands or in-laws; they had the freedom to come home.

Notice the use of the conditional clause. If a woman should have a bad husband or lose her husband, she would be free to go home. The Dravidian woman's freedom goes beyond the ability to extricate herself from a household of "complete strangers." She is free to leave her husband. It is as if the function of the "commonest" marriage in Tamil Nadu is to provide an escape hatch from marriage itself, to free women (and mothers in particular) from this institution.

Indeed, while in the field I observed that it is the women who are either widowed or casualties of bad marriages who most often arrange these uncle–niece marriages. I hasten to say, however, that such decisions are not entirely determined (if this is even the word) by practicality or extremity (although to be sure these factors do play a role). The very circumstances that leave women widowed or separated, or married to crooks and drunks and away from kin in the first place, "reproduce" in a generative kind of way the negation of marriage encoded in the matrimonial orientation described in this chapter. For to say, as my informants did, that you marry daughters close by so that they do not leave is in effect to work against the very meaning of marriage, which, throughout India and Tamil Nadu, is to send women away to another family. The full ramifications of this basic statement already prefigure the life situations just described and begin to indicate why a "close" alternative might be preferred by some women. Whether in theory or in practice there is nothing to indicate that "the commonest form of close inter-marriage" (Good 1996: 6) works in favor of marriage itself.

The argument that the Dravidian woman is primarily a mother and a sister rather than a wife is supported by a vast corpus of Tamil myths and rituals that show a woman resisting her conjugal role. Consider, for example, the narrative underpinning an eighteen-day festival recorded by Indira Arumugam in Vaduvir Natu (2011). Every year the goddess Pidari Amman must go back to her husband's house for the length of the celebration. As soon as the ceremonial procession departs, however, the goddess becomes "heavier and heavier," "almost impossible to lift" (2011: 249). Arumugam concludes: "Pidari Amman is clearly reluctant to leave her own territory to go to that of her husband's" (2011: 25). Conjugality, we might say, is not her thing.

The Brother's Duty (*Kaṭamai*)

Radcliffe-Brown (1952[1924]) once claimed that, in a patrilineal society in which the father is a distant and feared figure of authority, customs relating to the mother's brother are extensions of the close affective bond between mother and child (see Gillison 1987: 166). By "customs," Radcliffe-Brown meant marriage with the mother's brother's daughter, suggesting that in African societies it is natural for a man to want to form a marriage alliance with people who are warm and friendly, like his mother. Given that similar parental stereotypes/archetypes prevail in South India, it is tempting to apply this "extensionist hypothesis" to the understanding of Tamil marriage with the elder sister's daughter. After all, this girl stands in a position of the mother's granddaughter vis-à-vis the groom.

Jack Goody objected to Radcliffe-Brown's argument on the grounds that it "neglect(s) not only the existence of a cultural tradition, but also the standpoint of the senior generation and their hand in promoting these marriages" (1959: 63). Goody's point is pertinent to my ethnography. In Tamil Nadu, it is parents and not children who arrange marriages. When we look at the kind of marriage described in this chapter from the perspective of the mothers and daughters who conclude it for their children, we discern that the general association of mother and her brother is not simply produced by "life within the family in the narrow sense" (Radcliffe-Brown 1952[1924]: 29) nor is it associated with "love" as Westerners might define this emotion (in the context of their family dynamics). More critically, the identification between brother and sister, and their interests, is tied to dynamics of sublimation and to sacrificial action and the merit it accrues.

The brother who marries his elder sister's daughter, I want to suggest, performs a kind of sacrifice. In effect, the man relinquishes his sexual desire (he is not exactly "interested" in his niece), his autonomy and rank (he is encompassed by his elder sister and mother), his "right" to enter more profitable matrimonial transactions (he "takes less"), and his political role in public life (his ability to form "alliances" with other men), as well as his own independent line of descent (which merges with that of his sister/mother) in order to reclaim the family women (which is, once again, the common explanation for marrying a sister's daughter).

My interpretation is not as far-fetched, even psychologically, as it may seem. Scholars have long documented the close association of marriage and sacrifice in the Tamil religious tradition (Harman 1989; Hudson 1977). David Shulman (1980), in particular, has shown how Tamil myths[8] of the marriage of Siva to the goddess promote sacrifice as the central metaphor for divine matrimony, devotion and regeneration. The god offers his life in the form of a gift, with which he is identified, to his consort. The consort here is no submissive Sanskrit goddess, but a dangerous, often malevolent, feminine power, who entices "her husband to a violent, self-sacrificing death" (1980: 212), or slays him as he attempts to unite with her (1980: 224). The Tamil goddess, Shulman proposes, is the source first of death, then of a new flow of vitality as she rewards her victim, here the god, with rebirth from her womb (1980: 297).

The younger brother's sacrifice paradoxically develops the main theme of the great Bhakti tradition, a religion of passionate and total, agonizing, and struggle-ridden devotion that, according to scholars, arose in the Tamil-speaking region of south India in the fifth century C.E. to counter the kind of practical sacrifice just described. In Bhakti, the goal is not to generate the cosmos or fulfill some concrete need for life but to love and fuse with the god. As the great Indian scholar A. K. Ramanujan writes of Tamil-speaking saint-poets devoted to Visnu, who lived between the sixth and ninth centuries: "A *bhakta* is not content to worship a god in word and ritual, nor is he content to grasp him in a theology; he needs to possess him and be possessed by him" (1981: 116). Likewise, marriage to the sister's daughter is described in terms of joining, incorporation (*cērntu*—from *cēr*: "to join", "append," "admix," "cause sexual union"), which is also why a sister can demand and receive her *tampi*'s gifts offered in "love" without reciprocating.

The marriage discussed in this chapter also borrows from the folk or "little" tradition of South Indian religion. In fact, it aligns itself with the contradictory aims of Tamil patrilineage cults that, as I observed in the early 1990s in villages near the town of Gingee, culminate with the cutting of a chicken, goat, or pig and the subsequent apportionment of its carcass among kinsmen (Nabokov 2000; Arumugam 2011). I write "contradictory" because it is well known to scholars of South Indian society that, although the basic distribution of shares in the patrilineage cult (or honors, *mariyātai*) is socially integrative, it is also the object of endless disputes. More often than not, brothers and paternal uncles fight for the right to be first in receiving sacrificial offerings. Likewise, while the sacrifice described in this chapter is said to keep the birth family together, it also invites the assertion of divisive individual interests as sisters compete for exclusive "right" over an eligible younger brother. The fifty-year-old woman who cooked for us recounted how all three of her mother's sisters aggressively tried to prevent her mother from marrying her to the one and only brother they (the four sisters) had. When I asked why, she replied: "They didn't want my mother to have an advantage over them. A marriage like this allows a woman to go home as often as she likes and be close to her parents; sisters don't like it." Whether it is meant to incorporate the father's side or the mother's side, sacrifice in South India also serves to oppose and divide kinship relations. Likewise, a "marriage" intended to keep women together in the end drives a wedge between them. There is no avoiding such ironies.

Throughout this chapter I have endorsed the argument that an uncle–niece marriage is of a different sort from the other "right" unions reviewed so far. Its main orientation—women centered, consanguineous, inward, and sacrificial—is indeed unique. In conclusion I need to underscore, however, that what makes this preferential marriage different from the others is the mother's brother's exclusive matrimonial privilege. I will say it again: The man has absolute first right over his elder sister's daughter. Among the castes who practice uncle–niece marriage, he comes before the "right" boy: the bride's father's sister's son or the bride's mother's sister's son (in the latter case, theoretically, his elder brothers' sons, and his own son or sons). It would seem that the *tampi*'s devotional commitment to the women and his unilateral and unconditional generosity toward them entitles him to come "first" in marriage, including the usual "lawful" partners. But while the mother's brother is hierarchically superior to "right" men, all other men for that matter, he comes *after* the women (his mother, his elder sister) who clearly encompass him. In that junior and substandard capacity he not only defers to but also champions the preferential side as well as the "best love" of Tamil kinship: that of the mother (*tāy*). In fact, with his sacrifice and duty (*kaṭamai*), the mother's brother removes the other "side" from Tamil kinship: the husbands who are not needed and the fathers who turn into custodians and "friends." He especially eliminates the father's sister, as indicated by the fact that the women who participated in the survey mentioned earlier would refer to the paternal aunt as "other" (*aṉṉiyam*). It is as if the maternal uncle's actions served to promote the kinship of mother above the kinship of father—love over law (*muṟai*), ties of mutuality over ties of precedence.

5

THE UNBEARABLE CHAIN OF KINSHIP

Pācam is the love (*anpu*) between kinship relations (*murai*).
—Arulmori, age 55

Pācam is a net; you can't escape from it.
—Abi, age 21

Pācam never ends. It's a continuing story. It keeps on going. No one can stop it.
—Thangal, age 61

I've a different *pācam* for each of my relatives. My *pācam* for my father is different from the *pācam* I feel for my daughter.
—Minakshi, age 33

If a woman dies and her husband dies soon after, we call it *pācam*.
—Celvi, age 44

Human beings must have *pācam*. *Pācam* is what makes us human beings. Animals have *pācam*, too, so if we don't have *pācam*, we're lower than they are.
—Sridevi, age 25

At this point in the book it is time to clarify that most close-kin marriages in Tamil Nadu are not "preferential," as anthropologists say of marriage to either the patrilateral or matrilateral cross cousin, or the elder sister's daughter. Nor do they conform to the Tamil notions of "right," or "privileged," marriages that we have reviewed so far. It is fair to say that the castes that wed *contam* do so with kin on all "sides," in all kinds of "ways," and as often as possible. Hence, the genealogies I collected in the field are little like the elegant, symmetrical patterns typically used by anthropologists to represent Dravidian kinship organization. More like a confusing jumble of wayward arrangements that defy any notion of system, let alone preferential organization, my genealogical charts are nonetheless quite consistent with the images used by the Tamils to visualize or describe their kinship arrangements. Mayandi, in Chapter 3, spoke of the "unbroken chain" (*toṭarpu caṅkili*)[1] that entangles the Kaḷḷars of his village, a chain of loops that link and relink in roundabout and inextricable ways. And I have heard people comparing their kinship relationships to a Tamil dish called *iṭiyappam*. Anyone who has eaten a plate of these mushy and sticky "string hoppers," or spiral noodles, knows that it makes a perfect symbol of mixed-up jumble and confusion—anything but a neat structure.

There are many reasons for this. First, the reader will recall, not everyone in Tamil Nadu has unilateral matrimonial rights. Second, as I have discussed in Chapter 2, when the firstborn siblings and their firstborn children (or their designated successors) have married the "right way," brothers and sisters are free to marry their children outside the law, even on the other side of matrimonial "rightness," and this naturally upsets any tidy representation of matrilaterality or patrilaterality. Third, as I have already hinted in both Chapters 2 and 3, the elements of habit, emotional pull, self-interest (and sometimes plain circumstance) work against the implementation of matrimonial norms and therefore against clear-cut matrimonial orientations and patterns.

Hence, in real-life scenarios, close-kin unions exceed the totalizing worldview encoded in any anthropology of kinship, as well as the Tamil ideal of rules and rights. To study them, as I have already suggested in Chapter 3, we need to draw on a bundle of interrelated terms such as agent, actor, person, self, individual, subject, and what Bourdieu calls "strategy" (1977). I must point out, however, that the Tamils do not merely press goals, advance purposes, and play power games. In their capacity as kin, at least, I believe they also act on the basis of what I will call, for lack of better terms, the dread of being separated from people who are like them (*contam*) and of having to "join" with others who are different (*a<u>nn</u>iyam*). This is the basic explanation for marrying I recorded in the field. Whatever else brings people to wed kin (rule, right, game, power-play, circumstance, and so on), the need to be at home with one's in-laws, feel on par, equal, with them, is definitively a factor, and this works both at the level of cultural ideals and at the level of personal preferences.

In the genealogies I collected, all these factors express themselves in a marked inclination, even compulsion, not merely for a high degree of endogamy but also for relations that foster the convergence and overlapping of many different kinds of kinship relationships. The problem, and it is indeed a problem for some Tamils, is that when new layers of affinity overlay prior relationships of consanguinity (or vice versa), the results are not merely complicated, but "mistakes" (*tappu*) can occur. Structural superimposition is, of course, not the only source of *tappus*. Mistakes may also occur in the name of expediency, as when, for instance, a woman marries her younger sister to her son because both have some sort of physical handicap. The *tappu* here resides in the fact that, in effect, the young man marries a woman who is related to him as "little mother." But whatever the cause, it is important to note that a matrimonial "mistake" is outside the field of Tamil matrimonial law and its language of quasi-official rights. Hence, the Tamils call it *tappu*, meaning, "It shouldn't have happened," rather than *kuṟṟam*, which would imply that some kind "fault" or "crime" has been committed and the offenders ought to be prosecuted and punished.

Oedipus Again?

The mention of kinship relationships that are plainly "incorrect" or even "wrong" raises the specter of incest. This is a subject I have deliberately avoided until now, if only because this book is about marriage and not sexual intercourse between close relatives. Moreover, from the perspective of my consultants, the marriages reviewed so far, including the "mistakes" to be described in this chapter, are not tabooed. Finally, and perhaps more critically, I am reluctant to apply the Freudian theory of incest to my ethnography.

First, there is the weight of the allegation, the assertion of incest in and of itself. It is no small matter for an anthropologist, a foreign-born anthropologist at that, to allege that her subjects have incestuous desires, especially when they have no concept—or as Dumont put it, no "imagination" (1986: 202)—for something like an attraction to the opposite-sex parent. It comes down to the question of what anthropology is, and the role of the anthropologist, the Western anthropologist in particular. Do we, foreigners, go to the field with the aim of eliciting the "native point of view"? No matter how naïve, lofty, and hopeless it may sound, this still strikes me as a noble goal. Or do we go to tell our informants that, contrary to all appearances, *they* are the strangers, that they do not know themselves, and that it is our duty to tell them who they really are?

Second, the Freudian thesis of incest as a natural and universal human desire does not in point of fact account for the ethnographic facts I have recorded in Tamil Nadu. Quite simply, the marital (or kinship) patterns I present in this book fit neither the Oedipal nor the counter-Oedipal scenarios usually discussed in the context of South Asian scholarship. For the latter category, I have in mind A. K. Ramanujan's suggestion that many South Indian folktales suggest a reversal in the direction of violence familiar to us from the Greek myth, depicting not sons murdering fathers but rather fathers killing, castrating, or dismembering sons (Ramanujan 1983; Shulman 1993).

A case could be made that such an "Indian Oedipal pattern" is at work in Mayandi's comment that he took a woman (the elder sister's daughter) who, according to his caste's matrimonial law, should have gone to his own son. But before we speak of a father's feelings of jealousy and anger for his offspring's right to marry a closely related girl, let me repeat again that sisters and mothers are crucial, in fact central, to arranging the uncle–niece marriage. In my view this union rather emasculates husbands and fathers so that its underlying psychological complex can be neither the Greek nor the Indian Oedipus.

And what of Bronislaw Malinowski's argument (1927)[2] that in a matrilineal society that gives special valuation to the mother's brother, it is this man, and not the father, who is the object of Oedipal fantasies and rivalries? The majority of Tamil castes are patrilineal, yet on some occasions men would appear to begrudge the prominent role assumed by the mother's brother. Once, at a young woman's puberty ceremony, I noticed that her biological and classificatory "brothers" were clustered together at the periphery of the ritual space, looking sullen and resentful. When I reported this observation to Neelam (of Chapter 3), he explained that young men "envy" the *māma*, whose ritual role is to beautify and garland their sister with flowers. The lesson I took from his comment is that what is forbidden is no less desirable in Tamil rituals than it is in Freudian psychology. But I do not think that we can say that Tamil brothers harbor the "wish . . . to marry the sister *and* . . . kill the maternal uncle" (Malinowski 1937: 81, my emphasis). Recall that *appā* is a disciplinarian figure, and, as previously mentioned, Tamil literature (both classical and folk) has him pegged as his son's murderer (Ramanujan 1983; Shulman 1993). The *tāymāmā*, by contrast, is a confidant, an accomplice, a protector (even against the father at times). It is true that the Tamil mother's brother has the first right to take a man's sister, but in all castes he is the giver par excellence and in some castes (among the Kaḷḷars, for example) he is also the prototypical bride giver. Killing him would be like killing *ammā*; it would make no psychoanalytical sense.

At this point the reader may wish to point out that, if not substantiating men's "wish" to kill other men (sons, fathers, maternal uncles), my ethnography nonetheless demonstrates the presence of Oedipal feelings for mothers and sisters—as just suggested by my description of brothers' behaviors at puberty rituals. Because this fantasy of incest with the cross sibling is what Margaret Trawick's ethnographic study of Tamil family love (1990) puzzles over, I now return to her argument, first brought up in the Introduction.

According to Trawick, the love that links the four main relationships of the Tamil nuclear family has much in common with the Lacanian psychoanalytic theory of "incompletedness of being." In the mother–daughter, father–son, husband–wife, and brother–sister relationships, Tamil individuals experience themselves or/and the other person as lacking. "The father longs for continuity, but the son longs for independence." "The daughter longs for continuity, but the mother longs for independence." "The bond between brother and sister is strong but must be denied." "The bond between husband and wife is conflictful but difficult to sever" (1990: 158–184). Based on her reading of Lacan's work, Trawick suggests that the persistence of lack in the self and the other gives rise to a movement of desire, a desire to recapture the oneness that preceded the disunity and the associated experience of incompleteness. For her, Tamil cross-cousin marriage best lends support to her claim that "Lacan has hit upon some truths that Tamils have also discovered" (1990: 142), as this practice expresses the Tamil ideal: "Siblings live in their children, and in uniting their children, unite their own lives again" (1990: 177). Although Trawick does not say that the siblings' strong mutual love is sexual, she does trace it to the first object of their sexual desires, namely the mother. As she writes: "I am suggesting here that intense erotic love for the mother might under some circumstances be converted to intense attachment between brother and sister" (1990: 182).

It is tempting to adopt Trawick's insight that Tamil close-kin marriage derives from the nature of relations from within the nuclear family. But such relations, in my view, are far more complex than Trawick indicates and involve strong bonds that extend between mothers and daughters—not that "love" is absent from the Tamil brother–sister relationship I recorded. On the contrary, many consultants were very clear that they love their cross siblings more than they love their spouses. But, as I have suggested in the last chapter, the emotion that frames the uncle–niece marriage is not linked to the archaic feelings of childhood but to dynamics of sublimation and beyond that to sacrificial enactments. Moreover, the Lacanian notion of unfulfillment ("unspent desire") does not mesh very well with matrimonial institutions that have the coercive power of law and the force of "right" and "entitlement," as it especially does for Tamil sisters. Of course, there are all kinds of Tamil sisters: motherly sisters, compassionate sisters, energetic sisters, lazy sisters, selfish sisters, and so on. But what my ethnography reveals is that, when it comes to marrying their daughters to their brothers or their brothers' sons, Tamil sisters can be quite pushy (recall Virumandi's sisters, in Chapter 2). They also can be quite protective of their brothers' own matrimonial rights. To give an example of such behavior, once, at a puberty ceremony, I witnessed how a Kaḷḷar young woman reacted when the photographer, hired for the occasion, took pictures of the beautified girl and one of her male matrilateral cross cousins. This woman went to fetch her own unmarried brother who, in this case, stood in the category of "right boy" (father's sister's son) to the girl and ordered the photographer: "Take pictures of him and her too! He has *urimai*." Of course, to say that sisters seek only to control the ways in which brothers and brothers' children marry is grossly simplistic. But one thing is almost certain: The "love" in the sister–brother relation is mixed with a clear sense of "entitlement."

There is another reason why I cannot endorse the argument that Tamil cross-cousin marriage is a search for "completeness" on the part of the brother and sister. In my fieldwork experience, same-sex kin are very active in arranging marriage with *contam*. Here I am not simply referring to the mothers and daughters who conclude the uncle–niece marriage depicted in the last chapter. I am also talking of same-sex *siblings* who are key players as well. This becomes obvious when we move one generation up and examine the role of grandparents.

Two brothers, for example, may very well pressure their respective sons and daughters to marry their children to each other, so that the family property, lineage deity, memory of the father, and so on, remain undivided and in one piece. Another arrangement is possible. Let us suppose that the senior brother has a daughter who herself has a daughter. The junior brother is likely to press on the first woman that she is like a daughter to him, therefore like a sister to his own son, for we recall that the children of two brothers stand in the classificatory status of siblings. Hence the junior brother is in his right to demand that his "daughter" give her daughter to her "brother." Such male interest in uncle–niece marriage should not surprise the reader: Men, or rather brothers, also have their practical and emotional reasons for arranging a union that essentially works to prevent dispersal. Moreover, the two women of this hypothetical, but common, scenario are likely to welcome the arrangement as it will cast the daughter back on her mother's side of the family and thus work against straightforward conjugality.

The anthropologist Pauline Kolenda writes: "The relationship between sisters is not culturally emphasized, but sisters can maintain their relationships with each other, since travel for women is much freer for women in South India than in central or north India" (1993: 104). In my own fieldwork experience, married sisters not only visit each other on a regular basis, but they also strive to reside in the same neighborhood (or even the same house) if only because they too are involved, more so than brothers in fact, in arranging the very marriages that can help them regroup in the later part of life.

To be sure, the brother–sister bond is relevant insofar as it has priority over the husband–wife bond. However, same-sex sibling ties and filial relationships can be deployed to assert what I consider to be the main principle of Tamil kinship: a preference, framed as a "right," to *not* integrate or merge with others but rather to stay with people of the same sort so as to be at home with them and in control and possession of common resources.

The thing is, when grandparents, parents, spouses, cross siblings, and siblings all want to stay together by means of marriage, people end up locked in "chains" of kinship that bind them like "sticky noodles." As a result, they juggle multiple, and at times conflicting, kinship roles, some of which can be *tappu* and a real source of embarrassment. And herein lies another reason why any Lacanian notion of unfulfillment ("unspent desire") cannot apply in my research. The extremely endogamous patterns I have recorded in the field do not leave much room for "absence," "searching," and "striving"—all key concepts for Lacan and Trawick. They make instead for a field of rampant connections that at times results in flawed relationships, contradictory statuses, and incoherent roles. In such a kinship landscape the problem is not how people merge or "complete" themselves in others—for they have the matrimonial means to do just that in abundance—but how they can *undo* their inappropriate relations and recover the correct kinship oppositions. Before giving a feel for what it might be like to live in such a kinship landscape, the next section describes four ethnographic examples of muddled or even *tappu* marriages, each with a diagram, so as to make the discussion easier to follow.

Matrimonial Mistakes

In the first example (see Figure 5.1), an elder sister p1 and her younger sister p2 each have a daughter (p3 and p4), so that these two girls stand in the position of classificatory sisters. Usually the children of two sisters cannot marry, but here the senior women do not play by the rules. They marry the elder sister's daughter p3 to the younger's sister's grandson p5. Normally (but is there such a thing as a normal state of affairs in South Indian kinship?) this marriage would not take place because it is wrong (*tappu*) for a man to marry a woman who stands in the position of (classificatory) sister to his mother. In effect, p5 marries a woman p3 who is like a mother to him. The problem or *tappu* here is compounded by the fact that p3 is in a position of elder sister (*akkā*) vis-à-vis her husband's mother. Not that p3 is biologically older than p4 (and in the real-life example from which I draw this kinship scenario, she was not), but because her mother p1 is the senior sister in the preceding generation, she inherits that marker of precedence. The Tamils think it is a mistake for a wife to be of higher status than her mother-in-law because a daughter-in-law should not think of herself as better than her husband's family. But the greater mistake here is that a man marries a mother—a "big mother" at that.[3]

The chart in Figure 5.2 begins with three siblings: the first son p1, a middle daughter p2, and the last child, a boy p3. The sister p2 has two daughters, p5 and p6. She marries the first one, p5, to her eldest brother's son, p4, and the second one, p6, to her younger brother, p3. Now that the boy p4 and his "little father" p3 are married to two sisters p5 and p6, they become *cakalar*, or "like

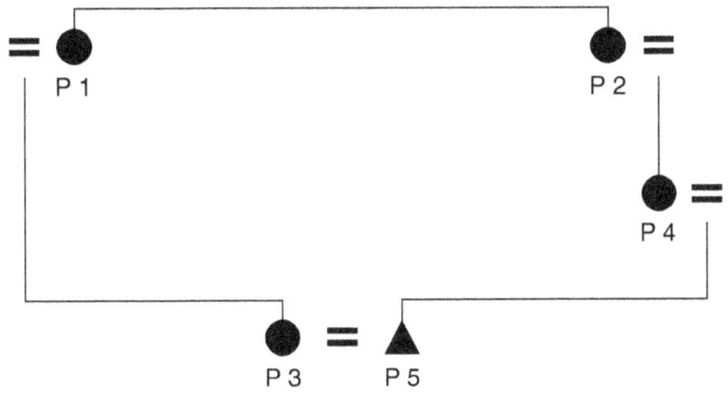

Figure 5.1.

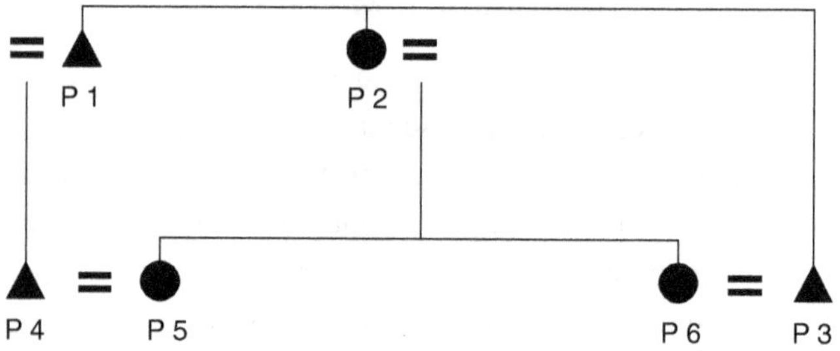

Figure 5.2.

brothers" (perhaps from the root *caka*, which means "with" "together," because that is what sisters' husbands are in Tamil).[4] In essence their respective marriages turn their filial and hierarchical relationship (classificatory father/son) into a classificatory sibling and more equal bond. In addition, p4 is related to his wife p5 in two ways. She is his father's sister's daughter *and* sister of his younger father's wife (*ciṉṉammā*). The latter status, begotten through the male line, prevails, and by extension his wife stands in the odd position of *ciṉṉammā* or "little mother."

The chart in Figure 5.3 starts with a sister p1 and her brother p2. The sister marries her son, p4, to the sister, p5, of her brother's wife, p3. Because p2 and p4 are married to two sisters, the maternal uncle, p2, and his sister's son, p4, (the two prototypical affines of Tamil kinship) become "like brothers." They still go by the affinal terminology, calling themselves respectively "*māmā*" and "*marumakaṉ*," but their children will relate as siblings because their mothers, p3 and p5, are sisters. The one man p2 will become "big father" (*periyappā*) to the children of p4 and p5, and p4 will in turn become "little father" (*cittappā*) to the children of p2 and p3. There is another twist: In effect, p4 marries a woman, p5, who falls in the category of "mother-in-law," for a maternal uncle's wife p3 is *attai* and her sister is also *attai*.

The final figure, Figure 5.4, is drawn from the genealogy of my Kaḷḷar consultant Mayandi (see Chapter 3), who is represented here as p5. But let us start from his father, p1, and his father's sister, p2. Mayandi's father p1 has four children (actually five, but the last son, not represented here, died at the age of fifteen): a daughter p3, a son p4, Mayandi p5, and another son p6. His sister, p2, has six children, but here I include only her boy, p7, and her girl, p8.

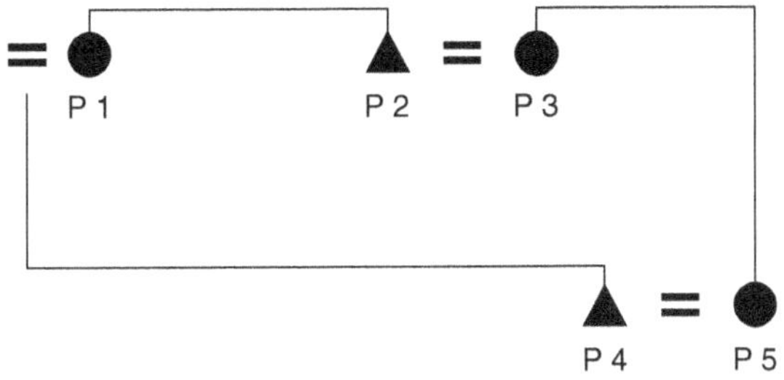

Figure 5.3.

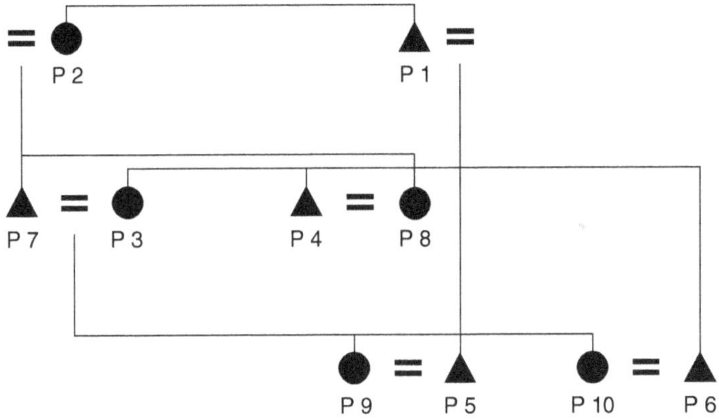

Figure 5.4.

The two siblings p1 and p2 marry his (p1's) first daughter, p3, to her first son, p7 (as is *muṟai* among the Kaḷḷars). Then, in an arrangement known in anthropology as "sister-exchange," they marry the brother's (p1's) first son, p4, to the sister's (p2's) first daughter, p8. The reader knows that Mayandi, p5, wanted to marry his "right girl," his mother's brother's daughter (not represented in this chart because the marriage did not take place). Twenty years later his sister, p3, persuaded him to marry her first daughter, p9. Then she went on to marry her youngest brother, p6, to her second daughter, p10. There is actually no real *tappu* here (except, of course, that the Kaḷḷars condemn marriage to the sister's daughter), but the reader can see that the relationships between Mayandi and his siblings are so unstructured, so entangled, that it does not make sense to speak in terms of the usual axes of kinship theory: "descent," or the ordering of genealogical connection, and even less of "alliance," which is the usual anthropological definition of marriage.

The Tamil people I worked with in and around the town of Madurai married very close, so close that at times their marriages "confused" or "jumbled up" their relationships in such a way that fathers and sons, or maternal uncles and nephews, became "brothers," and wives were also "little mothers" or "mothers-in-law." Of course, these arrangements were not considered "right" by any Tamil standard, but in virtually every genealogy I collected at least one "mistake" surfaced, reconfiguring all nearby relationships in the domino-like effect I have just described.

It seems to me that these ethnographic realities encourage us to think less about Western psychology and more about what it is like to be part of an inner movement that links (indeed, as the Tamils put it, "chains") people together in multiple, ambiguous, and at times very embarrassing kinship relations. I do not think that the people living in such kinship loops feel deficient in relationships. I surmise that instead they feel fettered and ensnared, as evidenced by the metaphor a woman used to describe her endogamous household: a rat trap (*eli mutaliya piṭikkum poṟi*).

It is likely that endogamy in South India involves at least as much rivalry, resentment, and violence as in the Oedipal myth of psychoanalysis. But the context that frames these relations generates its own specific pathos, drawn from a worldview in which arranging a marriage is the closest thing to what we call "family love." When people are married wrongly or with mistakes, they harbor not desire but deep resentment, and, as the next case study suggests, the dynamics of aggression are ultimately quite different from those depicted in the Greek or Indian Oedipus myth.

Thiagu

I first met Thiagu in 1989–1990 when I was studying Tamil at the American Institute of Indian Studies in Madurai. The seventeen-year-old son of a bookbinder, he would spend as much time away from his home as possible. My family adopted him, and he called me, the mother of a then ten-year-old daughter, "*māmi*" (which is the preferred Christian term for maternal uncle's wife). He did not speak English, but with his knack for understanding my broken Tamil, we managed to communicate. In any case I needed no words to enjoy his presence. A performer with a rich repertoire of Tamil movie songs and an artist with aesthetic sensibilities, Thiagu filled the air with lightness and beauty. The two ladies who prepared food for my family loved him, not least because he always complimented their cooking. When Thiagu was around, we had fun, ate well, and always learned something new because he had an eye and an ear for things that were not even on my ethnographic agenda: plants, parchments, markets, "traditional" houses, stories, photographs, and religious iconography.

Nineteen years later I met him again in the lobby of a hotel in Madurai. I could neither feel nor express the emotions of delight I had anticipated because the signs of his decline were unmistakable. Puffy and shaky, he looked so much older than his age. I wanted to cry at the toll that life had taken on him but managed to smile.

He had time, he said, about six weeks before he had to return to Madras (Chennai) where he now lived. Could we work together again for that period of time? "Again," he said, because years before he had helped me research my end-of-year paper for the language program at the American Institute of Indian Studies, which I wrote on the cult of the Madurai "black god," *Kaṟuppacāmi*. I agreed, but I soon realized that his idea of fieldwork had evolved. He still took me to "religious" people—a priestess of a sacred grove with long matted hair, a Dalit clairvoyant, and so on—but never for very long, thirty minutes at the most. In fact, quite often he would disappear as soon as we reached an ethnographic destination under the pretext that he needed cigarettes or gas for the motorcycle, but I knew he went off to drink. Yes, it was quite clear that he drank—the hard stuff, not beer.

He gossiped, too, intimating, for example, that my neighbor slept with her husband's younger brother or that the sister of so-and-so had been raped. Abuse, murder, vengeful tricks, and some elements of grotesque comedy or wry humor filled the plots of his stories. The prevailing tone was rhetorically exalted; he endowed everything with symbolic, mythic, or magic properties. Once, for example, he read my palm: "You've all these gifts," he said, "but you're like a cat walking on the wall with foul water on one side and someone ready to shoo you on the other. You can only walk on the wall." "Do you mean to say that I've no place to go?" I tried to follow. "You've a place to go," he replied, "but you're losing money." Thinking of my daughter's college tuition, I laughed his remark off, "I know where the money is going!" "You're not listening," he raised his voice, "Don't say that! It's happening. You're not thinking about what I'm telling you. You've got so many problems, but you want to escape. You're standing on the wall like that cat." "Am I not taking enough risks?" I asked. "You're taking risks. That's why you've got so many problems." We laughed, hard and long.

Once we went to Chennai together on the spur of the moment. The train was packed and, without confirmed reservations, we had to stand. Thiagu, who was not sober, immediately ordered the conductor to convert my wait-listed ticket into a foreign-tourist quota seat in the air-conditioned compartment. He made such a fuss that I went to stand in second class, leaving him cross-legged on the floor by the door to the AC compartment. He was still there when I brought him tea a couple of hours later, but now he was deeply engaged with another passenger squatting across him. The man (as it turned out, a chief officer of a Madurai police station) kept staring at Thiagu, whose own eyes were filled with tears that streamed down his cheeks. It did not take me long to realize that my friend was in a state of trance, in the midst of "decoding the signs" (*kuṟi coḷḷutal*) of this man's life. When, halfway through the trip, the conductor let us all into the AC car, the two men did not say a word to each other. It was as if they had never met.

I knew I was not getting anywhere but could not let go of Thiagu, needing his company in ways that I did not understand myself. Because it was neither productive nor safe to ride his motorcycle we spent an increasing amount of time in his ancestral home on the outskirt of Madurai, watching Tamil films and talking about marriage with *contam*. Without my or his realizing it, the ethnographic conversation quickly became private, even intimate—more quickly in fact than I would like to admit. In hindsight, though, I can plainly see that our conversations were bound to cross the personal line as one source of Thiagu's suffering lay precisely in the line of my study.

Because I did not think of Thiagu as an informant and because I was slow to discern that his experiences constituted "data," I seldom recorded our talks. As part of my ethnographic routine, though, I daily recapitulated our conversations in my field notes, drawing in genealogical format the many close marriages in his family—marriages that he evoked with so much bitterness. When he departed for Madras six weeks later, I was left with a maze of diagrams filled with holes and blank spaces. To fill in the gaps in my records, I paid numerous visits to Thiagu's widowed paternal aunt (*attai*) who, together with her daughter, offered genealogical information in a more linear narrative. I begin my account with these later facts, which amid silences and downright avoidance suggest the connections that ultimately entangle every member of this family in its history of violence.

WHAT ATTAI SAID

A strong looking woman who liked to play cards and dice, Thiagu's aunt (Attai) had both a sweet tooth and a remarkable genealogical memory. Perhaps because I usually showed up at her door with a box of *laddus*, *maladus*, coconut *burfis*, *jilabis*, or other Indian treats, she kindly agreed to walk me through six generations of her family history, from her grandparents to her great-grandchildren. She and her daughter patiently reviewed the many graphs my assistant Anand and I successively drafted, referring to our various working documents as *curukkam*, which means "abbreviation," or "abstract." In my discussion here I zoom in on the (mostly marital) relationships the two women themselves focused on. A brief note in advance: In their caste the "right girl" is the father's sister's daughter and the "right boy" the mother's brother's son.

Attai was ten months old when her mother succumbed to typhoid. Six months later her father remarried, leaving her and her brother (Thiagu's father), then two-and-a-half years old, in the care of their maternal grandfather. The old man raised his deceased daughter's children, eventually marrying them "on his side," specifically to two of his younger brother's children in an arrangement known in Tamil as *kuṇṭu mātti kuḻi mātti*, an expression that is also used when two players of the game *pallāṅkuḻi* ("fourteen pits") trade counters (beads or shells) on a wooden board that has fourteen pits in all.[5] I have heard Tamils say that they do not like the exchange of brides between two families, much as Louis Dumont reports, on the grounds that, if trouble arises in one of the two couples, "a quarrel or divorce will immediately be repeated by the other couple as reprisal" (1986: 205). But Attai herself brought up practical advantages: "I don't give anything, and you don't either." This statement reminds us that, decidedly, Tamil marriage with *contam* is less about reciprocity than a zero-sum game.

In this case, however, there was an additional layer of complexity. The maternal grandfather's younger brother was married to his younger sister's two

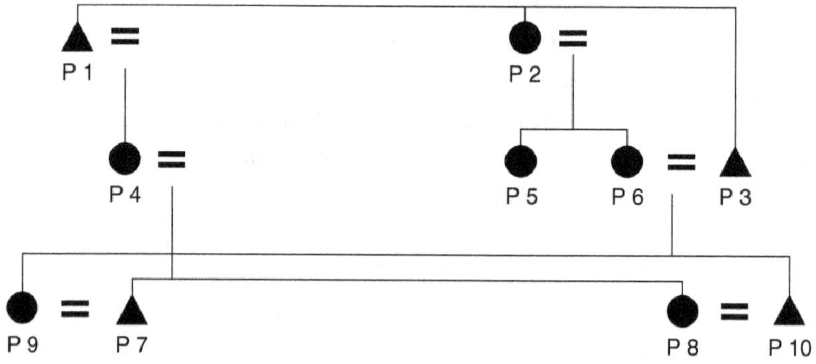

Figure 5.5.

daughters (one of whom was blind), so that Attai and her brother married a pair of siblings who were related to them in two main ways, and one of them, I will now show, was not "right" at all. Consider the diagram of these relationships shown in Figure 5.5.

At the first level, this chart depicts three siblings: a boy, p1; a girl, p2; and another boy p3. The first son, p1, has many children, but the only one depicted here is Attai's mother, p4, who died after giving birth to Attai's brother, p7, and Attai herself, p8. The second daughter, p2, marries her two daughters, p5 (who is blind) and p6, to her younger brother, p3. The first son, p1, marries his (deceased) daughter's children, p7 and p8, to his younger brother's children, p9 and p10. Because p9 and p10 are also the grandchildren of p2, all three siblings—p1, p2, and p3—"rejoin" at the third generation.

In effect, Attai p8 married a man, p10, who stood in the *ideal* classificatory position of mother's brother. The man p10 and Attai's mother p4 were "brother and sister" by virtue of being children of two brothers, p1 and p3.

Note that when we trace their relationship through his mother, Attai's husband is also related to her as her second-degree patrilateral cross cousin because both her mother p4 and his (either p5 or p6) are children of a brother, p1, and sister, p2.

Although *Attai* married properly, her brother, p7 (Thiagu's father), did not. Because his wife, p9, was his mother's (p4's) younger classificatory sister—they were children of two brothers, p1 and p3—she was "little mother" to him. To be sure, when reckoned through her mother's line (either p5 or p6), she was also his second-degree cross cousin, but it was the link through her father, p3, that prevailed. This was why Thiagu's father sometimes referred to his wife as "*citti*" ("little mother") *but he never addressed her that way* because that would have been too shameful for the couple.

Let me recap the main facts of Attai's account so far. A young mother dies, a father leaves, and two small children are left to the care of their maternal grandfather. This is not unusual: My field notes contain other examples in which a daughter's death leaves her father in charge of raising and arranging marriages for her children. That the man here chose to marry his grandchildren to his brother's children (and his sister's grandchildren) is also not that surprising. In many of the genealogies I collected, death jump-starts marriages between the immediate descendants of same-sex siblings—not a small thing to consider when we recall that, two to three generations ago, mortality rates were still quite high in Tamil Nadu (Guilmoto 1992). Finally, Attai's account confirms what my broader research shows, namely that the anthropological categories "cross-cousin marriage" and its associated polar opposites "affine" and "kin" do not begin to describe the many ways in which the Tamils marry or rather "chain" themselves in very closed, and at times faulty, circuits.

Attai got married at the age of fourteen. The year was 1959. Five years later, her husband, a truck driver, took his own life the day after his boss reprimanded him for having caused a road accident. Attai and her two small children moved in with her brother, Thiagu's father. Her brother's wife was away at the time; she had gone back to her natal home pregnant with Thiagu, as Tamil women then used to give birth in their mother's place.

Thiagu remembered growing up with Attai and her children. But Attai herself told me that her brother's wife (recall, her own "little mother" as well) kicked her out when she came home a few months later. Whether Attai continued living in her brother's house and in his care, or went off on her own as she claimed, working sometimes as a seamstress and sometimes as a coolie in the fields, I do not know. But the two siblings must have remained in close contact because years later they arranged for her firstborn son to marry her brother's eldest daughter, which further muddled the relationships in this family.

Although Thiagu maintained that his father had opposed this marriage, it is very likely that the man saw the practical benefits of a union that essentially would save him the cost of a dowry. But convenience, even if this was the motive, is no guarantee of happiness. Barely eight months into the marriage,

Attai's son killed himself. He "loved" another girl. Because I never had the heart to ask Attai to speak about her son's death and because Thiagu himself obsessively relived the events that led first to his sister's widowhood and then to her own suicide, I now switch to his version.

WHAT THIAGU SAID

"My father had to take them in," Thiagu protested, "He was maternal uncle to these children." According to him, it was because his father raised his sister's son like his own son that he opposed the marriage. As Thiagu said, "How was my father supposed to call the boy now? 'Son-in-law'? He couldn't do it." In Thiagu's version both his mother and Attai pressured his father, who eventually relented. As he recalled: "Attai would implore, 'Give your girl to my son,' and my mother, 'Give our girl to my brother's son.'" We recall that Thiagu's mother was Attai's (dead) husband's sister.

Thiagu was sure that the young couple never consummated the marriage. "When the spouse is like a sister," he reasoned, "there's no desire (*ācai illai*), no love (*kātal illai*). The man just doesn't think about it. He wouldn't know where to begin even if he were lying naked next to the woman." Thiagu added for my benefit that in such circumstances, parents or elder married siblings usually pressure the couple, locking them in a room together so as to force them to have sex—"compulsory sex," he repeated loudly. In this case, however, the family had no time to intervene; the young man took poison and died. "By the time my parents realized what they had done, it was too late," Thiagu lashed out angrily, "The boy was dead and my sister a widow."

Traditionally Hinduism has frowned on widows remarrying, and many still face discrimination and neglect, but in recent years the Indian state, and the Tamil state in particular, have created schemes and incentives to change their lot. Nowadays it is increasingly possible for a Tamil widow to remarry, especially one with a good job and dowry. Thus, Thiagu's sister went back to school to become a nurse; over time she obtained a coveted position in a government hospital, and the family found her another husband. Attai gave her consent, and the family offered a sizeable dowry. But what could have been a happy ending to a sad story did not come to pass. According to Thiagu, the new husband mistreated his sister. Five years later, she killed herself, leaving two young sons behind. For my friend, her death was no suicide. "*Murder*," he screamed in pain, "the dog never let her forget she was a widow; he killed her!"

Thiagu could not release himself from the memory of his sister's death, which tormented him in more than one way. "The moment she died," he would repeat, "I became a drunk! . . . I can't bear the thought of these two boys raised by her murderer!" He did not dwell on the two previous suicides: the first (but was it even the first in this family?) by Attai's husband and also Thiagu's mother's brother; the second by Attai's son, who was "like a brother" to him. But when he drank, he would return to the episode of his elder sister's death, and recounting it inevitably made him sob like a child. I learned from experience that going down this road was not good for him. But there was no stopping him, as he spoke furiously, binging on grief and lamentation. When I could not take it anymore, I would leave the house.

Suicide and Retribution

We will never know what exactly causes Tamil families to marry as closely as Thiagu's family did. But it is hard to believe that the reasons are anything but subtle, varied, and profound. The death of a daughter, a yearning to join and rejoin, love, convenience, pressure from relatives who hold kinship rights, and the wish for power all certainly factor in. It is just as likely that the elements of compulsion, the inability to separate, and the sheer dread of being outside one's kinship world—one's zone of comfort—push families into intertwinement.

In previous chapters I have shown how a society that equates endogamy with not merely equality but also "rightness" and "privilege" exacerbates patterns of childhood anguish evoked by the kin's opportunism, favoritism, betrayal, and withdrawal: junior siblings feeling excluded by their seniors, brothers feeling taken for granted, even "bossed around," as I heard one man say, by manipulative sisters, and so on. I have also highlighted the trauma that results from marrying on one's own without parents and elder siblings making the arrangement. This chapter's case study brings out a source of injury that is more specific to extreme endogamy. When someone is thrown into a marriage that muddles kinship roles, he or she feels not merely unappreciated or confused but deeply ashamed. In this context, the thought that "my wife is my younger mother" is sure to cause indignity.

Perhaps now we can understand why Tamils hang on to the one source of polarity, and therefore clarity, in their marriage practices: the principle of laterality. As I have already stated, husbands and wives fight hard over which side to marry their child on. One suspects that their sons and daughters would feel trapped or hounded like a "cat on the wall," but Tamil children are not left completely defenseless. They are socialized to choose between mother and father and play the same game of rank and exclusion as their parents. Consider the question repeatedly put to them at an early age: "Are you Daddy's child (*appā piḷḷai*) or Mommy's child (*ammā piḷḷai*)?"—as if this were an innocent game.

For Thiagu, however, the answer provoked risky and devastating consequences. If you side with or identify with "*appā*," as he did, "your mother doesn't love you." As he explained: "She gives you bitter chewing paste instead of milk; she betrays you and tries to do you in all the time." "She never loved me," he would say of his mother, an accusation that surprised me because, as I pointed out in the last chapter, in general *Ammā* is the source of love in Tamil kinship cosmology. Moreover, the literature on the Hindu tradition usually points to the cultural devaluation not of a boy but of a girl. This devaluation comes, however, with important psychological compensations in the particular attention given to a girl by her mother and by others in the natal household. The boy, by contrast, is often depicted as receiving disproportionate outpourings of possessive, nurturing, overwhelming love and demands that leave him weak, dependent, nonautonomous, and not very confident in his own judgment (Kakar 1978).

If Thiagu felt no kinship with his mother—"She is not my mother," "We are not the same color"—he strongly identified with his father and even looked like him. When I had first met him twenty years before, his father was a trickster, a raconteur, definitively a performer. But years of drinking had bloated the old man, who was also plagued with boils that never seemed to heal. Tragic memories weighed him down as well: the loss of his mother at a young age; a *tappu* marriage; and the suicides of—in turn—his sister's husband (and classificatory mother's brother as well), a boy he raised like a son, and his own daughter. Sick and estranged from the two most important women of his life, his wife and Attai (whom he had not seen in years), he seemed to take grim refuge in alcohol.

But Thiagu defended the old man:

> My father lived unhappily under the shadow of his wife and sister, who always competed to usurp power. My father was just a convenient pawn in their hands. Everything that concerned him—what he should eat, what he should do—became a bone of contention between them. If his sister took a stand, his

> wife would take the opposite one. My father didn't complain. Whenever he couldn't bear the fighting anymore, he just left the house.

For Thiagu, it seemed, his father did no wrong. The two women—Thiagu's mother, in particular, who in a bizarre kinship twist also stood as his father's own "little mother"—had engineered all the family tragedies.

Thiagu emphasized, however, that in his family individuals seldom vented grievances (*veḷippaṭai*) in the open. Instead they found quiet ways to "punish" (*taṇṭi*) the offenders. While in the field I witnessed many instances of this kind of silent rebuking behavior. Once the woman of a household where I lived for a few days in Madurai wanted to attend a ceremonial function in a nearby village. She asked her son to give her a ride to the central bus stop, but he turned her down. She resorted to asking a young man who ran errands for the family, but on the morning of her departure he failed to show up. Instead of looking for him or finding another way to get to the bus stop, she sat in the inner courtyard looking deeply unhappy. When I offered to pay for a taxi, the daughter told me to leave her mother alone because she was not feeling well (*maṉam cari illai*). To me it seemed that the woman deliberately missed her bus to punish both her son and the young helper. Her whole body language communicated the message, "See what you're doing to me! You prevented me from going on my trip!" But she never said as much in words.

The most dramatic expression of the behavior I am describing here is suicide—a painful leitmotif of this chapter's case study. This is not the first time, however, that I am led to reflect on how very common suicide is in Tamil Nadu. I concluded a previous publication with these lines: "A central entry of my field notes concerns the category 'suicide' (*taṟkolai*). The word runs through many pages of my notebooks like a sinister refrain" (Clark-Decès 2007: 109). I added, "In many Tamil family histories or genealogies I collected there was a threat of suicide, an anticipation of suicide, a memory of suicide and so on" (Clark-Decès 2007: 109). At the time I wrote these lines I was not aware that South India, particularly Kerala and Tamil Nadu, and Sri Lanka have reported the world's highest suicide rates (Mayer 2011).[6]

In a village located in the Tanjavur district, the German anthropologist Gabriele Alex observed that the loss of a job and income or the failure to pay one's debts or pass an important entry test become reasons to kill oneself (2008). But I am struck by her observation that in two of the four cases she analyzed "suicide can be a means of blaming other people and ascribing guilt" (2008: 69–70). As Alex explains: "If a man kills himself after his wife has committed adultery, she will be blamed by the community for his death; or if a man commits suicide for not being able to repay his debts, it is the money lender whom people will hold responsible" (2008: 70). Her logical conclusion is that in Tamil Nadu suicide "allows people to shift the shame and blame from themselves to others and regain their own good name" (2008: 70).

The great challenge for any anthropologist is to remain cautious about offering strong judgments of her own. But I must say that Alex's daring and paradoxical conclusion resonates with my findings.[7] In my field experience, suicide is a means of retribution. Thiagu's maternal uncle, Attai's husband, killed himself to shame the boss who scolded him after the accident. Attai's son took his life, from Thiagu's own account, not merely out of despair at being in a loveless marriage but also to get back at those who arranged it. It is also possible that Thiagu's own sister killed herself to shame her abusive second husband.

Such an objective in suicide offends against what we take as the standard of Western rationality (or the myth of Western rationality, I should say), but a logic of efficiency and self-maximization is not the only good or value in this world. Very different considerations prevail in Tamil Nadu, where reputation matters and where the possession of status is the highest good. In such a society besmirching a perpetrator's name or bringing him low with shame can be the source of immense gratification—regardless of the cost to oneself. The price may be as low as missing a bus and a ceremonial function and as high as dying. To some Tamils at least, the satisfaction of taking revenge against an enemy or someone responsible for one's suffering—a kind of wild justice—is worth any price.

It is not my intention to establish that Tamil families who repeatedly marry "within" are more prone to violence than those who do not. In fact, I delayed bringing up Thiagu's case in this book for fear that the reader would jump to the conclusion that dysfunctional marriages, thwarted marriages, "wrongly classified" marriages, and suicidal marriages are the norm. Not *all* Tamil marriages with kin are hopelessly confused and screwed up; many are "successful" and "correct," involving couples who achieve a balance of conjugal and familial satisfaction. But whether it represents a weak position or an act of productive power, the instinct to injure self and other is so strong in the case materials I collected that it is difficult for me to make the case that the life lived in highly endogamous families is automatically "loving." It is even more difficult for me to support the notion that people in these close relations entertain Freudian or Lacanian fantasies of incest. The people I introduced in this chapter did not need to fantasize about sexual attachment to parents and siblings; they were fettered to, and even "locked up with," these relatives. The central dilemma they faced was how to free themselves from the chain of kinship, how to release themselves from each other.

This language of fetters and chains is not mine alone. The Tamils use it. Associations of captivity and bondage surfaced in many of my conservations, as when married women complained that life with closely related in-laws was "boring," using this English word. "Nothing is new," they would say, "nothing ever changes; we keep on living with the same people." To be sure, every generation or so the processes of birth and death do recompose any household, adding a person here, subtracting another one there. But these women meant that life is boring when no "outsider" comes in. I detected a sense of ambivalence amid all the praise for marrying *contam*, a feeling that the family is strangled, even trapped, by its likeness and familiarity. As a Brahmin woman told me in English: "When you grow up in such a family, people know that your mother was a sick child. They know how your father lost money. Why your grandmother doesn't talk." What I understood her to say is that this kind of private history, built over generations, yields a kind of claustrophobia that has no cure. Not that this life is necessarily intolerable, but the plague of familiarity forces everyone to surrender to habit and repetition, binding them to the same traumas and patterns of deadly revenge.

6

THE WRONGNESS OF KIN

I've never liked my family, madam, I'm sorry to tell you. They never arranged my marriage.
—Kavita, age 44

In this world, there's so much to learn. I want to study and work and expand my brain.
—Abi, age 21

Even a cowherd asks for dowry and wants the wedding expenses taken care of by the bride's parents . . . In earlier times, the girl was enough; they needed the girl to help in the house, to light the lamp in their house, so they even gave gold . . . The groom's parents would come seeking an alliance . . . they would walk a hundred times up and down to our house.
—Sundari Ravindran 1999: 39

As already mentioned in the Introduction, when I returned to Tamil Nadu in 2007 I initially lived in a multicaste village located twenty or thirty kilometers away from the town of Pondicherry. The 1,600 or so people who resided there thought of themselves as "modern." Indeed, some key signs of development were visible: Children went to school, an increasing number of students headed to college, women gave birth in a newly built local dispensary, and just about everyone had electricity and a television. But the many vacant houses plastered with political posters suggested that not all was well in this changing village.

The expansion of factories in the area to manufacture leather goods, paper, textiles, chemicals, fertilizers, food, and sugar, as well as a distillery, had created high demand for real estate. Farmers who sold land to relocate to cities such as Pondicherry or Chennai profited, but those who stayed inherited an environmental nightmare in the form of industrial waste running into the irrigation canals and polluting the drinking water. Families who spent the proceeds of their land sale too fast found themselves not merely without income but also without leverage in a community where conflict was a fact of life. Not that the residents of the *cēri* (or Dalit ghetto, located at the margins of the village) fought with caste Hindus, for the man who led them had earned a reputation as a wise man. Everyone knew he was a man of consequence, a popular and respected leader who had made it his career to help people in distress. But party politics within the village itself were so contentious that the slightest issue became a cause for violence.

I had barely arrived in this troubled rural community when Abi showed up at my door and declared, in English: "I want a job." Small and bony with frizzy hair cut short, Abi immediately struck me as being far more outgoing and independent than the many housebound and shy Tamil girls I knew. There was no hard edge to her, but, as her introduction to me suggests, she was direct in her manners. I hired her on the spot and never regretted my impulse; she was very bright, although I must say that there was a price to pay for the privilege and pleasure of working with her. Whenever I was slow to understand something—a kinship chart, a term, whatever—she would scold me, saying "Auntie!" in a reproachful tone of voice. This tone, to me at least, meant, "How can you be that stupid?" Alternatively, she would ask, "Are you clear now?" or "Is it clear now?" It did not fret her that I was much older than she was, and a university professor in the United States. Not merely impatient and admonishing, she was actually more professorial than I am, often punctuating her speech with questions such as: "Am I not right, auntie?"

For her first assignments, I asked her to collect exegeses of words that were key terms in research. Many of the glosses I have offered in previous chapters—for example, *muṟai* ("rule"), *urimai* ("right"), *mām*ā ("maternal uncle")—came from the questions she put to relatives, neighbors, friends, and old teachers. Tucked in the word-for-word transcriptions in her notebooks are many little jewels of meaning that convey, for example, the expansive power in husband and wife relationships and the goodness of marriage. Consider these definitions that Abi collected among women who were more of less her own age:

> Marriage (*kaliyāṇam)* is joining in front of the community. It's an agreement before the community, a function that's done in a happy way. —*Vasudha, age 25*
>
> Marriage means cooperation of relations. —*Archana, age 21*
>
> Marriage is a relation that joins a man and a woman, a public relation that's recognized by society. —*Vasanthi, age 20*

> Marriage turns people into adults with responsibilities. Marriage changes a person. —*Celvi, age 20*
>
> The relation is thicker after marriage. —*Kavitha, age 21*
>
> Marriage makes a man and woman share everything. It's a lovely function in front of the community. —*Ananthi, age 23*
>
> Getting married is the greatest thing in life, so no one should speak badly about it. Marriage shouldn't be tainted. —*Dharuna, age 25*

One would be hard pressed to guess that such descriptions were collected in a corner of India that up until very recently used to practice a high level of consanguineous marriage. But then again, all the young women interviewed by Abi wanted to marry *a<u>nn</u>iyam*. It was as if marriage outside the kin group was, for them, what fieldwork is for anthropologists. As one told me, "If we go outside (*veḷiyē pō<u>nn</u>a*), we come to know a new culture." Like fieldwork, their arrival in a different world was bound to be awkward, but over time the initial cultural shock would wear off and it would be exciting to be out of one's element.

With this chapter we thus approach the subject of change in kinship, more specifically the decline of marriages with close kin. This decline—in both incidence and cultural value—has to be understood in light of the many changes occurring in Tamil society as a whole. Because some of these changes have long been in formation, in this chapter I first try to build a grid of causality that includes multiple forces impelling change. Or, because this sounds too much like a new functionalism, rather I seek to construct a matrix of intelligibility, one that allows for multiple points of entry into the causal and consequential questions posed by changing marriage practices.

Neither my method nor my materials, however, allow me to map current marriage practices onto changing features of social organization, as if they were mere reflections of new institutional arrangements. I will attempt to show how, for people living at a particular time and place, the world is not entirely determined by seemingly "objective conditions" such as large-scale historical forces and economic trends. Rather, the circumstances of one's life take on their seeming inevitability and naturalness from the very interpretations and reinterpretations of cultural ideas which allow circumstances to be grasped and understood—for the person living through them as much as for the anthropologist. To show that this work of interpretation provides the means through which new forms of value emerge, I will—in this chapter and the next—explore the transformation of Tamil marriage from the point of view of young people, acting subjects like Abi, as they navigate their way toward adulthood and, because this is the one most important marker of adult status among Tamils, toward marriage.

Three Explanations for the Decline of Consanguineous Marriage

I start from the kind of top-down sociological explanations that provide the framework for much analysis. A first explanation emphasizes the critical fact of demographic change. Between 1881 and 1921, according to the French demographer Christophe Guilmoto, the average number of children per Tamil woman was between 5.08 and 5.57 (1992: 25). Because these figures include widows and women who were sterile, Guilmoto estimates that in the latter part of the nineteenth century Tamil women must have typically given birth to at least eight children each (1992: 26). This number may seem very high by modern standards, but to Guilmoto it remains far below the conceivable maximum. Tamil wives then usually began cohabitating with their husbands right after puberty; however, two major factors prevented them from reproducing throughout the whole span of their fertile years. First, life expectancy at birth was short, especially for men, and because husbands were usually older than wives, a quarter of women between the ages of thirty and thirty-four were widowed and therefore less likely to be sexually active (1992: 31). Second, the short interval between generations limited the procreativity of women. A woman married at the age of fifteen could very well have a married daughter with small children by the time she reached the age of thirty-five (1992: 33). Guilmoto invokes the "complex of the pregnant grandmother," first introduced by David Mandelbaum (1974: 29–32), to suggest that, because women were ashamed to be with child at the same time as one of their daughters or daughters-in-law, they curtailed their sexuality (Guilmoto 1992: 33). I am not, however, convinced by this argument as it goes against the Tamil most preferential marriage, namely the uncle–niece marriage, which involves a mother marrying her son to her daughter's daughter.

Over the last few decades, improved living standards (better nutrition, health care, and education) and governmental public health and contraceptive campaigns have led Tamil women to change not only when they marry but when they become parents and how often. Even in the villages, women increasingly give birth to only two children on average. The drop in birth rates has had a major impact on the incidence of cross-kin marriage. Quite simply, smaller family size reduces the pool of marriageable relatives, as evidenced by Christophe Guilmoto's calculation of the statistical possibilities: "Some 50 years ago," he writes, "the average number of siblings and first paternal cousins was no less than 35" (2011: 32). "With three children per woman on average," Guilmoto adds, "everybody has on average eight paternal first cousins and siblings. However, this number reduces to three in smaller families (with two children per woman on average)" (2011: 32). The drop in birth rates also widens the gap between generations, so Bittles, Coble, and Rao are correct when they say that "the general reduction in family size throughout South India will make uncle–niece unions more difficult to arrange within accepted spousal age difference norms" (1993: 115). Nowadays the mother's brother is just too old for his niece (but not always, as the reader will soon see). While Tamil women ought to be younger than their husbands, people agree that ideally spousal age difference should not exceed six or seven years.

The second explanation for the current decline in marriages with close kin has to do with the medicalization of spouse selection in South India. Nowadays, anthropologists like myself do not often hear Tamils say, as they used to, that men transmit blood to their children and women transmit "love" (*uravu, pācam*). These cultural ideas about physical inheritance are no longer widely held, nor consistent (Good 2000: 326). Instead, a kind of pseudo-scientific discourse is fast replacing the old South Indian concepts of procreation, transmission of life, and the ethnophysiology of inheritance of blood and bodily fluids (for a review, see Good 2000). Today, Tamils say that a child receives 50 percent of his or her genetic makeup from the mother and 50 percent from the father, and that brothers and sisters share 50 percent of their genetics. They have heard that "consanguinity" between parents increases the risk of "silent" genetic defects showing up as birth defects or diseases in children (blindness, blood cancer, breathing problems). Many Tamils invoke these pieces of information to make the case that it is "scientifically *tappu*" to marry close kin.

In fact, brothers and sisters may share 50 percent of their genetic material, but that would be extremely rare because the combination of parental chromosomes is not a simple "blending"—half and half—but rather starts out as a random assortment, affected first by the variable selection of the parent's chromosomes that make it into their sex cells. Moreover, other biological factors or environmental conditions can account for what the Tamils call "imperfections" (*kuṟai*; this word is also used to describe a premature baby), and science has not yet proven that even the closest blood relationship between parents is directly injurious to offspring.[1] Yet notions of the dangers of consanguineous marriage, garbed in an aura of scientific authority, are increasingly common among Tamils.

The same pseudo-scientific notions pepper our own views of consanguinity. But because the Tamil discourse is linked to national agendas and desires for socioeconomic development,[2] what is communicated has its own logic and cultural twists—particularly lacking the moral dread of "incest" that would structure the discussion in a Western context. Village health nurses,[3] for example, condemn consanguinity on grounds that "relatives share the same blood type, and people with the same blood type beget children with *kuṟai*." Morning television shows and magazines broadcast the same message: It is best to marry *aṉṉiyam* (an "outsider") because he or she will have another blood type and that difference will work in favor of genetic fitness. These beliefs about blood type are widespread, indicating something else is at stake here other than strict scientific truth or medical guidance. Indeed, the *aṉṉiyam* in question is just as likely to have the same blood type as a relative, and there is no correlation between the parents' blood types and the genetic fitness of their child (in fact, it may be more advantageous or "selective" for a pregnant woman to carry a fetus with the same blood type as her own). Yet, in a survey I conducted among young people, the majority of the respondents believed that, because relatives share the same blood type, they should not get married.

I mention these findings not to ridicule village nurses or deride Tamil media but to suggest that the campaign against consanguinity in Tamil personal lives and amid Indian governmental programs produces truths and facts that do not conform to "objective science" but rather hew to an enduring worldview that shares the very conceptions encoded in the old marriages with *contam*. Relatives share the same blood type because *contam* share everything; they are the "same," as Neelam (of Chapter 3) liked to say, using this very English word. Taking note of these Tamil conceptions about relatives puts the emphasis not on the kind of ideas associated with state developmentalism and its scientistic discourses—in which there is no difference other than a time lag, as scholars of modernization once held, between the West and the "developing" world—but on the work of interpretation by means of which the Tamils create new meanings and practices.

It should be clear by now that I am arguing that the relationship between the "objective" factors of science, politics, and economics and the "subjective" realm of meanings and practices is not one in which the former is superimposed on the latter and determines its shape or content. I want to stress this because it is a point underappreciated by yet a third explanation for the transformation of South Indian marriage. I am referring to Karin Kapadia's argument that the rising prominence of dowry in village marriages in the early 1990s precipitated "the collapse of close-kin marriage" (1995: 58). In brief, Kapadia contends that an increasing availability of high school education and salaried employment led rural Tamil middle-caste men to want wives who, like them, would not work in agricultural fields. Women increasingly stayed home without engaging in economically productive labor, while their parents switched from the old "bride price" (*pariyam*) mode of marriage payment to "dowry" marriage (*varataṭcaṉai*) (1995: 57–58).[4] Dowries, the argument goes, attract educated and salaried young men, prospective husbands, whose regular paychecks over the long term will benefit daughters and the families from which they come. The ultimate cause of the change, however, is rising affluence and education.

There is no denying that in the last few decades the changing meanings of "dowry" have profoundly affected rural matrimonial arrangements and the status of village women (see also Mukund 1999). As a result, the category or type of relation that is "right" is increasingly determined not by genealogical specification (mother's or father's cross siblings' children, for example) but by class considerations. Indeed, financial standing and education can override any "rightness" (or "wrongness") in terms of kinship categories or marriage rules. The Tamils no longer ask: Is the groom related? Does the bride come from his mother's side or his father's? Is this marriage "right"? Those used to be the right questions, even if in practice they were often answered in the negative. The new questions are: How much did her parents spend on the dowry? How much gold did he receive? Does he have a government job? How much does he make? Class rather than kinship is the "preferential" criterion. Or, as Kapadia put it: Upwardly mobile families "marry in a 'modern' manner, for money and status rather than 'for love of kin'" (1995: 46).

I must point out, however, that the description of dowry as "new," purposeful, strategic—and in the best *economic* interests of the parents paying it and the daughter for whom it is given—loses its explanatory leverage once we recall Dumont's observation that, in 1950s, the expenses of a Piramalai Kaḷḷar marriage were "considerable" (1986: 252) and heavier overall on the wife's family. Again and again Dumont emphasized that Tamils said the father should invest double the amount of the bridewealth in his daughter's jewelry. The reader will also remember that Dumont mentioned that, before he arrived in Kaḷḷar country in the mid-twentieth century, a "reform" (1986: 238) had led to a reduction in the expenses borne by the wife's parents. The collection of money (*moy*) intended to "partially compensate" them was three to six times less than in the past (1986: 257). This leads me to suspect that the meanings of dowry extend well beyond the changing nature of men and women's work and beyond even the perception that it is a "modern" institution.

Moreover, the theory that dowry is the price paid for an improvement in the status of the girl does not quite stand up to latest developments. Nowadays Tamil women are catching up with men, increasingly finishing secondary education, graduating from college and professional schools, and finding employment in schools, hospitals, police stations, state government offices, and private industry. In other words, the gender gap in schooling and occupation is not as wide as when Kapadia conducted fieldwork, and yet this new trend is not exactly reconfiguring marriage payments. It is true that professional women (especially the women who have government jobs) pay less to acquire grooms having similar or higher qualifications (Fuller and Narasimhan 2008), but at the time of my main fieldwork (2007–2008) their parents still laid out significant sums of cash and gold. For example, the middle-class family of a young woman who had a master's degree in English offered in dowry fifteen gold sovereigns (each worth approximately 6,000 rupees) and 30,000 rupees in cash. When we take into consideration that the family in question lived on a monthly income of about 10,000 rupees, we are forced to ask why the groom should be "compensated" so lavishly for having an educated wife, if such compensation for the groom's rising economic status is the "modern" meaning of dowry.

Finally, Kapadia's argument conveys the impression that girls' families are caught in a kind of existential impasse, as if there is nothing they can do: They can only pay. It is true that exorbitant dowry payments place a huge burden on families, and this all the more so because the bride's parents are expected to keep on presenting money and jewels well into the marriage. But, in my experience, families are eager to give. They would "beg" a groom, as the lady who cooked for me once put it, to accept their gifts of cash and jewels. Likewise, Linda May observes, families "would not marry off daughters without dowry, even if [they] had the chance" (1986: 33). Dowry is linked with notions of standing and social prestige, so that, to quote May again, "A rich family would be slitting its social throat to give too little gold" (1986: 162–163). Of course, rank is no longer destiny in Tamil Nadu; it can be purchased, as Kapadia's own analysis of dowry payments suggests. But I believe that something else is at stake here.

The old marriages with *contam* used to establish social distinctions through the orchestration of exchanges. If you were equal to us, you had the right to take from us and the formalities of our transactions were (and still are) reduced to a minimum. "Modern" marriages to *aṉṉiyam* remain a critical means of status making, but through the opposite mode of exchange: a highly codified and ever inflationary language of giving that echoes that of the Kaḷḷar ceremonial collection of money (*moy* or *ceymuṟaihal*) discussed in Chapter 1. The wedding ceremony itself is an occasion to observe the semantics of this opposition as it plays out in lavish expenditure. Expensive silk saris and vessels are displayed in rows, price tags intact, impressive stacks of bills are publicly handed over to the groom, and the weight of the gold jewelry the couple parade is a constant and legitimate topic of conversation. Everyone openly talks about the amount of wealth changing hands, and the hype is heightened by the fact that families do not hesitate to boast, even exaggerate, what they give or receive—importantly, *to outsiders* and with no overt expectation of "keeping" it in the family. What I am saying is that it is not only new modalities of employment that are at issue in the preference for dowry-marriage. Rather, time-honored meanings of rank, inclusion or exclusion, and intimacy or distance played a vital role in the transformation of Tamil marriage payments. What is in evidence here, in light of the historical ethnographic data and the experiences I recorded in the field, is not so much a "shift" to, or an "inflation" in, dowry payments—though the meaning, timing, form, and tempo of marriage payments is altered—but a dynamic transformation that is as rooted in Tamil meanings and practices of social distinction as it is a result of "monetization" or "modernization" of marriage.

Abirama (or Abi, for short)

After two weeks of recording exegeses of the kinship categories I was interested in, Abi complained that everyone in the village was "fed up" with her questions, and so I gave her a new assignment. Instructing her on the mechanics of my camera, I asked her to take pictures of people doing things as opposed to standing straight or locked in frozen poses, as is often the case in Indian photographs. Abi followed my stipulations to the letter, and when she showed me the developed roll of film, it did not take me long to realize that all her pictures depicted relatives preparing or cooking food. Her captions underscored this as well:

> Here's my sister. She's packing the lunch that my mother has just prepared for her. This is what my sister does every morning just before she leaves for school. It's a daily scene.
>
> Here's my grandmother (mother's mother); she's cooking food for her grandchildren.
>
> Here's my mother's brother and his wife; they're squeezing juice for their children. They do this every day.
>
> Here's my mother's elder brother. He is cooking a big pot of *biriyani* rice. That's what he does for a living. He has a *biriyani* shop.
>
> Here is my grandmother (father's mother). She is making *badgis* (fried snacks) to sell in the little store she runs in this village.
>
> Here is another one of my mother's brothers; he's boiling a pot of milk in his teashop.

Abi concluded her presentation with the comment that "everybody in my family has a food shop." To her this was not much of an achievement, and her mission in life was to put an end to this fate. "In the future," she said, "I don't want my relatives to sell any food. I want them to be educated." She could have added "like me," for Abi held a college degree in chemical engineering and spoke English well. But she was less interested in calling attention to her own accomplishments than in reforming or, as she put it, "developing" her family. On her own account, she was not particularly successful in this effort. Her sixteen-year-old sister was failing tenth standard and near the point of dropping out of school. Moreover, Abi's relatives did not seem to understand the value of a postsecondary education for a woman. "Why are you studying?" they would tease, "Go to work!" Once, I asked Abi whether it was difficult for her to relate to her mostly illiterate family. She replied, "There are a lot of differences between us, but it's not difficult. I like these people very much."

She took no pictures of her father's two brothers, who lived two doorsteps away from her house. But I did not ask why, as my landlady had already volunteered that the three siblings "did not speak." Apparently Abi's father (the firstborn) had kept a larger share of the ancestral property for himself, and the two younger brothers regularly fought for their due. On one such occasion—about a month before my arrival—Abi's father, who was intoxicated, became violent and almost killed his youngest brother (according to my landlady). It was not the last time that I would hear that the man was a drunk. The whole village knew it.

Further on I will suggest that his addiction to alcohol placed a huge burden on Abi. Not only did she have to witness his abusive behavior and answer to the police when they made their inquiries about his outbursts, but the responsibility of providing for her mother and younger sister fell on her, too, as the firstborn with a college degree. Unfortunately, Abi was hard pressed to find a job, for, as Craig Jeffrey, Patricia Jeffery, and Roger Jeffery have rightly argued, the ability of young Indian people to benefit from higher education "depend[s] crucially on money, social resources and cultural capital" (2008: 208). A poor village girl with no useful social connections, Abi was never selected when she went for job interviews (whether in the public or the private sector)—which is why, of course, she had asked me to employ her. But before revealing the full scope of the situation she was in, I want to continue introducing Abi in the way I came to know her, through our ethnographic collaboration.

One afternoon when the monsoon was soaking the village alleyways and we could not go anywhere, I asked her to draw a chart of Tamil kinship relationships. The way I framed the exercise was something like this: "Americans have relationships between people that fit definitions of the English language term 'relative,' and these relationships are further classified into such categories as 'brother,' 'mother,' 'uncle,' and so on. My question to you, Abi, is do the Tamils have something equivalent to these Western concepts and, if not, how do they organize the relationships that are called 'relatives' in English?" I am aware that this was not the best anthropological assignment because it invited Abi to model her understanding of the Tamil cultural domain of kinship after mine, but in the field it is not always easy to come up with truly relativistic frameworks.

Abi did end up identifying a system of logical relationships among a discrete set of terms, which she mapped onto a genealogical chart. Her chart, which she titled "general things," emphasized lineal rather than affinal relationships, although I must say that in it "grandparents" and "grandchildren" were linked to each other independently of parents. Moreover, her chart began not with filial but with sibling relationships. Hence, instead of putting a husband and wife at the center of her chart and saying, "This man and this woman are the parents of these four children," she put a brother and sister at the center, noting that the first boy she marked out was brother (*cahōtarar*) to the first girl, and she in turn was sister (*cahōtari*) to him. The reader would note that this placement undermines my argument that anthropologists need to "de-center the brother–sister relation from South Indian kinship," but Abi's main intent was to give me a crash course on "general things," not to walk me through the full intricacies of Tamil marriage with *contam*. And to fully convey her baseline understanding of Tamil "right" marriages, she had the first boy and the first girl of her chart marrying their children together and duplicated this pattern for the second boy and girl.

Because Abi did not represent the four siblings' spouses (or any sibling's spouse for that matter), the impression conveyed was one of autonomous or spontaneous reproduction, as if generations of siblings succeeded one another on their own without any marital or affinal connections. This impression was only compounded when Abi returned to the subject of terminology. Children had names for "father" and "mother" and for parents' siblings but apparently none for these siblings' spouses. In Abi's chart and running commentary there were neither wives nor husbands; "cousins" had only one parent, not two. That is, relatives in the position we would call "cousin" had a mother or a father who was first and foremost a sibling to ego's mother or father, but no other parent who was *only* defined as "spouse." Abi's consistent use of curved arrows to trace the relationships she drew produced a bounded enclosure, one more hint that in her representation Tamil kinship sustained itself on its own, without any "outside" contribution.

One of the things I have learned during the years I have conducted fieldwork in Tamil Nadu is that people represent their culture to the anthropologist from their own perspectives, with their own vested interests in mind, infusing their account of the culture's abstract "meaning" with specific, felt significance drawn from their own lives and existential dramas. Notwithstanding the fact that Abi had correctly rendered Tamil "right" marriages with insiders, our subsequent conversations led me to understand that her suppression of marital ties was not entirely informed by "culture."

The Things We Talked About

As we got to know each other better, Abi confided that she was under pressure to marry her mother's youngest brother, who lived in a nearby village. This man was around twenty-five or twenty-six, so the difference in age was not great, but Abi wanted nothing to do with him. Like an increasing number of rural women, she felt that children of related parents were bound to have problems, whether mental or physical. She had heard health workers talk about these complications on TV. And like the young women interviewed by Narasimhan (2006: 96), she regarded marriage with relatives as a "backward" aspect of village life that she wanted to move away from. But the main problem with her proposed spouse, she lamented, was that her *māma* was not educated. He had completed only the eighth standard, which meant he had dropped out of school at the age of fourteen. Abi predicted what would happen were she to marry him: "We won't make a good match. Lots of misunderstandings will come. We'll argue constantly. Every time I'll say something, he'll disagree and insist he's right. I want to tell my mother what will happen to me in this marriage, but she doesn't understand."

Most Tamils would agree with Abi: Her *māma* would not be right for her as they obviously were not of the "same level," as they say of couples unequally matched in terms of economic and symbolic status. What made matters worse in this case was that it was the woman, namely Abi, who was of the higher level. It is quite all right for an educated Tamil man to be married to a woman with little schooling, but the reverse is unthinkable. A man should not be placed in a subordinate position in the family by being married to a girl who trumps him in terms of class or education. He should be her equal or superior but not her inferior. A twenty-three-year old man interviewed by Sundari Ravindran echoed my consultants' feelings on this subject when he described the basis on which he selected his bride: "I had seen seven girls before this. Didn't approve of any. Either the girl was too talkative or much better off than me. These kinds of matches don't work. They won't respect you. With this girl, she was suited for my status, and more importantly, she liked me. So I knew she would be obedient" (1999: 38).

I never asked Abi's mother, who every now and then cooked breakfast for me, why she was determined on marrying her daughter to her brother. But to my talkative landlady the motivation was clear: "He'll take whatever is given to him." Indeed economic considerations were very likely to be at work here.

Abi's parents could not afford a large dowry, and the mother's brother—an uneducated worker in a family food shop—had no business asking for much gold and cash. It was a match made in the heaven of convenience.

I was surprised by the relative ease with which Abi was able to reject her parents' proposal. Indeed, Abi had an unusual amount of freedom for a young rural woman, coming and going in and out of the village, as she liked and on her own. Usually a girl at the stage between puberty and marriage is subjected to strict surveillance; her parents must know everything: where she goes, what she eats, who she talks to, and so on. There are strict restrictions on her visibility, mobility, and above all on her interactions with men. A girl who wanders around alone in the public sphere is extremely vulnerable to gossip.

Abi's strength and autonomy were also evident in the very way she reacted to her parents' wishes. She did not threaten to take poison—the suicide threat of choice for youngsters who wish to stop their parents' negotiation—nor did she flounce around, weeping and refusing to eat. Instead she managed to convince her parents to "save," as she put it, the maternal uncle for her younger sister—a time-honored solution to the delicate problem of turning down a relative who has a matrimonial claim. The unwilling side does not disentangle itself from the family obligation; instead it finds a substitute.

As I came to learn over time, however, Abi's relative freedom was predicated on one critical condition: She had to work. As long as she made money and supported the family, her father tolerated her outspokenness and her rounds to nearby villages and the town of Pondicherry—for her work for me, for interviews, and to see friends. But as the next section suggests, when Abi was unsuccessful in her search for secure salaried work, her father could be ruthless.

Abi's Diary

Knowing that our collaboration was temporary, Abi kept looking for employment during the month we worked together. Unable to capitalize on her educational qualifications, she found only poorly paid family jobs; for example, occasionally operating the phone booth owned by her senior maternal uncle. Because she was still unemployed when I left for Madurai, I offered her 200 rupees a week to keep a dairy in Tamil. At the time I did not expect much to come out of this exercise (at the most I thought Abi would write about what she was doing from day to day), but I nonetheless encouraged her to be introspective and record her feelings, hopes, worries, and happy and sad experiences. When I met her in Pondicherry a month later, it was clear that she had taken no pleasure in this assignment. "I've nothing to say," she pleaded, "I hardly have time or energy to keep a journal. I'm looking for a job. Besides, what's there to tell?"

Indeed, at first she wrote as if she wanted to confirm the ultimate pointlessness of both the assignment and her life. Here I quote some of her entries:

> *October 11, 2007.* All I did today was to go for a job interview in Pondy. Nothing's happening in my life.
>
> *October 14, 2007.* I went to my friend's house from 2:00 pm to 8:00 pm and came home.
>
> *October 18, 2007.* In the morning I went to work at my [elder and married] maternal uncle's phone booth [in a nearby village]. I like to help him out. Then I went to Pondy for a job interview. I caught the last bus and didn't get home until 11:30 pm. There were no cars on the road then. I was tense because I didn't get the job, so I called my [girl] friend.
>
> *October 21, 2007.* I went to work at the phone booth, and my four maternal uncles joined me. They teased me, and we laughed together. My [eldest] *māmā* gave me a parcel of rice *biriyani.*
>
> *October 23, 2007.* Nothing's happening in my life.
>
> *October 25, 2007.* I went to work at the phone booth. On the path to my mama's village my cycle's front tire got punctured, so I walked half of the way. My *māmā* gave me a parcel of *biriyani* rice.
>
> *October 28, 2007.* I spent the afternoon with my [girl] friends in Pondy. We went to the Sunday market and a bookstore. On the way to the beach we bought ice cream. Everything was great. We talked about our lives. At 9:20 pm I caught the last bus back to my village, and my mother scolded me: "Where were you today? You didn't work, so where were you?" I lied, saying I went to interview for a company called "Priya," which is my friend's name!

The entries for the month of November 2007, however, suggest that journal keeping became a one-way conversation that she initiated in difficult times. Now Abi mainly wrote on bad days, and the records for that month suggest she had many of those:

November 26, 2007. I went to interview for a job in customer care at one company but didn't get the position. I hate my life. I'm not lucky. My timing is bad; nothing's right now. I pray to god.

November 27, 2007. I went to see my [eldest] *māmā*. Because I still don't have a job, he called me "unlucky girl." This comment upset me very much. But the more I think about it, the more I know he's right. I'm unlucky. I don't want to pass my bad luck to my [girl] friend so I'm not calling her.

November 29, 2007. My dad woke me up: "Hey dog, wake up! You're an unlucky girl! Get up! Look for work!" He turned up the sound of the TV very high. He increased the volume so as to torture me. I cried all day. My father had never done this to me before. My parents think I'm useless. But my dad shouldn't do this. He should console me and tell me he'll always be there for me. I cried a lot on that day. I was tense. My mother remained silent. She didn't defend me.

We read these lines together, and at the mention of her mother Abi lashed out: "She's afraid of her husband. She never opens her mouth in front of him. Because he dominates her, she can't defend me. I hate my life totally. There's no one to take care of me. I feel very bad. The only person who thinks about me is Priya, my [girl] friend. My family doesn't do anything for me, but Priya takes care of me. I live only for her."

A middle-class young woman from Pondy, Priya was everything Abi wanted to be: smart, fashionable, and modern. The two had met in college, where Priya took it on herself to tutor Abi, who had not had the chance to study in an urban-based, private English-medium high school. "She's very intelligent," Abi would say of her friend, "and helped me reach the 80th percentile of my class." Priya, who perhaps benefited from her family's social links with private entrepreneurs, was then working in an engineering firm in Coimbatore, making a very nice salary of 13,000 rupees a month. The two young women talked on their cell phones three or four times a day, and Abi lived for these conversations. Actually she depended on Priya for everything. As she once said: "She taught me how to dress, how to speak correctly, how to behave as a guest in other people's houses; she has changed me a lot. She encourages me when I fail and helps me be strong."

Eventually Abi did find a job as a "software technician assistant" in an e-publishing company in Pondicherry. From 2:00 pm to 10:00 pm, six days a week, she entered data for a salary of 2,000 rupees a month. The pay was abysmal, and I was upset to learn that she would not be compensated during the training period. But Abi was not complaining: "There's no need for money," she told me, "all I need is love." Besides, she assured me, "I'll soon be making a lot of money, 20,000 rupees." During this time she wrote two entries that caught my attention.

> *December 3, 2007.* I went to the job training with my dad. It has been a long time since my dad accompanied me anywhere. Not since my school days. I was happy. My dad bought me a note pad.
>
> *December 6, 2007.* At 11:00 pm my friend Oli called me from Chennai. He went there to look for work, but because he doesn't know anyone there, he's lonely and distressed. I put him in touch with someone who can help him. Oli and I went to tenth standard together; we were the best students in the class. I was first and he second. We're friends because we're in the same situation. Our fathers drink, and our mothers cry. I don't have words to express our situation. Our lives are very difficult in this village. Our parents always fight, and there's no place to hide. We both dream of getting out. Oli is just like me. He has to support his family, a younger brother and sister. He and I can't afford to make any rash decisions. We have to carefully plan our lives for the next five or six years so that we don't have to come back here. I hope he'll manage in Chennai.

Abi's Marriage Is an Issue, Again

Two days before Christmas we met in Pondy, but our time together was marred by the news that her family was pressuring her to marry a man who was "old" and had once been married before. Abi was in tears: "I'm twenty, and he thirty-two, and I don't want to be a second wife. I'm not mature enough for marriage. I don't ever want to get married." The issue this time was that Abi's parents had agreed to marry her younger sister to the mother's brother, whom Abi had earlier spurned. But, for her sister's marriage to take place, Abi, who was the firstborn, had to marry first. Tamil families hardly ever marry daughters out of age order for fear that people will speculate over why the older daughter is still single. Is there something wrong with the girl? Are there problems at home? Abi's parents settled for an "outsider" who was in no position to ask for much gold. He made a decent living, working in the accounting department of an electricity company a few kilometers outside Pondicherry, but his first wife had left him for another man.

Abi knew she was in trouble. It would not be easy to persuade her parents to turn down this particular marriage. They were poor and eager to marry off her younger sister, and who knew how many more outsiders would be willing to marry Abi on the cheap? My young friend's reaction was to take on an additional job in Pondicherry. She worked in the mornings at one of the city's many public phone booths and in the afternoons at the e-publishing company. Leaving home at 6:00 am, she seldom returned before 11:00 pm. "Work helps my mental state," she wrote then in her diary—for, without my prompting, she continued to keep her diary:

> *December 28, 2007.* I can't even speak to my sister; she only thinks about getting married. I'd like to educate her, but she isn't interested in going to school. My sister likes marriage. She's a village girl. My sister is a coward. I can't speak to my father because he is a drinker, a MAXIMUM [she wrote this English word in capital letters in the Roman alphabet] drinker. I hate every man because of my father. I don't want to get married because I don't want to end up like my mother: beaten up by my husband. That's my main fear. I could speak to my mother, but she keeps on bringing up the topic of my marriage, so I avoid her as well.

When I read these lines with Abi, I tried to defend her mother, but Abi was not in the mood. "Yes, my mother loves me, but she loves my sister more. She wants me to marry so that she can marry her younger daughter. My mother has always taken better care of her. I like Western cakes, and my sister likes Tamil sweets, so guess what my mother buys at Deepavali [the "festival of lights" celebrated in the fall]? And she expects me to eat these sweets! I'm still waiting for my cake. It's the same with clothes. She doesn't buy me jeans and T-shirts. She buys me stuff I don't wear." When I ventured to say that at least she had the freedom to come and go as she wanted, Abi let out: "That's true; no one cares if I come home after 11:00 pm. But if my sister isn't home by 5:30 pm, my mother is very upset." "I hate my life," Abi kept saying that day. "Nobody is on my side. Except for Priya, no one cares for me."

The next day was the Tamil New Year, and Priya arrived from Coimbatore. In the early evening we all went out for soft drinks, and Priya poured out "practical advice" for her friend. "Because this man is old and black," she warned Abi, "he'll feel insecure with you. He'll be jealous, perhaps not right away, but in ten years, for sure, he'll become obsessively jealous." Priya threw out another argument: "People will say that you married an old, black man, and if your husband is to hear these words, he'll automatically beat up your friends." She repeated the word "automatically" for the sake of emphasis. She covered her mouth, mimicking the way people maliciously talk about the personal or private affairs of others, so we could see for ourselves the gossip, its banality and inevitability in day-to-day life. Even Abi laughed.

This was the last time I saw Abi. I did not have the chance to see her again before I left the field a few months later. Then, for at least two years she sent me e-mails variously entitled: "To Make You Smile," "Very Important Aunty," "ABCD of Friendship," "Good Morning," "Wish You a Happy New Year," "Unbelievable but True," "How Is Your Project Going On?" In 2009, she wrote: "My Sweet AUNTY . . . My sister's marriage will be held on coming 25th May." It seems that, somehow, she had managed to evade or block her own marriage with the "old," "black" man. The last I heard from her was in early 2010. She was then working in Chennai, and her e-mail ended with the following upbeat quotation: "The future you see is the future you get!" I have no idea what has become of Abi since, but I like to believe that one day she will succeed in getting what she sees.

The New Rights and Wrongs of Marriage

The results of a survey I conducted in Abi's village suggest that the practice of marrying close kin is not obsolete yet. According to my data, 103 of 348 married couples residing there were related. Such percentages, however, are lower than those reported in prior studies. In 1966, for example, an extensive study of 3,433 outpatients in a pediatric clinic at the CMC hospital of Vellore (Tamil Nadu) indicated that "45.3 per cent of [the patients'] parents were related to each other" (Reddy 1993: 118, citing Centerwall and Centerwall 1966; see also Centerwall et al. 1969). And in 1978–1979 the anthropologist Govinda Reddy noted that in the Nellore Taluk of Andhra Pradesh, consanguineous marriages constituted 42.92 percent of the total of 480 marriages he recorded (1993: 38).

The statistics I documented drop further when we turn to the next generation. Of the ten young unmarried women that Abi arranged for me to meet in her village, only one (excluding Abi herself) was preparing to wed with kin. This sample, I admit, is very small, but the villagers themselves confirmed that the old preferential marriages were on the wane, especially marriage between uncle and niece. Indeed, as far as I know, only one young girl in Abi's village (excluding the Dalit population) was married to her maternal uncle, which puts us far behind the numbers produced by Reddy in 1978–1979. Of 422 consanguineous marriages he recorded in Nellore (Andhra Pradesh), 185 were between uncles and nieces (1993: 120). What Anthony Good once called "the commonest form of close inter-marriage" (1996: 6) is fast disappearing from South Indian kinship.

We can understand why Abi's mother was pushing for Abi to wed her youngest brother. This would give her the opportunity to frequently visit the village located about seven kilometers away in which her five younger brothers lived in three separate households. Given that her husband was a "maximum drinker" and violent, it made sense for her to return home and establish one household where she was sure to get support.

Abi herself rejected the arrangement on two grounds. Her first objection is one that I often heard in the field: It is "scientifically wrong" to marry a relative. We note, however, that Abi's position on consanguinity was not rigid. "Wrong" for her, the maternal uncle was perfectly "right" for her younger sister. In my fieldwork experience the same double standard operated in marriage with cross cousins. Firstborn children, particularly firstborn sons who had enough clout within the family, increasingly "saved" "right" boys and girls for younger siblings who had less voice. It is impossible to miss the irony here: What used to be the privilege of those who came first in life is now the "right thing to do" for those who come last. The scales may be reversed, but these marriages continue to be associated with rank, or rather birth order, in the kinship hierarchy.

Abi's second, and main, objection was that the maternal uncle was unsuitable, uneducated in particular. Here Abi was not merely voicing "modern" ideas of spousal equality; she was also drawing on old matrimonial ideas of spousal compatibility (*poruttam*) that are predicated on notions of homogeneity or similarity between spouses. Recall that it is because *contam* used to be the same that they were best to marry, and it is because *aṉṉiyam* used to be different that they were not. As the informant already quoted in Chapter 2 said: "We don't give the elephant to the cow." Essentially, what Abi predicted was that she and her mother's brother would stand in a position of *aṉṉiyam* vis-à-vis one another. Hence all the problematic emotions associated with marriages with people who are not of the same rank would creep in: feelings of being inferior, of being snubbed, and so on. Because she was more educated than her husband, therefore inappropriately related to him as superior, he would compete with her and battle with her all the time. Notice what is happening here: When kin are outsiders, there is no point in giving them priority.

In respect to the obvious underqualification of her mother's brother, Abi's predicament was not unique. There is often (though not always) something wrong with the relatives whom poor girls like Abi are fixed up with. The grooms are physically challenged; they drink, or their fathers drink; perhaps they reside in a remote village where no young girl in her right mind wants to live; or they have many sisters to marry; and so on. There is bound to be something that is unattractive in their situation, otherwise their parents would give in to the temptation to seek the large dowries available in marriages between nonrelatives.

It was not merely the maternal uncle but the institution of marriage itself that Abi objected to. I did not have to probe deeply to understand why. Her alcoholic father was prone to explosions of violence in and out of the house. Alcoholism, which has already come up many times in this book, is very much in the increase in India (Prasad 2009), in the South in particular, and also plagued many of her friends' households, not merely that of her schoolmate Oli. Abi grew up witnessing the behavior of several drunken fathers and the suffering of several abused mothers, and she was afraid to be beaten up by a husband. As she poignantly said, "That's my main fear."

"Dravidian" women, I have argued in Chapter 4, have long tried to escape dysfunctional conjugality or conjugality tout court. What was distinctive about Abi was that, at least when I met her, she wanted out of her family and her village, too. There is no doubt that she was preparing her escape. Recall what she said of her friend Oli: "He and I can't afford to make any rash decisions. We have to carefully plan our lives for the next five or six years so that we don't have to come back here." That she had no more need of marriage than of kinship surfaced the day she announced that she wanted to adopt and raise a child on her own—actually, not quite on her own, because in her dream world Abi lived near Priya. This was, as she knew, an unrealistic scenario. As she said, "We're not boys, we're girls. Anything can separate us: husbands, parents, and jobs." But Abi's wish for a family that was constituted neither by marriage nor by a web of blood-relations—unlike the very "undeveloped" family she had depicted in her kinship diagram—said it all:

She wanted out of *contam*. To me this wish, not merely Abi's rejection of her mother's brother, points to a big change in Dravidian kinship. This change, we note, is driven neither by demography, nor by fear of consanguinity, nor even by the rising cost of dowry, but by a process in which young people like Abi who live in particular circumstances, gaining from social opportunities (education) and losing on familial situations (a drunk father), come to imagine themselves and their futures in novel ways.

7

LOVE IN THE TIME OF YOUTH

The first love will always be with us.
Poem by Mohan, age 27

Tamil people don't like to feel inept; it makes them very uncomfortable. They'd rather marry kin than feel awkward.
—Abi, age 21

Whenever I tell American friends or my French family that I am writing a book about the decline in preferential marriages with close kin in Tamil Nadu, they react to the news that there is such a decline with relief, as if I were announcing that the World Bank is succeeding in eradicating poverty in India. In their opinion, a reduction in consanguineous marriages can only be a good thing. This reaction must be understood in light of the fact that Westerners (and North Indians, too[1]) have very specific hang-ups about consanguinity. It is fair to say that "marrying-in" is, to us, what marrying outside the caste is to most Hindus. It evokes dread—with the difference that our fear is not rooted in notions of purity and pollution and misalliance but in our widely held belief that marriages between closely related kin, such as first cousins, pose a biological risk to offspring (Ottenheimer 1996).

Usually the people interested enough to continue talking about the topic of my research assume that the decline of South Indian close-kin marriage must be caused by the emergence of love marriages. This is not a wild supposition. The few social scientists who write about changing marriage practices in India have brought up the waning power and authority of older generations over younger family members. Youth in India today, they argue, are increasingly free to choose their own spouses on the basis of affection and love.[2] Thus, in 1985 the scholar Katherine Hann wrote that "the pressures that are leading to a breakdown in the incidence of relation marriage" include "imitation of Western life-styles," "the gradual increase of 'love marriages,'" and "a gradual erosion of caste traditions" (1985: 66; also see Conklin 1973). In the time since Hann wrote these lines, anthropologists have been evermore eager to map the arrival of globalization on the Indian subcontinent and to locate the practices and energies that link Indians with the First World (and its forms of consumption, recreation, and entertainment). Thus, they have not been that inclined to question the claim that the new South Indian youth is increasingly an individual who marries as "Westerners" do.

It is true that a growing culture of individualism, free choice, and consumer aspiration means that ideals of youth autonomy and self-chosen marriage—as well as lower family size—are increasingly prominent in South India (see Nisbett 2004; Rogers 2005; Lukose 2009; Nakassis 2010). Television stations stage debates on the relative merits of "arranged marriage" versus "love marriage," and such programs tend to impart the lesson that all individuals (including women) have the right to be free and equal and to enter social relationships based on consent.[3] Moreover, the premium put on education and salaried employment nowadays means that youth—especially young men—can now talk their parents into approving their choice of partner by stressing similar degrees, interests, and professional opportunities (Fuller and Narasimhan 2008). At least, as we saw in the case of Abi, they can talk them out of an unwanted matrimonial arrangement on the basis of a lack of similarity on these and similar criteria.

But it would be wrong to overstate the incidence of self-chosen marriage in Tamil Nadu. Fuller and Narasimhan clearly state that "arranged, [caste-] endogamous marriage still remains the norm, both ideally and statistically" (2008: 737). Guilmoto warns that there are no hard data to suggest otherwise: "While arranged marriages widely predominate, the rise in the incidence of marriages by personal choice (so-called 'love marriage') in both urban and rural areas of the country remains unfortunately a matter of statistical uncertainty" (2011: 35). This is not to say that romantic unions never take place, nor that marriage for young people is only pragmatic and absent of considerations of love (see also De Munck 1996), but merely that, for the most part, parents (in consultation with astrologers and marriage brokers) continue to look for, and find, spouses for their children. The basic explanation for this is that marriage is too important to be left to chance individual attraction—in fact, a child's marriage is the most important and often the most expensive decision a South Asian family ever has to make. No one ever argues that sentiments should not exist within a marriage, and in fact the question of whether the members of the prospective couple like each other is increasingly taken seriously. But in general, Tamil people take it for granted that marriage is a social contract and that the best way to secure the couple's social (but also personal and even sexual) suitability (*poruttam*)[4] is for parents to select the spouse *and* arrange the match (see also Mody 2002: 226). This basic assumption runs through Tamil literary and popular cultures. When the main character of R. K. Narayan's well-known novel *The Bachelor of Arts* finally finds the courage to declare, "I shall marry this girl and no one else," his mother exclaims, "Do you think marriage is a child's game? We don't know anything about them, who they are, what they are, what they are worth, if the stars and the other things about the girl are all right and above all, whether they are prepared to marry their girl at all . . ." (1954: 69).

The young men and women (all born after 1980) I met in and around the Tamil town of Madurai in 2007 and again in 2009 wanted their elders to select their spouses. For them, an arranged marriage was a sign of parental love. It was because families cared that they looked for the best possible bride or groom for their child. Hence sons and daughters were bound to appreciate their parents' care and effort. As one young man put it, bluntly: "I don't want to find a bride on my own. I don't want love marriage. If I were to choose a girl on my own, I'd offend my parents. If the bride of my choice weren't to adapt to my family, it'd be terrible." This young man's conclusion that "it's best to leave the choice to my mother" echoes the sentiments of many young Indians. In her study of college students in Mumbai who came from low-income families, Leena Abraham also notes: "Although some of the students did favour 'love marriage,' the general opinion was against it" (2004: 232). Her further finding that "girls preferred 'arranged marriages' to 'love marriages' as the latter was seen as an arrangement beset with enormous insecurity" (2004: 232) is consistent with mine. The young Tamil women I met in Abi's village also said that a girl in a love marriage would have neither the support of her husband's family nor that of her natal family; if her husband mistreated her, she was on her own. For the very same reasons, "none of the . . . girls," Linda May knew in Madurai in the mid-1980s, "wanted to go out and find herself a husband" (1986: 131). For them, as for my young informants, a marriage contracted against the wishes of parents was a risky proposition, which perhaps explains why the young people who do fall in love often do so with someone who fulfills the criteria the family expects in a marriage partner (but not always, as we will see in this chapter): a "home-loving" girl, for example, or a girl who does not talk back.[5]

If most marriages continue to be arranged, however, the average age at which they are contracted has risen considerably over the last few decades (Guilmoto 2011: 34). Nowadays, even in the villages girls do not marry before the age of twenty-one or twenty-two, although they seldom marry past that age, so as to prevent people from asking if there is something wrong with the girl or if there are financial problems at home. The situation is different for men. Ideally, men marry between the ages of twenty-seven and thirty, but some remain bachelors into or beyond their thirties. For one thing, there is less pressure for men to marry. Moreover, many things can derail their marriage (Moreno 1989), the main one being that, by the time they reach their late twenties, many still do not have a steady job. This holds true for educated men as well. This is not the place to analyze education, strategies of mobility, and the Indian job market, but Jeffrey and the Jefferys' argument that in rural western Uttar Pradesh "power and inequality mediate people's access to educational 'freedoms' [and] . . . employment markets" (2008: 31) applies equally to Tamil Nadu. There, too, it takes capital, connections (caste, class, and kinship), and often bribes to move toward secure employment. Recall how a poor, young village woman like Abi spent days searching for a job, only to eventually land a position that was not particularly rewarding.

A top-down analysis, however, is not enough to explain the often-considerable delay of marriage for Tamil men. The youth I met were complicit in this development, if only because they were neither bereft of cultural notions regarding social status nor untouched by the matrimonial values of their society. Their views—which, I may add, were quite conservative—on standing and respectability—prevented them from taking on what they considered to be undignified forms of work. Even uneducated or unemployed sons of low-status families did not want manufacturing or, especially, agricultural jobs, which are nowadays "reserved" for women and Dalits (ex-untouchables). This kind of employment was too demeaning for them.[6] As for sons of middle-caste families—a staggering diversity of landowners, civil servants, professionals, and aspiring entrepreneurs—they aspired for clerklike positions. If they could not find occupation in an office, or were not qualified for it, they spent large amounts of time out of the house in all-male groups, socializing, not thinking about the qualifications (education, employment, social networks, social standing, and so on) they would need to marry and raise a family (see also Osella and Osella 2006: 43–45). These unemployed men also remained bachelors for long periods of time—part of a process known as the "prolongation of youth" and one that is now considered a global phenomenon (Cole and Durham 2007; Jeffrey and Dyson 2008).[7]

During the transitional period, many youth experiment with intimacy and nurture "love interests" that, like the "flirtations and romances" documented in Kerala by Osella and Osella (2000; 2006), rarely develop into the founding of a conjugal couple unless the "love" at stake is "right" or meets their parents' approval. I do not want to give the impression that premarital love is a new or "modern" feature of Tamil society. All one needs to do is read the classical Tamil poetry of emotions and of interiority (*akam*) to realize that such love was anthologized as early perhaps as 2,000 years ago (Hart 1979). Nor do I wish to convey that Tamil youth all pass through a sequence of stages that are predictable or uniform on their way to adulthood. The experiences of the two men introduced in this chapter emphatically suggest that they do not. But I hope to show that discourses fetishizing individualistic notions of "choice" and self-chosen marriage do more to obscure than illuminate the ways in which Tamil young men love and marry.

Mohan

Born in 1980, Mohan was twenty-seven when I met him in the same village that Abi (the young woman introduced in the last chapter) hailed from. Round, with a black head of wavy hair and soft brown eyes, he came across as quiet and loyal. Like other members of the local *patayachi* caste, his once relatively highly ranked family was falling behind a rising "middle class." This category is very slippery in the Indian (or any) context, and many scholars have discussed the problems of definition and identification of this class (Donner and De Neve 2011; Mazzarella 2013; Baviskar and Ray 2011). For a significant number of consultants, however, "middle class" was a clear-cut descriptor of social identity—one that was tied to bureaucratic work in the state or public sector, specific household goods, and above all a secure material lifestyle. In the cities, they explained, the middle classes were those who possessed government jobs, concrete houses, and upholstered furniture. In the villages the people who worked for the state might also till the land—theirs or that of others—so that the distinction between public servants and farmers was blurred. But for my informants the one factor that distinguished state employees (clerks, teachers, police officers, nurses, and so on) from mere landowning castes was the pension they received on retirement. This steady income was a major mark of middle-class status.

Mohan's father had retired from a foreign textile firm with a lump sum of 50,000 rupees. But the money was gone, spent on the marriage of Mohan's younger sister. The family had a little "wet" land but could never depend on agricultural revenues because more often than not the old man was too drunk to grow anything, let alone the most prized crop of paddy.

It was thus up to Mohan, the firstborn son, to support his parents and his younger brother (who could not hold a steady job because he suffered from chronic migraines). Mohan had thought of selling the land to the developers who were fast industrializing the area around his village. But he had seen what happened to farmers who gave in to the temptations of fast cash. They spent it on expensive weddings and then starved. Besides, Mohan was not sure he could stop his father from drinking the proceeds of a sale. So, for the time being he was holding off. He did work, but like many young men who fail the exam for the Secondary School Leaving Certificate (SSLC) at the age of sixteen, he had no good professional prospects. The year I met him, however, he had found temporary employment with an NGO implementing an awareness program on environmental degradation for local farmers and in the process was learning how to type on a computer.

Because he lived close to the house I rented, he would give me rides on his motorcycle to the little town nearby, so I could place phone calls to the United States. Once I asked him to type up a few letters for me in Tamil, and when I came to pick up his work I saw on his office desk a folder tagged "*putu kavitai*" (which means "new poetry"). This genre of poetry breaks the rigid rules set down in classical Tamil literature, allowing more freedom of expression. When I asked about it, Mohan simply compared it to haiku, a type of descriptive yet compact poetry from Japan. Because I looked interested, he lent me some of his poems.

Like haiku poets, Mohan used simple words and grammatical constructions, and his poems were short, usually no longer than three or five compact lines. Because my appreciation for literary Tamil is limited, it is impossible for me to assess the quality of his poems, and I certainly cannot tell how much work went into them. Perhaps they took no work at all. But what is clear is that, unlike haiku poets, Mohan did not make poetry from whatever occurred to him in daily life. I see in the few poems he showed me no preoccupation with the trivial nothings of life. He seemed to write only about what moved him, or rather what feelings persecuted him. The specific theme of his poetry was love, but always a love that is not reciprocated or that is long gone. The point is the absence of the loved one, and the point is bleak.

First Day
From the very first day you were mine in my mind.
You left me in sorrow.
At the time of love, you appeared like the sun and disappeared.
You inflicted pain on me. You made me suffer.
Your life is in your hands.
Why did you not take me with you?
From the very first day I needed you.
You played in my life and left.

The Dream
Life is a dream.
We are dreamers of the delight.
Thinking you were there, I peeked.
I don't understand why you deceived me.
I have not seen the depth of the sea; you forced me to see the depth of your heart.
I thought I needed you, and you went off my mind.
You were my world and left me with feelings only.
My life became a dream. You were its embryo.

I was sure these poems verged on the autobiographical, but I refrained from asking questions. "There aren't any happy experiences in your poetry," I once took the liberty of saying to him. Mohan replied, "That I loved her in my heart is my great joy." On another occasion I ventured to suggest that the love he wrote about was in his mind; the girl was most likely unaware of it. Mohan simply retorted, "No, she knew."

Over the next few weeks, as Mohan dropped by now and then to take me to town, I learned that he and the young woman he wrote about had exchanged furtive glances and secret notes for about two years, until she married another man. This all had happened more than four years before I met him, but he was still composing love poems, fixated on a relationship that was long gone. My feeling is many Tamil young men keep looking to the past for love, as is inevitable in a society in which women move more quickly into marriage and its associated maturing experiences.

Mohan himself would have liked to marry, but his matrimonial prospects were weak on all fronts, as he had little education and no permanent job. Nor could he readily get together the 100,000 rupees minimally spent by men of his caste on a wedding—on the silk saris for the bride and her female relatives, on the rental of a reception hall, and on the band and the feast for 2,000 to 3,000 guests. Mohan's father's addiction to alcohol also weighed heavily against his marriage prospects. As he said in a matter-of-fact voice, "When he drinks, my father is a bad man. Who's going to give a girl to that house?"

His mother pressured him to marry her brother's daughter, but Mohan kept giving excuses: "I don't want to marry now"; "I don't have money"; and so on. From what I understood, he was not interested: The girl was "right" from a jural perspective, but she was uneducated and poor, therefore not likely to come with a good dowry. Mohan thought she would make a good match for his younger brother whose chronic and crippling migraines made him even less eligible for matrimonial gifts of cash and gold. There was no point in dispensing advice such as: "Never mind money!" "Never mind gold!" "Have a simple marriage with a girl you like!" Mohan lived in a world in which giving and receiving dowry played a central role in commanding respect from others and in one's own sense of self-worth. This explains why he had spent the whole of his father's pension check plus borrowed money, a total of 125,000 rupees, on his sister's wedding. "The groom's mother asked for gold chains," he said with a proud smile, "and we gave. They asked for a small bike, and we gave a big bike." When I registered my surprise at his lavishness, Mohan felt compelled to explain, "I've only one sister, I wanted people to say that we did well by her."

Over time I came to understand that respect[ability] (*mariyātai*) was the most important thing to him. As he liked to say: "A man's life is not worth living without honor (*māṉam*)" (also see Anandhi et al. 2002: 4403). The problem was that the kind of regard Mohan was after was out of his reach. He could not marry because he had no permanent job, but he had no regular employment because, like most village youth of his caste level, he spurned both agricultural (even on his own land) and manufacturing (once a source of pride for his father) work, and he was not competitive in the white-collar job market. He embraced his society's ideals of how a man should live (with propriety and distinction) and marry (with dowry) but lacked the necessary capital (schooling, professional competence, and so on) to reach them.

It took me a while to appreciate his dilemma. From the outside, Mohan projected an image of a well-adjusted young man—at home in both modernity and tradition. Like the college students who worked or mingled at the new Internet center in the nearby town (where he would drop me off), he was style conscious and was always dressed up in tight pants and crisply ironed shirts. He also possessed all the right badges of consumerism: He had a cell phone and a motorcycle, and he was learning to be computer literate. But Mohan was also conservative, and he took many of his ideas of what it meant to be civil, moral, and up-to-date from religion. In fact, he embodied these ideas, as he often bore a dot of ash and red vermillion powder in the center of his forehead, the ash symbolizing purification through worship and the red symbolizing Sakti, the power of the South Indian goddess.

Of course, Mohan was not as much of a "goody-goody" as I make him out to be. For one thing, he had a sense of humor. The night before Deepavali, the Hindu "festival of lights," for example, we rode back from town amid loud explosions of firecrackers that made the streets sound and smell like a war zone; the air was thick with sulfur. When I shouted from the back of his motorcycle that firecrackers were illegal in most American states, Mohan simply replied "Does everyone in your country not have the right to own a gun?" (thus pointing out my insinuation that Americans knew better than to fire rockets off, at least in the middle of the main street).

But Mohan respected his elders, particularly those who commanded respect. His best friend was a successful Christian fellow forty years his senior. I must say that at first this man, whom I refer to as Amadeus, got on my nerves because of his propensity to talk about his financial position: the amount of his pension, the cost of his house, the money he spent on his daughter's marriage, the price of the many gold chains and bracelets he was buying as a future dowry for his grand-daughter, and so on. The public appraisal of one's possessions, however, is a legitimate topic of conversation in Tamil Nadu (see also May 1986: 163–164). One gets used to being asked by strangers how much one paid for rent, a sari, or a pair of sandals. Besides, Amadeus came to my rescue on more than one occasion: If the fridge repairman did not show up, if I ran out of cooking gas, or if the water pump broke down, it was Amadeus whom I (or rather, Mohan) called. I depended on him not only for practical help but also for social entertainment. Over wonderful meals at his house he would offer his analysis of Tamil class dynamics. The lecture was always the same: "The rich don't have anything to worry about; the poor are resigned to their lot; *but*," and I can still hear the stress in that conjunction, "the middle classes are at risk of falling behind." Each time he said this, Mohan nodded positively, for he knew from experience that money was transforming the meaning of social inequality in his village.

I want to remind the reader that Mohan hailed from the same village as Abi and faced similar life circumstances: He too was the firstborn in his family, he too had an alcoholic father and a younger sibling to support, and he too held unfavorable marriage cards. Another commonality is that both chose not to exercise their matrimonial "rights," preferring instead to hand them down to younger siblings for more or less the same reasons: Their marriageable kin were unsophisticated and disadvantaged; in short, inadequate.

But here the similarities end, for these two young people could not have been more different in their outlook. Abi longed to get out of the village, and local opinion did not seem to have any special hold on her. She also eschewed traditional roles, be they gender, marriage, or familial roles. She did not even seem to care for boys or romance. I once asked whether she thought that her friendship with her former classmate, Oli, could grow into the Tamil love called "*kātal*." Abi's answer was a categorical, "No." And she added: "A lover expects something from a girl. Friendship isn't like this. We don't expect anything from our friends." Anyway, from what I could tell, Abi was fixated on her friend Priya, who brought a much-needed "outside" perspective into her life.

By contrast, Mohan was rooted in his world, valuing anything in life that touches on proper masculine conduct and sentiments (love poetry, daily worship, respect for elders, deference to social norms, and so on). Such a disjuncture between his and Abi's stances in life do not merely point to the varieties of youth experience in Tamil Nadu. It also suggests that feminine and masculine roles, formed of cultural ideals, social position, and personal circumstance, ensure that Tamil youth neither grow up nor marry like their peers in other cultural and social contexts, whether in the West or anywhere else.

More "Notes on Tamil Love"

I did not go to Tamil Nadu to research young men's personal experiences of love. I was not even interested in the subject of premarital romance. Rumors that college-aged male students often fell for "figures," an English term that does not refer to girls with attractive body shapes (as one would surmise), but girls with fashionable clothes and other such tokens of consumer culture, did not exactly pique my curiosity. Nor was I very patient with Raja, one young man I encountered whose experience could be reduced to this story line: "I love her, and she loves me, but my parents won't let us marry." Call me callous, but I wanted to say to Raja, a second-year undergraduate student in commerce, "You're only twenty; your parents know best." It was actually difficult to relate to the qualities Raja liked best in his sweetheart. He told me, "She's peaceful (*amaitiyaṉa*) and never looks at other boys. There isn't another girl like her." Again, call me cynical, but I could not empathize with this infatuation that, apart from being freely chosen, was not otherwise at all progressive. Raja's choice of girl was rooted in the ideal of a woman who is demure and self-effacing.

What I know of Tamil love I learned on the side, mostly from young men (like Mohan) who gave me rides or ran some errands for me. In the ordinary course of affairs we did not talk about personal lives (either theirs or mine). But, over the months, as I got to know them, our conversations turned to the topic of their relationships with the other sex. I hasten to say that such a mode of confiding conversation is not natural to Tamils; their culture opposes such sharing of personal problems. But talking to a foreign ethnographer, one who weeps easily at that, is not normal conversation.

When they referred to love between men and women, these youth and their friends used the word *kātal*, explaining that *aṉpu*, also glossed as "love" in English, was a more general and inclusive category (see Trawick 1990 on feelings of *aṉpu*). You felt *aṉpu* for a god, for friends, and for family, but *kātal* for the girl you saw on your way to school every morning, for example, or by the riverbank on hot evenings. I write "girl" and not "wife" because for my young unmarried consultants the defining feature of *kātal*—secret intimacy—was opposed to the public and institutionalized relationship of a married couple. My parents choose my bride and their requirements and criteria mediate my affection (*pācam*) and desire (*ācai)* for her. But I personally "arrange" my *kātal*. This distinction was clearly communicated to me when a married man nervously said in front of his wife, "I don't know about *kātal*." Somewhat confused—how could a husband deny loving his wife in her presence?—I reported his blunt admission to the middle-aged lady who cooked for me. She laughed at my naivety, explaining: "*Kātal* means meeting a girl on one's own, having the opportunity to be close to her, sharing feelings and so on. This young man was not about to disclose a *kātal*-like experience in front of his wife!"

I would maintain that our Western idea of "falling in love" and Tamil notions of feeling *kātal* are not the same. But, to be sure, my young informants produced all the symptoms and behaviors that would suggest something fundamental here, something that all human beings share after all. "*Kātal*," they explained, "comes on its own, catching us unaware." The mind may be slow to grasp that this is it, but the body is immediately affected and unable to perform its basic functions. "When we feel *kātal*," one youth stated, "we don't feel like eating." His friend nodded in agreement, adding, "*Kātal* won't let me sleep." Besides such overpowering, disruptive, and dumbfounding side effects, I encountered notions of an irresistible urge to be with the loved one. "I feel like going around the place where she lives," someone volunteered, "and I pace before her house slowly, sometimes twice, in hopes of catching a sight of her." Another young man shyly reported, "I follow her at a distance on the evenings when she returns home from the river."

Although *kātal* is said to be "a great feeling," young men were of the opinion that it "could drive you crazy." The main problem was that, once caught by *kātal*, you were compelled to do things you would not ordinarily do, and the Tamils often compare *kātal* to a state of possession or stupor (also see Trawick 1990: 113). You can mock the person rapt by love, but you have to pity him as well, because, as one eighteen-year-old put it, "*Kātal* is permanent intoxication (*mayakkam*); we can't come out of it."

Kātal is all the more overpowering in that it is, by convention and by nature, nondiscursive. Of course, one does not talk to parents about *kātal*. But expressing it to the loved one, or rather "proposing" it, as the youngsters I knew put it in English, is no less difficult. "To feel *kātal* is easy, but declaring it is hard," one confided. The reason is not merely that "the girl may make fun of me or turn me down," although this prospect is a strong deterrent in and of itself. Communicating love is "hard" because the process inevitably provokes unwanted and uncomfortable feelings of *veṭkam*.

To translate *veṭkam* with the English word "shyness," does not begin to convey the inhibition most Tamils—whether young or adult—feel when they meet someone for the first time. The experience is one of acute anxiety, the kind of apprehension that may be closer to what we call in English "stage fright." As someone put it: "All I can think about is 'will I perform well'?

'What will the person think of me?' 'Will I live up to his or her expectations?'" The fact that the Tamils also feel *veṭkam* when they make a mistake or when someone scolds them only confirms that first encounters in Tamil Nadu are associated with feelings of ineptitude, inadequateness, awkwardness, and so on. If the reaction to a casual meeting is one of painful self-awareness, imagine the dread youngsters feel when they communicate *kātal* to someone whom they obsess about. The young men I met could not bring themselves to take such risks. As one confided, "When we get to talk, I feel like asking her so many things, but I don't dare. I don't know what to say." Many enlisted the help of trusted friends or younger sisters or simply relied on the safe technology of cell phones and text messaging to say, "I love you."

What complicates the "modern" love encounter is that nowadays youth from different castes, classes, and localities comingle in public spaces such as schools, streets, and malls. Their encounter with the otherness of "outsiders" (*an̲n̲iyam*) can be stimulating, as Abi's friendship with Priya suggests. But in a society organized by relations of avoidance and deference with elders and superiors and marked by emotions of extreme touchiness when it comes to one's social standing, socializing with strangers can also be a potential source of embarrassment, anxiety, and anguish. The feelings of self-doubt and inadequacy that may plague individuals then are bound to questions (as I have already pointed out in this book about interfamily relations) such as: Am I behaving the right way? Am I up to their level? What do they think of me?

The experience is all the more agonizing and troubling when men meet women who are cosmopolitan and sophisticated. It is not simply that young men expect women to be submissive, for many have to reckon with strong sisters and mothers—women who take orders from no one. But normative models of masculinity require men to display *āṇmai* ("manliness"), even a kind of machismo and swagger. So when a young woman is cleverer or simply more assertive than her "boyfriend," his experience can be very confusing, even crippling.

Sunil

I met Sunil in Madurai one month before he graduated from Kamaraj University's law school in 2007. He was a very thin young man with very dark eyes and a wide, taut mouth. His starched cotton shirts concealed bony sharpness, not flesh. His English was excellent, but because of either nervousness or insecurity he sometimes stammered. Because he did not practice law yet, he agreed to act as my guide and assistant, but for reasons I explain in the following paragraphs our relationship turned out to be mostly social.

Sunil loved his ancestral village, located on the banks of the Vaigai River about thirty kilometers outside Madurai. I could see why. Brimming with stands of graceful plantain trees, the lush landscape reminded me of the beautiful backwaters in nearby Kerala. Sunil's family owned 1,000 coconut trees, and by my calculation the plantation was profitable. On average each tree yielded 240 coconuts a year, and at the time of my fieldwork a coconut fetched 2 rupees on the wholesale market and 5 rupees on the street.

Beautifully tiled, and with windows well situated to catch the passing breeze, Sunil's ancestral house invited conviviality. On a given afternoon it was not unusual to find his two younger brothers and their friends sprawled on the floor, watching cricket on TV, while his many sisters' daughters played games of pretend. Sometimes the girls would act as the operators of a medical dispensary, giving injections, using plastic syringes without needles, to anyone who happened to have the bad luck of being around. If the boys resisted their urgent care, the girls would hurl commands at them: "Be quiet!" "Do what I say!" Once I asked one of the girls, aged ten or eleven, whether she was the nurse or the patient, and she replied in English with a self-assured tone of voice, "I am the doctor; my younger sister is the nurse." It was hard to resist these little spirited beings.

Sunil might have had everything going for him: a prosperous plantation, a beautiful family, a good name in the village (thanks to his grandfather's long tenure as local headman), and a law degree; but he was not well. In fact, for most of my fieldwork he was suffering through a major breakdown, and we were not able to work together.

It was a simple exercise, which he himself initiated, that clued me in: A girl was the cause of his crisis. A stack of index cards on which I had written categories pertaining to my research triggered his revelation. Perusing the pile, Sunil immediately removed the cards bearing such words as "modernity," "maternal uncle," and "dowry"—words that did not, he said, connect with his life. He then held the cards for "friendship" and "change" and launched into a personal narrative. "My friends try to change me," he began, "they want me to be better." "My problem," he went on, still using the cards as props for his story, "is that I rush to make 'connections' and end up feeling 'disappointed' and 'angry.'" Selecting the Tamil words for "love" and "shame," he then said something like: "I am 'ashamed' that I once 'loved' a woman who only thought of crushing me."

I did not see him for quite a while after this. He would call and set up a time to meet but fail to show up. One day he invited me to have lunch at his house, and because I arrived early we went for a walk along the nearby riverbank. We talked about small things until he pointed to a shrine I could hardly see because it was sunk in a trough of sand and surrounded by shrubs. "I owe something to that god," he said in a serious tone of voice.

It was only then that I learned Sunil had taken five years (instead of the usual three) to complete law school. "I had to take a leave because I was too depressed to study," he volunteered, adding that when the time came for him to take the bar exam, he vowed to the god we were facing that he would sacrifice a goat were he to pass. Sunil then extended this pledge to ten other river gods. "When you're afraid," he laughed, "you don't worry about logic."

We kept seeing each other socially. I went to hear him present a case in court, celebrated Poṅkal with his family, ate out with him, and so on. And as I got to know him better, Sunil began to talk about the "girl," who "almost destroyed" him "in the span of ten months."

He was twenty-seven and in his second year of law school when he met her. At the time, his experience with women was limited. He had attended a men's college, and the only young women he knew were his sisters and neighbors. "This girl was new to me," Sunil said, "She not only came from a different caste but was smart, free, funny, and popular. Everyone thought she was the best." He managed to spend time with her every day after class. But negative emotions colored these moments. He was nonplussed by the young woman's expectations that he should at all times appreciate her looks, mannerisms, smart talk, and so on. He was "disgusted" with the way she called attention to herself and "frustrated" with her "power games"; he often felt "small and stupid." Yet he could not bring himself to end the relationship, and the realization that he had grown completely emotionally dependent on her, "addicted" as he put it, greatly distressed him. As he recalled: "Once we exchanged harsh words. She used crude language and cried. I thought she was ashamed and about to apologize, but instead she walked away. That night I couldn't sleep. All I could think was, 'My god, she's going to leave me. My god, what am I going to do with myself?' At 2:00 in the morning I called her cell phone. I couldn't get through. I waited, called again but couldn't reach her. By 8:30, I couldn't take it any more. I rushed to her college, hoping to catch her before her first class. She was so happy to see me in the pathetic state I was in. I couldn't speak, I was shivering, and she delighted in the power she had over me."

In their descriptions of young people's premarriage romances in the nearby state of Kerala, anthropologists Caroline Osella and Filippo Osella report that at first conversations are more like confrontations. "The overall effect is that of a battle of wits or verbal duel" (2000: 195). But when a girl signifies her willingness to pursue the romance, a boy "will drop his aggressive and hostile teasing manner [and] now takes the part of humble and ardent suitor, whose happiness (indeed, whose life) totally depends upon the favours of the beloved" (2000: 199). According to Osella and Osella, then, "two aspects of *love* and, indeed, of masculinity—assertive aggression and supplicant tenderness—mark boys as ambiguous creatures and place them at opposite ends of two different hierarchical dyads with respect to girls" (2000: 201). They conclude that neither boys nor girls hold a permanent advantage in the process of romance: "Dominance, control and relative status remain fluid, as power continually oscillates, and neither roles nor hierarchy can be fixed or maintained" (2000: 201).

In Sunil's account, power clearly remained with the girl, and he comes off as emasculated in more than one way. Premarital romance in South India tends to be nonsexual (see also Osella and Osella 2000: 196), but if sexual intercourse does take place, it is assumed that the young man initiated it. In Sunil's case, however, the pressure was reversed. In the account he gave, the girl made the first move, and he took on the normative gender role generally attributed to women: He resisted. "That was the only power I had," he said, adding, "We didn't have sex." According to Sunil, though, the young woman found a way of punishing him. "She made me say, 'I love you,' and that's all she wanted."

He went on:

> When she called to say goodbye, I cried. I cried in the street. I cried for a long time. I thought she was joking. I couldn't imagine she wouldn't come back. I kept dialing her number for the next six months, and she'd answer with poise and completely in control. I'd get mad. I kept calling for no reason. I knew it wasn't right. I was behaving like an uneducated man. I'm not supposed to act like this. I've a good life, a good family, but back then I couldn't tell right from wrong. I started to drink. I drank hard and a lot. I don't mind telling you, Isabelle, because that's the truth. I don't want to give a false picture of

> myself. Between the ages of seventeen and twenty-seven, all I drank was tea. But when I stopped seeing that girl, I became an alcoholic. I drank hard for two years, so hard that I had to drop out of law school. My family didn't understand why I was so irresponsible. Once I drank the whole night with a rickshaw driver and passed out under a tree by the [Madurai] temple. In the early morning a college friend passed by and recognized me. He made me talk, and I told him everything. "That girl is a whore," he said. I pleaded, "Don't say this; it hurts." But he kept repeating, "That girl is a whore. She has broken many hearts." He took me to a restaurant, fed me, and paid the bill. Then he drove me home and stayed with me for a couple of days.

Taping this sad story was Sunil's idea, not mine. He spoke with the clarity and determination of a trauma survivor who wants to go on record and testify. By the time we recorded this conversation he was better but deeply demoralized. He could not find a job, his married sisters were mad at him, and his name was associated with alcohol.

More painful to him was the fact that his behavior had cost him the one cousin he had wanted to marry since he was a teenager. The two families were well matched in terms of status and wealth, and according to Sunil the young woman felt the same way as he did. "We talked only twice," he said, "but you don't have to talk to know these things." Instead of Sunil (who stood in the position of her maternal grand-mother's brother's son), however, the girl married her "right" boy (her father's sister's son). This marriage must not have been all that "preferential," for six months later she was back living in her mother's house. Had Sunil been well then a matrimonial agreement might have been possible, but this was when he was drinking hard and "there was no question of marriage then." Eventually his cousin remarried, and Sunil came to regret the missed opportunity. "I lost her twice," he remarked with sadness. Two years later, when I saw him again, he had found intermittent work in a law office in Madurai, and his family was still trying to arrange a marriage for him.

The Remainders of Love

In his wonderful study of his childhood village of Béarn in Southwestern France, Pierre Bourdieu observed that in the 1960s a new class of bachelors emerged. As young women were quicker than men to assimilate the urbane values and lifestyle associated with the nearby growing town, they increasingly married out, and some male peasants remained single (2004). For Bourdieu, the rising rates of bachelorhood in Béarn were not simply a result of outside forces, overtaking the world in which rural men lived and made their choices. Rather than being wholly encompassed by a cultural clash between country and city—beyond their control and knowledge—these men embodied their "unmarriageability" in *habitus*, a concept that Bourdieu variously defined as "attitudes," "dispositions," and "tendencies." Thus, at local balls—then the only socially approved opportunity for meetings between the sexes—these men adopted and actually amplified the very behavior that disqualified them for marriage. On the rare occasion that a girl would lead a bachelor onto the dance floor, as Bourdieu describes the scene, "he stands firm, embarrassed and delighted. Then he goes once round the floor, deliberately accenting his clumsiness and heavy footedness . . . and looks back laughing at his mates. When the dance is over, he goes and sits down and will not dance again" (2004: 3). To Bourdieu, these and other bodily displays of shyness and gaucherie suggested that these peasant men were conscious of their standing and unmarriageability.

The Tamil rural society in which I worked in 2008 was also changing. The specific dynamic forces tearing at the social and mental fabric of village life were various, including the closing of the gender gap in education, a rise in the age of marriage; the prolongation of youth, the devaluation of agricultural work, the sale of land to industrial developments, changing types and amounts of marriage payments, the commodification of social relations, the rise of alcoholism, and so on. All these changes produced conflicts and contradictions that affected everyday life, specifically marriage practices.

The comparison with the Béarn of the 1960s only goes so far. Unlike French peasants, almost all Tamil villagers eventually do get married, no matter how disadvantaged they are, because in South India the social category of "bachelor" is virtually nonexistent. Moreover, Tamil "romance" rarely results in marriage, so matrimonial success has little to do with dating savoir-faire and everything to do with family standing, the amount of dowry offered, and levels of education and employment, particularly of the husband but increasingly of the wife as well. But there are similarities.

Much as in Béarn in the 1960s, whole categories of men in Tamil Nadu are currently disqualified or disqualify themselves from the matrimonial competition. The line between active and passive, disqualification or disadvantage, is not always clear. Young men like Mohan are not simply "waiting" for the resources necessary to marry (Jeffrey 2010). They are waiting to marry well because they inhabit a world in which masculine success depends on enacting the "right" forms of Tamil sociality. Their "choices" and lifestyles are not, as some social scientists are inclined to imply, radically cut off or liberated from history and local culture but are lived through in accordance with social norms. That honor, in particular, matters to these young men is evident in the fact that most do not elope with the girls for whom they feel *kātal*. They want their parents to arrange their marriages.

Young Tamil men, however, are conscious of their unmarriageability. They may not embody it, for Tamil bodies (unless under the influence) are not readable in the manner of the French peasant bodies that Bourdieu observed. Tamils, in general, aim to contain and hide rather than express emotions (see also Trawick 1990: 93). Moreover, the factors working against Tamil rural youth cannot all be reduced to the simple paired oppositions between village/ unsophisticated and city/fashionable used by Bourdieu. Most Tamil rural youth identify with, or at least emulate (with varying degrees of success), the styles and trends of the city, even of Indian modern public culture.[8] But in their poems and conversations with the foreign ethnographer, both Mohan and Sunil regretted in private that they were not suitable grooms.

At no time, however, did they act according to the newer models of the possessive liberal individual, promoted in much social science as the end-point of a single, homogenized world culture. To be sure, both Mohan and Sunil felt some kind of *kātal* for a young woman, but, despite the very modern-sounding plot that structures their stories ("boy meets girl," and a smart and powerful girl in the case of Sunil), the experiences they recounted either in poetry or ethnographic time do not strike me as indexing a Western-like (which more often than not stands as a metonym for "global") sensibility. In his inclination to write verses after he lost his girl, Mohan expressed himself in a language that has deep roots in Tamil literary culture. Recall how the Kaḷḷar man Mayandi of Chapter 3 also turned to poetry *after* his right girl was wedded to someone else. That the unavailability of the loved one remains integral to the "new" love poetry composed by contemporary youth like Mohan casts doubts about the erasure of the "local" and "tradition" that is constitutive of much of globalization studies. It also suggests that the expression of present-day *kātal* *still* requires feeling deeply about loss and sorrow—a far cry from American happy ending love stories.

A landowner from a respectable and entrepreneurial rural family outside Madurai, Sunil's particular premarital experience undermines another assumption of the uniform meta-narrative of modernity and globalization, namely that the spread of love is causing the decline of Dravidian marriage. Love nearly wrecked Sunil, leaving him—ironically, we might add—to regret that he had also lost the chance to marry his close kin. It is fair to say that for him, and other young men I talked with in Tamil Nadu, marriage with *contam* remained *preferable* to other unions, including and especially love marriage.

CONCLUSION

The Present Is Not Another World

We can develop *uravu* with unknown people.
—Abi, October 2007
Uravu is at the basis of human life.
—Mayanti, February 2008
First *uravu* is mother. Only through mother
do we come to know about father.
—Srinidi, September 2008

The main process of change documented in this book concerns a radical reformulation of marriage and family life in Tamil society. Endogamy, in the precise sense of close-kin marriage, continues to be a critical feature of South Indian kinship organization as the Tamils still marry *contam*. But the percentage of young people marrying preferential spouses—"right spouses"—or spouses with matrimonial rights is falling if only because, as indicated in Chapter 6, India in general, and South India in particular, is entering uncharted territory in demographic history. Although rural society is slower to embrace this change, preferential kin marriage is disappearing as a characteristic of the Tamil family in both town and village. My goal in this book has been to offer a cultural framework for understanding the old pattern of preferential marriages and to interpret their decline through the point of view of subjective perspectives.

I began by pointing out that we seldom encounter the Tamil word *contam*, the closest gloss to the English word "kin," in the classical descriptions of Dravidian kinship. Instead, theories sprung from the linguistic fantasies of nineteenth-century missionaries, and scholars such as Bishop Robert Caldwell, Lewis Henry Morgan, and W. H. R. Rivers focus on more formal terminology or on its structural "expressions," without following the general kinship vocabulary or considering, at the theoretical level at least, the kinds of explanations South Indian people provide of their own matrimonial arrangements. This is too bad, at the least, because in these very terms and local explanations there is also, I have attempted to show in these pages, a theory of what marriage and kinship mean for many Tamils.

Contam, I have suggested, is connected to notions of sameness. To the degree that *contam* is opposed to *aṉṉiyam*—which signifies "otherness"—there is not only a concept of identity or homology at work here but also a fundamental role of kinship in defining and managing alterity: who is "in" and who is "out." Sameness, I have also shown, does not merely mean that kin share the same substance, or blood, although that too (Good 2000: 326)[1] but that they are (in principle, at least) equal in status. Such parity in turn entitles *contam* to transcend the kinds of give-and-take exchanges that in most contexts of Tamil social life can degenerate at any moment (symbolically or literally) into relationships of subordination and superiority. More critically, it gives kin the right to make ownership claims, and such a privilege, which is exercised on the basis of that very social equivalence, I have argued in this book, is a major reason why the Tamils preferred, and still prefer, marrying kin.

The word *muṟai*, another critical Tamil word for "kinship," brings out an entirely different, in fact opposite, dimension to South Indian endogamous practices. Within the kinship group, *contam* are broken down into relations (mother, father, sister, brother, and son) that are endowed with varying quasi-legal rights, and specific relations are "righter" or/and have exclusive marital "rights." In the priority given to firstborn daughters and sons and in the unilateral rule or preference, we discern the association of marriage (and its potential for making *campantam* or "relation," for procreating life, for generating continuity, and so on) with precedence, asymmetry, and therefore hierarchical distinctions between "same people." If marriage to *contam* normalizes a social order that privileges relations of likeness, marriage to the right people favors relations of difference and rank. The important quality the latter union confers is the precedence and superiority of those who possess marital rights over those who do not. In addition to a conception of kinship, and by extension sociality at large, that honors the higher status of a relatively small privileged class, there is also a critical notion of hereditary aristocracy. The kin who occupy a particular temporal order (the firstborn) or "side" (mother's or father's) are expected, even required (think of the Kaḷḷars), to intermarry. In fact, it is moral and legal for them to do so. Hence, the right marriage not only introduces distinctions among people who by all accounts are most alike, it also legitimizes, in theory at least, a concept and practice of institutionalized inequality.

This concept does not exactly invalidate Claude Lévi-Strauss's theory of the "elementary structures of kinship." Each of the three Tamil preferential marriages (from the man's point of view: marriage to the mother's brother's daughter, the elder sister's daughter, and the father's sister's daughter, the latter of which this book has somewhat neglected) does privilege a particular field of exchange and comes with its own cosmology, sociology, and psychology. Marriage to the mother's brother's daughter offers the opportunity to create a wide network of alliances and a thriving, if risk-prone, social life rich with opportunities for speculation, which perhaps explains why it is favored by such enterprising and expansionist groups as the Kaḷḷars (as well as the Gounders, studied by Brenda Beck [1972]). Marriage to the elder sister's daughter, by contrast, makes for a narrow or "restricted" kinship terrain that shuns conjugality and affinity and the connections with "others" they necessarily entail. The category *muṟai*, however, clarifies that a logic of privilege and elitism organizes the exchanges involved in Tamil "right" marriages. Hence, Dumont was onto something when he linked the fact that Kaḷḷar sons of "senior" wives did not intermarry with those of "junior" wives or of illegitimate unions (1983: 44) to broader "Indian," social conceptions, classifications, and assumptions underlying caste. But the priority he (and just about all scholars of Dravidian kinship) gave to the system of categories generated by the terminology, and Sanskrit texts, prevented him from pushing his insights into the selective and discriminatory aspect of Dravidian marriage.

Another reason why the structuralist focus on exchange, emphasizing its formal consequences for social solidarity, does not quite capture the meanings of "right" marriages has to do with the subjective dimension of Tamil kinship rights. "*Urimai*," Thiagu's father told me in English, "is power"; the power, one may add, to declare you as my equal and to claim as mine, without compensation, whatever you own—property and relations. Not surprisingly, such an absolute leverage comes with a totalizing orientation, and the sense of expectation and entitlement brought by the anticipation of one's due it is only too real: Take my *urimai* away, and I'll kill you (my brother or sister); or, as we saw in Chapter 3, I'll live with a sense of loss and tragedy for the rest of my life. Exercise your *urimai*, and I (your child) may kill myself. The emotional cosmology of Tamil kinship can be quite stern.

The binding edge of this kinship world is even more pronounced among the Kaḷḷars, for whom the distinction between "rights" and "obligations" is blurred. This is most visible in the strongly prescriptive character of their marriage rule, which is couched as law. In this phrasing we discern that the Kaḷḷars are not quite the masters of their lives they claim to be. Families are *required* to do the "right thing" even if this means "joining" with brothers or sisters of lesser status or wealth. A distinct political theory, I have explained in Chapter 2, justifies this requirement: one that condemns the development of permanent inequalities between siblings. When chance prevents correct families from "doing the right thing," marriage privileges ought to rotate to the nearest, best kinsperson. Of course, this is only a theory, for in practice the question of how families actually take turns in marriage is likely to remain open ended for people who see most social situations as opportunities to produce gain or loss of status. The reader will recall how Kaḷḷar ceremonial collections of money, for instance, regularly mount into contests of one-upmanship, where each party seems to contribute in the hope that their rival cannot reciprocate their prestation or counterprestation. In Kaḷḷar society, it seems to me, the equal quality of two (or more) parties is up for grabs at any moment so that social parity is more a platonic ideal, a utopia of community, than the working order.

But enough about men. In this book I have also suggested that Dumont's ethnographic focus on the Kaḷḷars led him to overlook what used to be the most common and most valued marriage in South India. Marriage to the elder sister's daughter, I have argued, is arranged by, and for the sake of, women, the very gender group ignored by French structuralists. Here I am not merely suggesting that the South Indian women who marry a very close kinsperson are better off than the North Indian women who marry outside of both the kin group and the local group. To the degree that the uncle–niece marriage gives a measure of freedom to Tamil women, it supports the old comparative correlations of consanguinity in the south with women's relative independence and conjugality in the north with women's subordination. But the "advantage" I am talking about here is not one of power but status. Quite simply, the important relation conferred by the uncle–niece marriage is not parity or interchangeability of possessions, as is the case of Tamil endogamy in general, but superiority. The mothers and daughters who arrange it end up living in a household headed by a man who is de facto inferior to them, their son or younger brother.

It would be mistaken, I think, to interpret the *tampi*'s acceptance of his low position in this predominantly female household in light of the argument recently put forward by Marshall Sahlins (2013). In his new book: "What Kinship Is—and Is Not" (2013), Sahlins proposes that the basic "idea of kinship" at work in a variety of ethnographic contexts "is 'mutuality of being': people who are intrinsic to one another's existence" (2013: 2). Something like this does frame the relationship between brothers and sisters in Tamil Nadu and is in fact the reason given to the anthropologist when she asks why the "right" partners must be the children of a brother and sister, rather than the children of two brothers or two sisters. Inevitably she is told that the brother and sister share love, feel each other's sorrow and joy, and so on.

But Sahlins's notion of "intersubjective belonging" (2013: 2), however appealing it may be, leaves out the all-critical dimension of exclusivity that, as I have repeatedly emphasized throughout these pages, frames Tamil preferential endogamous unions, especially that of marriage to the elder sister's daughter. The brother steps in not merely to keep women at home near him, which is the common explanation for marrying a sister's daughter, but to put them (in particular, mothers and elder sisters) before men (fathers and older brothers). In essence, the *tampi* sacrifices his masculinity, autonomy, and higher rank in the household to give these women first place in the world of kinship, the world tout court. His sacrifice pays off. In exchange of his devotion, the man—much like the prototypical Indian worshipper (Fuller 1992: 72–73)—merges with the "deity" of Tamil kinship: mother. Such identification makes him superior to all other men, including fathers, as evidenced by the fact that he and only he possesses the absolute matrimonial right.

Notice what is happening here: The sphere of activity predominantly associated with men—competing for honor and coming first in life—derives from the brother's sacrificial relationship to the mother and her daughter. I say "brother" and not "younger brother" because I believe that this statement applies to all the mothers' brothers regardless of their age relative to the mother.

Tamil men's mode of sociality, I have shown in this book, develops out of their duty (*kaṭamai*) to either marry their uterine nieces for less or marry them off with great munificence. In the latter case, we have seen, men must generously advertise their sisters' daughters' readiness to marry. They must also go into debt to provide large amounts of cash or/and gold toward the cost of their weddings or/and dowries. Even an ultrapatrilineal and masculine group, such as the Kaḷḷars, requires the mothers' brothers to spend all that they have on doing the "right things." It is fair to say that the public life of these Dravidian men (their economic exchanges, social relations, and political moves) is completely encompassed and determined by their avuncular duties. This basic fact unifies all three preferential marriages I have described in this book, all Tamil marriages for that matter. Whether a marriage is conducted according to one set of rules or another, or no rule at all, it impels the bride's mother's brother(s) to act selflessly. The man's generosity sanctions his identification with the mother—the other one-sided giver of Tamil kinship—and the principle of superiority she represents. In this way we see that the source of a man's social life and privilege lies in his association with the mother's "side."

In this book, however, I have also argued that it is not accurate to characterize South Indian kinship by means of clear-cut axes (mother's side, father's side) and crystallized ideas (sibling and gender hierarchy, and so on). Because the "right" marriages are associated with privilege and plain power, their field of action includes dynamics such as compulsion (let's marry more children together), repetition (let's marry again), imitation (let's marry like them), competition (let's beat them to it), exclusion (let's not marry them), resentment (why did they not marry us?), and so on. As Chapter 5 suggests, the result of all that compulsive "joining" is a jumble of relations of affinity and consanguinity that place people in confusing, ambiguous positions. Only a few are plainly *tappu* and therefore tormenting, as when fathers and sons become classificatory "brothers," for instance. Yet most invalidate the formal models of "kin" and "affine" that for so long set the agenda for studies of Dravidian kinship and also undermine the high premium put by the Tamils themselves on "order" (*muṟai*) and classification. In the abstract, the orientation of marriage with the right spouse is inherently dyadic and discriminatory, but its practical applications are anything but tidy or categorical.

Finally, the last two chapters have documented how the change from marriage with *contam* to marriage with *aṉṉiyam*, a change that itself operates within the conceptual universe carved out by these very Tamil categories, is currently refiguring Tamil family life. The old kinship orientation based on blood relations is in the throes of changing to a kinship axis constituted by conjugal ties. The family you marry into is becoming more important than the one you are born into.[2] Another way to say this is that, nowadays, consanguinity has less social and emotional force than conjugality. This message is encoded in a Tamil synonym for *aṉṉiyam*, which is none other than the English word "private." When the Tamils say that so-and-so marry "private," they mean that the conjugal couple, who have no other ties of relationship to each other, is on its own (its own "island," as Mayanti once put it), for their families (their parents' siblings in particular) have fewer obligations toward the couple.

In these pages I have been wary of the argument that "modernity" is responsible for the demise of kinship practices such as Tamil right marriage. There is good reason to be guarded about the use of such broad explanations. Consider, for example, what happened to the modernizing paradigm used by many historians in the mid-nineteenth-century and through which they accounted for the many transformations in northwestern European family life from the 1700s through the mid-1800s. A century later, historians presented evidence suggesting that change had begun long before 1700. Indeed, the nuclear household—the touchstone of putatively "modern" family arrangements—had been common since at least the 1300s; individualism and the autonomy of younger generations could be traced back to the thirteenth century in England; and late marriage and widespread celibacy had been evident since 1000. In short, northwest European family life never underwent a dramatic, datable, transition from "traditional" to "modern" forms. The grand historical modernization narrative turned out to be a "myth" (Thornton 2005).

The kinship transformation I have discussed in the last two chapters also most likely predates modern times. It may very well have begun as early as in the thirteenth century. This was when the great Chola kings encouraged "linkages" between temples dedicated to Puranic gods, especially Siva, and localized shrines devoted to the tutelary deities of dominant caste groups (Stein 1980: 325-331). Such a directly political process of linkage culminated in an explosion of festivals celebrating the marriage of the Tamil goddess (and her multiple forms) to the Sanskrit god Siva. The divine wedding is ritually reenacted every year, to this day, in the center of Madurai, during the full moon of the Tamil month of Cittirai (April–May), and this ritual prefigures the structural and historical kinship conflicts analyzed in this book.

When the goddess Meenakshi marries Lord Sundareswarar ("beautiful deity" or Siva), another festival celebrates the journey of the god Vishnu (known locally as Alagar, "the beautiful lord") from his temple, twelve miles to the north of Madurai, to the Vaigai river bordering the old city. As Meenakshi's brother, Alagar is expected to attend the wedding ceremony, but no sooner does he reach the riverbed than he learns that the wedding has already taken place. Insulted, he refuses to enter the city and angrily goes back to his temple (Hudson 1977; Harman 1989; Fuller 1995).

In his description of this festival, C. J. Fuller suggests that "the complete absence of any ritually constructed connection between [Sundareswarar and Alagar] . . . express[es] a negative or non-existent relationship between the two divine brothers-in-law" (1995: 22). To me, however, it is not affinity that is "accorded practically no symbolic value" (1995: 24) in the Madurai festival but consanguinity. Its narrative—the story of a brother who does not make it to (in other words, who is excluded from) his sister's wedding to a Northerner—would seem to announce the failure of brothers to prevail over husbands. In other words, it would seem to herald the advent of conjugality. The reader should not be surprised that such an anticonsanguineal proclamation stands at odds with the anti*conjugal* story, recorded by Indira Arumugam (2011), some 125 miles away from Madurai. In this tale, a wife cannot bring herself to visit her husband, let alone live with him—and this situation is consonant with the anticonjugal practices I have discussed in this book. There is no contradiction here, as a more formalistic analysis might presume. Given the centrality of marriage in people's lives, and the frequency with which they become involved in debates over the rightness or propriety of marriages involving *contam* or *aṉṉiyam*, it is inconceivable that they should not have a whole repertoire of seemingly contradictory narratives available to justify the particular feelings and interests raised by one or another set of marriage-related practices.

Myth may prefigure the present, but—as suggested in the last two chapters—historical processes such as the decline in birth rates, the medicalization of consanguinity, the development of dowry, and the prolongation of youth have certainly accelerated the decline of Dravidian kinship. I have hinted that such developments should not be studied as forces that are exterior to individuals and therefore unknown to them. In fact, if there is one continuing analytic thread throughout this book it is that ethnographic investigation should be able to offer adequate explanations at the level of meaning, even if all the precise causal links or formal consequences are obscure (as they always to some degree are). Such a stance has led me to place the information given to me by the people I worked with, as well as their accounts of their own experiences, at the center of most of my chapters.

Of course, ethnographic documentation involves value judgments, too, and depends on the specific viewpoint of the investigator. This can give the impression that the discipline is imprecise and fuzzy and that ethnographic accounts are merely a summation of an indefinite range of phenomena from an indefinite number of points of view. I hope to have shown that, quite to the contrary, our focus on actors and their perceptions of the world—which has its roots in Max Weber's sociology and which carries through into modern anthropology by way of Clifford Geertz—responds to a "real" and forceful element of the world. More importantly, this focus contributes to the understanding of social change as it is lived and experienced.

At the very least, I hope to have shown that the meanings and narratives I collected have some traction, some compass, and especially some lasting gravitas in the modern world of my informants. Old Kaḷḷar ceremonial gift giving, and its bloated, speculative derivatives, remains a thriving precedent for and alternative to today's banking practices. The violence that ensues when kinship rights are denied is now mediated, and no less powerful, in modern courtrooms. The former association of marriage and rank has found new means of expression in the current escalation of dowry. The passion—both loving and agonistic—that circulated within families and in marriage exchanges provides a model for much of the emotion that is felt in "modern" or "love" marriages. Finally, missed opportunities, obligations, and "wrong" marriages still haunt the putatively individualistic youth of contemporary Tamil Nadu and grip their lives with notes of tragedy and loss. It is no wonder that the standard opposition between the "traditional" and the "modern," with the latter supposedly replacing the former wholesale and canceling it out in a continuously accelerating process of change, is foreign to my consultants' real experience and worldview.

The reason why it is important to resist the notion that change in Indian marriage patterns "just happens" from outside—as response to and emulation of neoliberalism and modernity—is that this reproduces a style of thinking that is quite old in anthropology, but no less naïve for its antiquity. This notion of external change always implies that change is progress, that the transformation from a society organized by kinship, endogamy, and patriarchal norms to some kind of "modernity" constitutes a step toward a better world. This reifies change as a leap forward, something like a movement from otherness and backwardness toward a known end-point, which is sameness and the modern. This progressive conception raises all sorts of issues for the anthropologist.

It is true that when this ethnography has carved out the small personal histories within the larger account, we have heard stories that support the notion of matrimonial progress. For some readers, perhaps, the happiest part of the book is when they meet Abi, who "resists"—by working harder—her parents' attempts to marry her against her wishes. But Dravidian women, this book has shown, have long found ways to resist conjugality. Besides, Abi's attitude toward tradition fluctuated. "Wrong" for her, the maternal uncle was perfectly "right" for her younger sibling.

This book has also presented accounts that reveal a more disturbing complexity, yet still challenging any notion of victory over traditional (that is, repressive) structures. Sunil's "love" for an "outside" girl crippled him for years. Mohan was mired in his youth and bachelorhood because he wanted his peers and elders' esteem. Recall that, in the name of respect and respectability, he spent his father's entire retirement check, plus a large sum of borrowed money, on his sister's wedding. And Mohan is not likely to get out of debt very soon. A maternal uncle, he has still the duty of giving gifts to his sister's two daughters until they marry. This much has not changed: For the time being, a Tamil man is still defined by such avuncular duties.

The big transformation, we have seen in Chapter 6, is that nowadays marriages are increasingly arranged with outsiders who come into the conjugal relation with achieved identities rather than ascribed ones. These new accomplished grooms take more than the "right" boys of the past, and their families have ways to make bride givers feel small. They certainly complain a lot: The bride is too short, the food served at the marriage feast is skimpy or not good, the gifts at the wedding (clothes, jewels, utensils) are of mediocre quality, and so on (Appadurai 1981, 1985). The problem, now, is that the bride's parents and brothers (the Mohans of this world) have no rights, no leverage, and no power. All they can do is to *publicly* endure these humiliations, acting as if they did not hear their affines' endless recriminations and demands for services—carrying bags, for example—that usually only servants perform. The Tamils have known this all along, and said it multiple ways: A marriage in which one has no "rights" is risky and potentially debasing. But for the sake of upholding social distinctions and of keeping sisters "above" brothers, they will suffer. Tamil preferential marriage may be on the decline, but its basic meanings of "rightness" and sacrifice are not.

NOTES

INTRODUCTION

1. In Muslim law, all first cousins both on the paternal and maternal sides are outside the ambit of prohibited degrees in marriage. Usually Muslims prefer to marry patrilateral parallel cousins (children of the father's brother). In Sri Lanka, however, they marry cross cousins (children of the mother's brother or the father's sister) (De Munck 1996; McGilvray 2008; Hussain Khan 2003) and in Tamil Nadu, uncles and nieces as well, thereby conforming to the "Dravidian" kinship paradigm described in this book.

2. David Schneider's influential work, *A Critique on the Study of Kinship* (1984), marked a turning point in the anthropological discussion of kinship. After a lifetime working on the subject, Schneider came to believe that his profession's obsession with "kinship," "the idiom of kinship," and "the kin-based society" was a serious ethnocentric mistake brought on by biologism. His attack destabilized the confidence held by kinship theorists but also opened a vibrant new theoretical vein for discussing the realities of nature and culture and the realities of kinship (and gender) within each.

3. Morgan's book, *System of Consanguinity and Affinity of the Human Family* (1871), was to complete the task to which philology had aspired but not completely succeeded: namely to show the unity, and Asiatic origin, of the American Indian languages (Trautmann 1984: 422; 1987). Such projects were not new, but Morgan's original contribution was to focus on the collection of kinship terms. His research included four summers traveling in the American Midwest and questionnaires sent to mission boards located in Indian areas elsewhere in North America. By a confluence of luck he discovered that the Ojibwa Indians had a similar terminology to that of the Iroquois, even though they spoke a completely unrelated language. This encouraged him to extend his research to other Indian tribes, and by mid-1859 Morgan was convinced that throughout North America there was a fundamentally uniform system by which relatives were named and classified (Trautmann 1987; Kuper 1988). Now he was ready to broaden his comparative work to Asia.

To this end he invited an American missionary to prepare a schedule of kinship terms for two south Indian languages, Tamil and Telugu. Morgan chose these two languages because one of his contemporaries, the well-known Sanskrit scholar Max Müller, had speculated that "Dravidian" languages were related to those of Native

American tribes. Morgan was overjoyed to discover that, like the Iroquois, the Tamils merged lineal kin (for example, parents) and collateral kin (parents' siblings) in ascending and descending generations so that the word *father*, for example, also referred to the father's brother and other relatives as well. He contrasted such a "classificatory" system with the "descriptive" kinship terminologies of the West, terminologies that introduce the word *uncle* to distinguish father from the father's brother, and concluded that the conflation of kinship terms indicated a lack of understanding of degrees of blood relationship (Trautmann 1987; Kuper 1988). To put it simply, in Morgan's view users of classificatory kinship terminologies did not distinguish between the father and the father's brother because they had no knowledge of biological paternity, and such ignorance in turn clearly proved that Indians of North America and Dravidians of South India once lived in a state of primordial promiscuity (Trautmann 1987; Kuper 1988). It was actually Morgan's friend and biographer, the Reverend Joshua McIlvaine, who first surmised that "classificatory" kinship terminology indicated a lack of knowledge (about fatherhood, for example) that could only be characteristic of "primitive society" or rather "primitive promiscuity" (Trautmann 1987; Kuper 1988: 59; Parkin and Stone 2004: 6). His influence led Morgan to revise his manuscript and chart the fifteen stages of "the development of family types" (1871: 481). The last stages of humanity's social development corresponded to the monogamous marriage of the "civilized nuclear family" and the final "overthrow of the classificatory system of relationship" (Morgan 1871: 481).

4. Although scholars have bickered about this or that aspect of Dumont's demonstration, they have also stuck to the same view (Yalman 1962; Scheffler 1977, 1984; Trautmann 1981; Good 1981; Rudner 1990; Trawick 1990; Parkin 1996a, 1996b).

5. From a structural perspective, matrilateral cross-cousin marriage is superior to its patrilateral counterpart; the latter has less potential to produce social cohesion because its exchange cycles are shorter (the direction of wife exchange is reversed in each successive generation).

6. There seems to be some consensus among South Indian ethnographers that the mother's brother's daughter marriage is preferred to the father's sister's daughter marriage (Beck 1972: 253; Trawick 1990: 177; Reddy 1993: 144), but in my opinion the jury is still out on this subject due to insufficient data.

7. Good drew on Rodney Needham's tripartite model of social reality (1973), proposing to study "marriageability" at: (1) the "statistic-behavioural level," or the demographic, marital, residential, and other observed patterns; (2) the "jural level," or the marriage rules; and (3) "the categorical level" or the kinship terms (1981: 108).

8. Of the fifty-eight unions Good documented, six (or 10.3 percent) involved marriages with the father's sister's daughter and five (or 8.6 percent) with the mother's brother's daughter. The corresponding figures for his entire sample of 144 unions were eighteen marriages (12.5 percent) of each type (1981: 119).

9. As early as 1914, F.J Richards—at that time the British collector of the Bangalore Cantonment—noted that in some castes of South India, a boy "has a preferential right to marry the daughter of his sister" (1914: 194). At the Congrès International

des Sciences Anthropologiques et Éthnologiques held in London twenty years later, in 1934, A. Aiyyappan presented a paper that aimed to "invite attention to a form of enjoined marriage less known outside Indian than cross-cousin marriage, and, therefore, very little studied—the marrying of one's own sister's daughter" (1934: 281). In 1972 Brenda Beck reported that, in the Koṅku area of Tamil Nadu, "Marriage with the ZD [sister's daughter] is generally warmly approved . . . [and] is, in fact, a more frequent marriage statistically than a match with a [cross cousin]" (1972: 249). Her data show that 5.9 percent of the 525 marriages she recorded were with the actual mother's brother's daughter, 5 percent with the actual father's sister's daughter and 6.5 percent with the actual elder sister's daughter. She concludes, "Of the three types of marriages considered, ZD [sister's daughter] is clearly the most popular, while MBD [mother's brother's daughter] runs second, and FZD [father's sister's daughter] unions are generally the least frequent of the three" (1972: 253). Good's own data are somewhat consistent: Of the 194 marriages he recorded in Tirunelveli, 5.6 percent were with the mother's brother's daughter, 6.3 percent with the father's sister's daughter, and 8.2 percent with the elder sister's daughter (1980: 484). But the Indian anthropologist Govinda Reddy's statistics on this last union are even more striking: Of the 979 marriages he recorded among three communities residing in the Nellore district of Andhra Pradesh State, 18.88 percent (or 185 marriages) were of the uncle-niece type (1993: 36). See also McCormack 1958; Rao 1973; Kapadia 1995; and Annoussamy 2003.

10. This figure is actually not much lower than the one reported by the National Family Health Survey conducted in 1992–1993, which indicates that "about 35 percent of [South Indian] women were married [then] to their blood relatives" (in Audinarayana and Krishnamoorty 2000: 192).

11. The word *Tēvar* literally means "lord." It has been adopted as an honorific by the Kaḷḷars, the Maṟavars, and the Agambadiyars and is used more generally to refer to the people of these castes.

12. That Sanskritic kinship was hierarchical and Dravidian kinship egalitarian was most effectively brought to the fore by Kathleen Gough's comparison of marriage preferences in a multicaste Tamil village (1956). Her study revealed that, whereas Brahmin families opted for matrilateral cross-cousin alliances that "reinforce already existing asymmetrical relationships," non-Brahmin (and therefore less Sanskritized) castes and landless laborers favored patrilateral or uncle-niece unions that "reverse such relationships" (1956: 844). Because Tamil non-Brahmins were prone to return a bride in the same generation (sister exchange) or in the next generation, a young bride was very likely to end up with folks who were equal to hers (see also Deliège 1987: 225; Kapadia 1995: 49; and Nishimura 1998: 121). If anything, Gough's study justified the division of India (whether locally or nationally) into separate "culture areas" by types of kinship organization. In this respect, she went against Dumont, who espoused the contrary notion. For him, India was one and unified rather than many and disjointed. He argued that the seemingly disparate kinship terminologies and marriage prestations of South and North India in fact pointed to a common structuring principle that was Sanskritic—and therefore hierarchical—in origin (1966).

13. The cross-sibling bond is indeed the most idealized bond in Tamil family life. As the Tamil scholar Indira Peterson (1988) has shown, the plots of many South Indian myths, films, and novels underscore that there is no stronger love. In general, though, sibling relations receive more attention among South Asians than among North Americans (Nuckholls 1993; Kolenda 1993; and Seymour 1993).

14. Dumont himself recorded a legend in which a Kaḷḷar ancestor was made to marry a girl who was both a Muslim and his granddaughter (the daughter of a daughter from a previous liaison with a Muslim woman) (1986: 151).

15. According to Goody, the Church had a strong interest in encouraging heirlessness and thus securing money that previously was kept in families, for in the early medieval period it was no longer a world-rejecting sect but was becoming a great institution that needed resources to support its clergy (for a critical review of Goody's argument, see Shaw and Saller 1984).

CHAPTER 1

1. The Kaḷḷars are predominantly found in the southern districts of Tamil Nadu and share the honorific title Tēvar (literally "lord") with two other putatively martial and related castes, the Maṟavars and the Akampaṭiyar. These three castes—also known as "people of the three clans" (Mukkulatar)—make up the most populous caste of Tamil Nadu.

2. Before British rule, kings and chieftains of the southern Tamil country periodically recruited Kaḷḷars to fight wars against local or foreign powers (Thurston and Rangacheri 1987 volume 3: 61; Dumont 1986: 13; and Pandian 2005: 5). According to Dumont, the Kaḷḷars from East of Madurai were "charged particularly with missions of harassment, with raids on the enemy's rear, with destruction and plundering" (1986: 13). Their martial and marauding traditions must have posed a serious threat to British troops because in 1755 army battalions engaged in at least five brutal campaigns against the Kallars near the town of Mēlur, massacring several thousand men, women, and children in a violent effort to force their submission (Pandian 2005: 6).

3. As the anthropologist Nick Dirks documents, the Kaḷḷars of Pudukkottai were clearly exempted from this mode of colonial classification because Pudukkottai was a princely state that, although under British suzerainty, retained some limited domestic autonomy from 1800 to 1947 (1987: 205).

4. There is no denying that the "Criminal Tribes and Castes Act" of 1911 wronged the Kaḷḷars, subjecting them to intensive police surveillance, techniques of intimidation, and judicial discipline. According to the historian David Arnold (1979), Kaḷḷar men were fingerprinted and required to remain in their villages after a specified curfew at night. In April 1920, he notes, "Fourteen piramalais of the Perungamanallur village were killed resisting registration under the Criminal Tribes Act" (1979: 158). Arnold further argues that the British themselves drove the Kaḷḷars to crime by forbidding them to practice their "traditional" watchman occupations and imposing economic policies that exaggerated the effects of drought and dearth on them (1979: 162–163). For this historian, crises such as the 1876–1878 famine caused the Pramalai Kaḷḷars of the Ti-

rumangalam taluk to lose 15.6 percent of their population over a period of ten years (1979: 156), leaving them no choice but to steal and collect "custodian" (or *kāval*) fees for the return of stolen cattle. Nor did the British help the Kaḷḷars make the transition to farming. In the village Mēlnāṭu located to the West of Madurai town, Arnold writes, "Land ownership was quite insufficient for their maintenance, especially as village tanks, which ought to have provided irrigation water, had been empty for most of the previous ten years due to drought" (1979: 157). Thirty years later, Dumont observed that the Kaḷḷars of that area were still poor farmers who mostly owned dry lands without irrigation networks (1986: 95).

5. Pandian (2005) recounts a widespread mass movement against the Pramalai Kaḷḷars of rural Madurai in late 1895. He writes:

> In village after village, cultivators swore by their ploughs to suspend Kallar watchmen and appoint men from other cultivating castes in their stead . . . All transactions with Kallars were halted. Kallars were prevented from drawing water from common wells. Village artisans, barbers and washermen were prohibited from serving Kallar households. Merchants were forbidden from selling them "the necessities of life," and discourse or "friendship" of any kind with Kallars was banned altogether. Massive regional meetings spread the movement to hundreds of villages, and countless Kallar households fled the region in fear of arson and robbery (2005: 2–3).

To Pandian, a colonial administrative survey sparked the anti-Kaḷḷar movement as it asked local *ryots* why they employed the Kaḷḷars as watchmen instead of farmers like them. To him, this question seized on both native and colonial constructions of the Kallar as a people predatory by nature and fomented the movement.

But certain historical developments complicate this scenario. As Pandian himself indicates, many of the Pramalai Kaḷḷars evicted by the assemblies in the Dindigul, Palni, and Periyakulam Taluks were recent immigrants from southern Madurai. It is very likely that these new settlers were poor and hungry because, as the historian David Arnold suggests, "The terrible famines of 1876–78 had forced countless Kaḷḷar families to move north and west [of Madurai] in search of livelihood" (1979: 34). It is also likely that the Kaḷḷars expanded into territories north of the Vaigai River by means of banditry, which was for them a time-honored method for acquiring political power and legitimate authority. Edgar Thurston's observation that "the people who suffer most at the hand of the Kallars are the shepherds (Konans or Idaiyans)" (Thurston and Rangachari 1987 Volume 3: 65) also throws light on the critical incident that caused "the entire anti-Kallar social body [to rally] against the entire body of Kallars" (Pandian 2005: 22). According to Pandian, "the movement reportedly began as a reaction to a Kallar man who had enticed away a shepherd woman and her daughter" (2005: 2). If this man kidnapped the two women, as the Kaḷḷars raided livestock in general to exact ransom and ratification of their protective services, it is likely that the cultivating castes of the area needed no administrative survey to join the shepherds on June 9, 1896, when 10,000 men assembled in the village of Nellore in Dindigul *taluk* to set fire to all the Kaḷḷar houses.

6. "Couples," because married children increasingly live on their own right after marriage, a fact that has contributed to the proliferation of ceremonial prestations.

When married children do not live under one roof, eat food cooked in a single kitchen, worship and hold property in common, they do not make or take "joint" contributions to life-cycle ceremonies. They give and receive *ceymuṟaihal* on their own. We should not exaggerate this trend. More than sixty years ago, Dumont noted, "The [Kaḷḷar] family type is not the joint family found elsewhere in India, but the nuclear family" (1986: 130).

7. Dumont discounts the influence of orthodox Hindu ritual on Kaḷḷar marriage, so there is no hint that the forms of negative reciprocity he describes are related to the Brahmanical concept of marriage as meritorious "gift of a virgin" (*kaṉṉikā-tāṉam*), which is ideally performed as a sacrifice to the gods with no expectation of worldly return.

8. Naturally, the colonial literature is replete of examples of such vindictive "acts of self-mutilation or self-destruction." Edgar Thurston, for example, noted that a Kaḷḷar man or woman would tear his or her distended lobes to compel his or her adversary to do the same and that a man could murder his wife and children so as "to have the atrocious satisfaction of compelling his adversary to commit the like murders in his own family" (Thurston and Rangachari 1987: 312).

CHAPTER 2

1. In his monograph on the Pramalai Kaḷḷars, Dumont did note that "a kinship relationship can always be expressed in two ways: in the form of murei, 'order, rule, custom,' a classification which broadly indicates the appropriate type of conduct; or more precisely, in the form of sondam, 'propriety,' and analytic description of the individual relationship" (1986: 301). Unfortunately, Dumont does not expand on these two key concepts, which he mentions in passing as if to illustrate the fact that the Tamils have categories for the subject of his chapter on kinship nomenclature or terminology (see also Rudner 1994: 177–178; and Kapadia 1995: 39–40).

2. Anthony Good, who had studied these prestations in three Tamil villages, explains, "These [shares] usually contain two components, *varattu campaḷam* ('income-salary') and *māṉiyam* ('honour, respect')" (1991: 37). The former, he was told in English, is given "for labour" (1991: 39). The latter is not given in exchange for work but in recognition of "the special qualities by virtue of which an expert is able to fulfill his or her function" (1991: 39). In other words, *māṉiyam* honors the caste-specific knowledge associated with a specialization or profession (1991: 39–40; see also Reiniche 1977). Good's report is consistent with my field data, except that in Kaḷḷar country I observed that the salary (also called *kūli*) component is not paid in the fields in front of everybody but at home in the form of paddy or cash, or both.

3. Instead of the numeral "first," the landlord actually says "lābam," which, according to the Fabricius, "is an auspicious term in counting while measuring grain and is synonymous with [one])" (1972: 87).

4. Tamil puberty rituals vary in length, complexity, and importance from caste to caste. Some last seventeen days, others less; some are elaborate and others simple. Because Tamil young women no longer marry immediately after reaching puberty, nowa-

days the ritual is performed over two phases. The first phase (essentially a purifying phase) takes place a few days after the girl first menstruates and the second and main phase (*caṭaṅku*) when her parents are ready for her to be married (see Good's detailed description of this ritual: 1991: 97–110).

5. Among non-Brahmin castes residing around the town of Madurai it is the girl's mother's married elder brother (or her mother's own maternal uncle) who brings the cir (see also Kapadia 1995: 95). But, according to Anthony Good, the main officiant at a female puberty ritual practiced by Hindus in three Tirunelveli villages is a female cross cousin of the pubescent girl (1991: 1, 97–110).

6. From the Tamil village of Aruloor Kirin, Kapadia notes that brothers give cīr (gifts of clothes, cash, and jewels at a young's woman puberty ritual) to offset the loss of their sisters' share of parental property (1995: 21–22). Although I do not dispute that the ceremonial gift of beauty and prosperity constitutes some kind of compensation to sisters who until recently did not inherit from fathers (Dumont 1986: 289–290), I do not think that a sociology of reciprocity (and its concomitant notion of debt) is adequate to understand the puberty cīr. As the last chapter already suggests, and as Chapter 4 will confirm, the maternal uncle is the giver par excellence. His constant munificence, I argue later in the book, is to be understood in terms of his identification to women, the mother in particular.

7. See also Dumont 1986: 209fn9; and Rudner 1994: 224–225.

8. My information here contradicts that of Dumont, who noted that, among the Kaḷḷars, "In principle the obligation is to provide a partner for each eldest son of sisters and for each eldest daughter of brothers" (1986: 207; his emphasis). As he explained:

> Suppose, for example, that three sisters are born in T and marry respectively into A, B, C. One son of each, and only one, must receive a wife from T. More specifically, he must receive a daughter of one of the three sisters' brothers in T. If there are three brothers, they will provide wives in their own birth order to A, B and C respectively. If there is only one brother, however, and he has three daughters, he will be obliged to give them in marriage to his sisters' sons in A, B and C respectively. If there are five brothers and all have daughters, in principle, the last two will have a right to marry their daughters to one of the extra sons of A, B and C. Not only are other children (brothers' sons, sisters' daughters) involved in other alliances, but once the obligations have been fulfilled, even children of the relevant sex may be married freely. (1986: 207)

Dumont further repeats, "While eldest children's marriages are strictly regulated, younger children's marriages seem free, as a sort of irrelevant addition" (1986: 207). Similarly, from the area of Koṅku Brenda Beck notes,

> Once one brother has married a girl of the correct genealogical specification, then the other brothers have no further claim upon other girls in the same category. Some informants say it should be the eldest brother who makes such a marriage and the younger ones who are "free" to marry elsewhere, but no one would argue over this fine point as long as one of several brothers will consent to take the urimai [muṟai] girl. (1972: 238)

The men and women I worked with were categorical: Only pairs of cross siblings, especially the first pair (and not all firstborn children of sisters and brothers), are required (or rather entitled) to practice a higher degree of endogamy, and the following unmatched siblings can marry however they want.

9. British scholars and administrators loved to report on this age discrepancy, especially if it worked against the groom. For example, the British museologist and ethnographer Edgar Thurston noted, "Among the Kammas of the Tamil country, the bridegroom is sometimes much younger than the bride, and a case is on record of a wife of twenty-two years of age, who used to carry her boy-husband on her hip as a mother carries her child" (1906: 51). Thurston read in the Madras Census Report of 1891 that, among the Tamil cultivators called Kongas, "Marriage with a maternal uncle's daughter is looked upon as the most desirable union, and this frequently results in a boy of seven or eight being married to a girl twice his age, who lives with her father-in-law until her husband grows up" (1906: 52). Thurston adds that "this custom is said to be dying out" (1906: 50), but on the next page he reports, "Among the Reddis (Telegu cultivators) who have settled in Tinnevelly [in Tamilnadu] a young woman of sixteen or twenty years of age is frequently married to a boy of five or six years, or even of a more tender age" (1906: 52–53). The British focused on the more aberrant details of "South Indian weddings." But my Kaḷḷar consultants confirmed that in the past neither seniority nor physical handicaps could free a man from the obligation to marry a "right girl."

10. Actually, at nonpublic fights, the rams are deliberately enraged (by forcing country liquor into their mouths or throwing chili powder in their eyes, ears, and mouth).

11. Dumont observed that in the early 1950s the Kaḷḷars paid an "indemnity" that was equivalent to the "minimum amount in cash paid by the groom's family to the bride's family" (1986: 209).

12. Brenda Beck also noted that matrimonial "rights are reinforced by magical sanctions that are dangerous and can bring bad luck if they are violated" (1972: 249). Similarly, the French medical anthropologist Brigitte Sebastia reports the case of a Tamil woman who thought her brother bewitched her because she had not respected his matrimonial rights (2007: 243).

13. This fact did not trouble my narrators, who pointed out that in every generation one marriage ought to perpetuate the relationship between the brother-sister's families, even if this meant reversing the rule (also see Dumont 1986: 211–212).

CHAPTER 3

1. Bourdieu elaborated a practice-based model that refers analysis to the reasons actors employ to justify their matrimonial strategies and the many ways in which they adapt to varied situations. For him the marriage of a son or daughter was to be interpreted as the equivalent of a "move" in a game of cards. The father who aims to choose the best deal possible always has the freedom to play with the rules, and this sense of game playing and advantage seeking clearly appears in negotiations. Hence, for Bourdieu the relative low incidence of so-called preferential marriage among Arabic or Berber societies (about 5 percent of all matrimonial unions) was not surprising. The self-interested and therefore open-ended actions carried out by particular agents mean

that matrimonial practice cannot be reduced to a simple application or execution of the rules (1990: 18).

2. In her research on the civil war in Sri Lanka, Margaret Trawick notes that the word *viḷaiyāṭṭu* is a combination of two roots: *viḷai*, which means grow and flourish, and *āṭṭu*, which means movement or dancing (2007: 11). She notes that the epitome of Tamil play, "the dance of growth and flourishing," is the sexual and dangerous play between male and female gods, "dangerous" because its heat can destroy the universe (2007: 11).

3. Mayandi's mother's brother's wife was also his father's mother's brother's daughter.

4. As already noted in footnote 1 of Chapter 1, both castes are predominantly found in the southern districts of Tamil Nadu and share the honorific title Tēvar (literally "lord") with the putatively related Akampaṭiyar.

CHAPTER 4

1. The common explanation is that the age disparity between a man and his younger sister's daughter would be too great.

2. Good's argument draws on the work of Edmund Leach (1951) and Jean Carter Lave (1966).

3. As Shulman defines this psychology,

> What counts is, first and foremost, the inner emotional reality, which abrogates the normative divisions between living beings. Shared sensation, especially of great intensity—especially sensation focused on or derived from loss and separation—becomes a form of self-transcendence. (1993: 14)

4. To be accurate, my consultants did not say that a father and daughter have no desire for one another. They simply stated that any sexual relationship between them was *mocam* ("bad").

5. Answers to this survey qualify Margaret Trawick's depiction of the Tamil bond between mother and daughter as being deeply unequal and unreciprocal (1990: 169).

6. In the area of Koṅku, Brenda Beck noted, "People say . . . 'a man has a very strong right,' implying that the woman's claim is less" (1972: 238). But, in my field experience, sisters, mothers, and daughters have *urimai*s as well, and the elder the woman is, the stronger her right, for we recall that in the Tamil world seniority always establishes priorities.

7. Pauline Kolenda's comparison of regional differences in household organization went on to list the specific variables enhancing women's "bargaining power" over husbands in the south (1987 [1967]). Subsequent social scientists placed even greater explanatory weight on the South Indian system of kinship and marriage. According to Tim Dyson and Mick More (1983), in particular, this system accounted for differences in key demographic indicators (in terms of fertility, mortality, and sex ratios) and in levels of "female autonomy" between North and South India. The complete picture of regional differentiation in kinship practices also included the higher prevalence of dowry marriage in the north and women's customary rights to inherit land or to be

apportioned land as dowry in the South (Agarwal 1994). At all stages of the argument, Patricia Uberoi rightly notes, the basic premise was that the family system in the South was qualitatively and experientially different from that in the North, "*at least from a woman–centered perspective*" (2008: 57; her italics).

8. Shulman's sources consist of the corpus of *Purāṇas* associated with particular shrines in the Tamil *śaiva* tradition.

CHAPTER 5

1. In the early 1970s, Kenneth David also noted that the Tamils who lived in the Jaffna penisnula of Sri Lanka used the "chain image" to represent both alliance and descent relations (1973: 528).

2. Comparing the patriarchal society in which Freud developed his psychoanalytic theories with the matrilineal society of his ethnography, Malinowski noted that a Trobriand man feels ambivalent and resentful not toward his father (for whom he has warm feelings), but toward his mother's brother, who raises him, disciplines him, and from whom he inherits his wealth. As he writes: "The ambivalent attitude of veneration and dislike is felt between a man and his mother's brother, while the repressed sexual attitude of incestuous temptation can be formed only towards his sister" (1927: 80). Malinowski adds, "In the Oedipus complex there is the repressed desire to kill the father and marry the mother, while in the matrilineal society of the Trobrianders, the wish is to marry the sister and to kill the maternal uncle" (1927: 80–81).

3. This marriage is likely to be rare, for the simple reason that a woman who stands in the position of elder sister to a groom's mother is usually too old for him. In this particular case the wife was only two years older, a relatively small age difference by our Western standards, but one that would not be acceptable for most Tamils, who nowadays at least like the bride to be younger than the groom.

4. From the nearby state of Andhra Pradesh, the French anthropologist Olivier Herrenschmidt also notes that men who marry "true" sisters become classificatory brothers (2009: section 28).

5. I thank N. Ganesan for pointing out to me that this expression has its origin in the South Indian variant of the *mancala* game.

6. In 2005, according to the National Crime Record Bureau, the official agency responsible for suicide data collection in India, Kerala had an estimated suicide rate of 27.7 per 100,000. The same year suicide rates in the other South Indian states were as follows: Karnataka 20.7 per 100,000, Tamil Nadu 18.6 per 100,000, and Andhra Pradesh 16.8 per 100,000. The union territory of Pondicherry had the highest suicide at 52.1 per 100,000 (Soman et al. 2009: 262). According to Tom Widger, "suicidal behaviour" also occurs "at unusually high rates" in nearby Sri Lanka (2012: 2).

The most notable community-based studies on suicide in India have emerged from Tamil Nadu, where researchers report that from 1992 to 2001 suicide was the leading cause of death for the age group fifteen to nineteen (Aaron et al. 2004). The rate for boys was 58 per 100,000 and for girls 148 per 100,000. In other words, suicide was the cause of about 25 percent of all deaths in young men and 50 to 75 percent of all deaths in young women. Jayaprakash Muliyil, the principal of the Christian Medical College in Vellore that compiled these statistics, suggests that the explanation for the different ratios lies in the gender bias against the girl-child in Indian culture and society. Young women are driven to suicide when there are conflicts at home or when they fail school exams, cannot marry the boy they love, or feel that the process of coming up with the money required to marry them off places a huge financial burden on their families. Jonathan Spencer's argument that, in the village of Sinhala Buddhists in central Sri Lanka where he worked in late 1980s, suicide arose as a response to conflicts involving hierarchically unequal parties also sheds light on these grim statistics (1990; but see Widger 2012). At least it seems plausible that young Tamil women, who are much less likely to face up to senior relatives than are men, express themselves (their problems, fears, grievances, and frustrations) by means of suicide.

7. See also the work of Jeanne Marecek on youth suicide in Sri Lanka (1998). She draws the very same conclusions and has vivid examples from the Sinhalese side.

CHAPTER 6

1. The most important physiological effect of consanguineous marriage is to intensify any or all inheritable family characteristics or peculiarities, by double inheritance of a recessive (or dominant) gene. Studies conducted among consanguineous populations indicate that a minority of families experience the adverse effects associated with inbreeding (Bittles et al. 1991, 1993). Govinda Reddy's detailed study of three castes in the Nellore District of Andhra Pradesh emphasizes the role of cultural variables, such as income level, level of education, age at marriage, and so on, influencing consanguineous marriages and their cumulative biological implications, and which, according to his data, point to higher rates of fertility and mortality than for nonconsanguineous unions (1993: 144–145).

2. The spread and growing popularity of the scientific discourse of genetics and its supposed warnings against close-relative marriage is an example of what the sociologist Arland Thornton calls "developmental idealism" (2005). Thornton argues that the modernizing paradigm used by mid-nineteenth-century historians to account for the transformations in northwestern European family life from the 1700s through the mid-1800s was integrally linked to this "developmental idealism," a vision that presumes that modernized family forms represent not merely change but moral progress. Although modern historians went on to present evidence suggesting that change had begun long before 1700, Thornton maintains that many developing nations have appropriated the four key components of developmental idealism:

1. Modern society is good and attainable;
2. The modern family is good and attainable;
3. The modern family is a cause as well as an effect of a modern society; and
4. Individuals have the right to be free and equal, with social relationships being based on consent. (2005: 8)

I suspect that something like "developmental idealism" is fueling the Tamil discourse against close-kin marriage.

3. The extensive rural network of primary Health Care Centers (HSC) or subcenters (an HSC caters to 5,000 people) has been an important conduit for spreading governmental conceptions of the modern family—a family characterized by late marriage, exogamy versus endogamy, conjugality rather than consanguinity, low fertility, and healthy children who go to school rather than engage in economically productive labor. Nurses working in village Health Care Centers do not merely monitor pregnancies, provide antenatal care, and record pregnancy outcomes, and so on; they also promote family planning agendas and advise against close-kin marriage (see also Chakrabarty and Guilmoto 2005).

4. Perhaps the first to note the dramatic transformation in South Indian marriage payments was Scarlett Epstein (1973: 194–199). On her first field trip to the South Indian state of Karnataka in 1955–1956, Epstein noted that the full responsibility for arranging a village wedding and meeting most of the expenses rested with the groom's family. In 1970 this had completely changed, with the bride's family now assuming the wedding expenses and paying dowry (in the form of gifts and payments) to the groom's parents, a development that Epstein saw as an additional sign of Sanskritization among farming castes, especially richer families (1973: 194). Her interpretation made sense because the model of Sanskritization was then widely used by social scientists to indicate a process of upward mobility in an otherwise "traditional" or static social system. According to ethnographers working in the early 1960s and 1970s, Indian lower castes attempted to eat, dress, and pray (and, according to Epstein, marry) like Brahmins (or other upper or dominant castes) to raise their rank in the caste system (Srinivas 1956). In the 1980s, the Sanskritization model became, as Kalpana Ram complained, "singularly inappropriate to describe the kind of transformations" of the new Tamil neoliberalizing economy (Ram 1991: 186–187). Note, however, that its basic underlying assumption reappears in Kapadia's attempt to link marriage payments with women's work and overall upward mobility (see the summary of her argument in the text).

CHAPTER 7

1. As already indicated in the Introduction, North Indians disapprove of marriage between close kin of any type. In fact, the classical model of their kinship system, Hindu law books, specifies a very extensive and genealogically deep range of exogamous prohibitions on both the mother's and the father's side (see Uberoi's summary in 2008: 65–67). The widely held North Indian opprobrium for consanguineous marriages complicated and delayed postindependence legislative efforts to formulate a comprehensive Indian marriage code. North Indian lawmakers who drafted the Special Marriage Act of 1954 and the Hindu Marriage Act of 1955 supported their prejudices with scientific studies of the potential risks of consanguinity for the genetic composition of a population. Patricia Uberoi notes that even those who spoke in defense of South Indian close-kin marriage "did *not* seek to contest the eugenic argument." She adds, "They simply argued that such marriages should be legally permitted in a 'transitional' society until such a time as people could be 'educated' into *voluntarily* giving them up," or the customs declined in the natural course of time (2008: 75–76; her italics). According to

Uberoi, it took a lengthy process of political lobbying, negotiation, and compromise to amend the two Marriage Acts' provisions regarding "prohibited relationships." In 1963, the legitimacy of Dravidian marriage practices was granted on grounds of "custom" and "usage," but the legal license granted to such marriages continued to be undermined by scientific or eugenic arguments against them (Uberoi 2008: 70–84).

2. The historian Rochona Majumdar (2009) has recently challenged the notion that arranged marriage is an authentic marker of traditional Indian life. She demonstrates the modern constitution of this key familial institution by reconstructing the ways in which Western liberal values (in particular, companionate couples and love marriages) have evolved in the context of colonial Bengal to produce a reconstituted Hindu joint family, based on a couple bound together by an arranged marriage and continued through a lineage of male heirs.

3. Public debates about marriage and family are far from new in Tamil Nadu. Mytheli Sreenivas documents how women-centered magazines published from the 1890s to the 1940s developped a novel paradigm of conjugal emotion that challenged existing patriarchal norms of family life (2008: 17). This emergent print culture, however, condemned not the institution of arranged marriage per se but loveless relations between husbands and wives. As Sreenivas writes: "This critique marked the components of companionship (particularly affection, pleasure, and romantic love) as the "natural" atributes of married life" (2008: 95).

4. See Daniel (1984) for an analysis of the Tamil category *poruttam.*

5. When I state that self-arranged unions are not desirable in Tamil Nadu, I do not mean that Tamil married couples do not end up feeling for each other something that "we" in the West and increasingly "they" in India call, in English, "love." As far as I can tell, many Tamil couples have an affectionate and intimate relationship (see Trawick 1990). Most parents actually arrange marriages in the hope that the bride and the groom will be happy together [see footnote 3]. What I simply mean is that it seems to be the common presumption that love should not precede marriage (see also Mody 2002: 225). For a comprehensive review of the numerous idioms of love in South Asia, see Orsini 2006; for a comparative study of "love" and "arranged" marriage in India, see Kapoor and Sen, who found "no significant differences . . . between these two types of marriage with respect to marital adjustment" (2002: 126). For a description of the complex interactions among law, publicity, and intimacy, see Mody's work on love marriage in Delhi (2002).

6. In a study of changing notions of and practices of masculinities in a Tamil village located in the Chengalpattu district, Anandhi, Jeyaranjan, and Krishnan note that even, "Dalit youngsters keep away from agricultural work . . . while their parents consider owning and cultivating land as an important indicator of their social status, the Dalit youths take special pride in stating that they do not know how to till the land" (2002: 4400).

7. Contributors to Jeffrey and Dyson's edited volume (2008) show how global and regional economic and social changes delay or prevent youth from achieving culturally appropriate forms of adulthood; the contributors address this phenomenon in the United

Kingdom, United States, India, Germany, Tanzania, Sierra Leone, South Africa, and Bosnia-Herzegovenia (2008: 5).

8. For a study of Tamil youth concepts of style and status, see Nakassis (2010). Nakassis focuses primarily on college-age youth in Madurai and Chennai.

CONCLUSION

1. Anthony Good, however, notes that, "the empirical evidence for Indian and Sri Lankan Tamils . . . is that most people do not habitually speak about kinship in terms of blood . . . and may even, as I found, deny its relevance when the question is explicitly put to them" (2000: 326).

2. According to the historian Mytheli Sreenivas (2008), this transformation began in late-nineteenth-century Tamil Nadu when merchants and Western-educated professionals began to carve out new models of "family" and "economy" that linked monogamous conjugality with notions of capital formation and capitalist relations. Although landed classes tended to reject these links and favor joint ownership by agnatic kin groups, visions of the conjugal family became the ground for debates about nation and national identity that began in 1920. Sreenivas, however, shows that the politicization and rationalization of conjugal norms did not automatically translate into lived experience, for example into growing affective ties between husbands and wives.

REFERENCES

Aaron, Rita et al. 2004. Suicides in Young People in Rural Southern India. *The Lancet* 363 (9415): 1117–1118.

Abraham, Leena. 2004. Redrawing the Lakshman Rekha: Gender Differences and Cultural Constructions in Youth Sexuality in Urban India. In *Sexual Sites, Seminal Attitudes: Sexualities, Masculinities and Culture in South Asia*, edited by S. Srivastava, 209–241. Delhi: Sage.

Abu-Lughod, Lila. 1986. *Veiled Sentiments Honor and Poetry in a Bedouin Society*. Berkeley: University of California Press.

Agarwal, Bina. 1994. *A Field of One's Own: Gender and Land Rights in South Asia*. Cambridge, UK: Cambridge University Press.

Aiyyappan, A. 1934. Cross-cousin and uncle–niece marriages in South India. In *Congrès International des Sciences Anthropologiques et Ethnosociologiques*. Compte-rendu de la Première Session, London: Institut Royal d'Anthropologie.

Alex, Gabriele. 2008. "When You Are Feeling of No Use Any More: Explaining Suicide in Rural Tamil Nadu," in *Good Deaths, Bad Deaths*, edited by Gabriele Alex and Suzette Heald, Special Issue of *Curare* 31:1.

Anandhi, S., J. Jeyaranjan, and R. Krishnan. 2002. Work, Caste and Competing Masculinities: Notes from a Tamil Village, *Economic and Political Weekly* 37 (24): 4403–4414.

Annoussamy, David. 2003. Le mariage entre oncle et nièce dans le Sud de l'Inde. In *Etudes en Hommage à Eugène Schaeffer*, edited by Gauthier Bourdeaux and Susy Berthier, 63–75. Paris: Emile Bruylant.

Appadurai, Arjun. 1981. Gastro-Politics in Hindu South Asia. *American Ethnologist* 8 (3): 494–511.

———. 1985. Gratitude as a Social Mode in South India. *Ethos* 13 (3): 236–245.

Appadurai, Arjun, and Carol A. Breckenridge. 1976. The South Indian Temple: Authority, Honor and Redistribution. In *Contributions to Indian Sociology* (N.S.) 10: 187–211.

———, guest eds. 1987. Public Culture. Special Annual Issue, *India Magazine* (New Delhi).

Arnold, David. 1979. Dacoity and Rural Crime in Madras 1860–1940. *Journal of Peasant Studies* 6(2): 140–167.

Arumugam, Indira. 2011. Kinship as Citizenship: State Formation, Sovereignty and Political Ethics among the Kallars in Central Tamil Nadu. PhD thesis, Department of Anthropology of the London School of Economics.

Ashokamitran, A. 2007. *Star-Crossed.* Translated from Tamil by V.Ramnarayan. Chennai, India: New Horizon Media.

Audinarayana, N., and S. Krishnamoorthy. 2000. Contribution of Social and Cultural Factors to the Decline in Consanguinity in South India. *Social Biology* 47(3–4): 189–200.

Barnard, Alan, and Anthony Good. 1984. *Research Practices in the Study of Kinship.* London: Academic Press.

Baviskar, Amita, and Raka Ray, eds. 2011. *Elite and Everyman: The Cultural Politics of the Indian Middle Classes.* New Delhi: Routledge.

Beck, E. F. Brenda. 1972. *Peasant Society in Koṅku: A Study of Right and Left Subcastes in South India.* Vancouver: University of British Columbia Press.

———. 1974. The Kin Nucleus in Tamil Folklore. In *Kinship and History in South Asia*, edited by Thomas Trautmann, p. 1–27. Michigan Papers on South and Southeast Asia, 7. Ann Arbor: Center for South and Southeast Asian Studies, University of Michigan.

Bittles H. Alan, William M. Mason, Jennifer Greene, and N. Appaji Rao. 1991. Reproductive Behavior and Health in Consanguineous Marriages. *Science* 252 (5007): 789–794.

Bittles, H. Alan, J. M. Coble, and N. Appaji Rao. 1993. Trends in Consanguineous Marriage in Karnataka, South India, 1980–89. *Journal of Biosocial Science* 25: 111–116.

Blackburn, H. Stuart. 1978. The Kallars: A Tamil "Criminal Tribe" Reconsidered. *South Asia* 1(1): 38–51.

Böck, Monika, and Aparna Rao. 2000. *Culture, Creation and Procreation: Concepts of Kinship in South Asian Practice.* New York: Berghahn.

Bouquet, Mary. 1996. Family Trees and Their Affinities: The Visual Imperative of the Genealogical Diagram. *The Journal of the Royal Anthropological Institute* 2(1): 43–66.

Bourdieu, Pierre. 1977. *Outline of a Theory of Practice.* Cambridge, UK: Cambridge University Press.

———. 1990. *In Other Words: Essays Toward a Reflexive Sociology.* Stanford, CA: Stanford University Press.

———. 2004 [1962] . *The Peasant and His Body*. Adapted by Loïc Wacquant; Richard Nice, trans. *Ethnography* 5(4): 579–599.

Busby, Cecilia. 1995. Of Marriage and Marriageability: Gender and Dravidian Kinship. *Journal of the Royal Anthropological Institute* 3(1): 21–42.

———. 2000. *The Performance of Gender: An Anthropology of Everyday Life in a South Indian Fishing Village*. London: Athlone.

Caldwell, Robert. 1856. *A Comparative Grammar of the Dravidian or South Indian Family of Languages*. London: Harrison.

Centerwall, R. Willard, and Siegried A. Centerwall. 1966. Consanguinity and Congenital Anomalies in South India: A Pilot Study. *Indian Journal of Medical Research* 54: 1160–1167.

Centerwall, R. Willard, et al. 1969. Inbreeding Patterns in Rural South India. *Biodemography and Social Biology* 16(2): 81–91.

Chakrabarty, Manisha, and Christophe Z. Guilmoto. 2005. An Analysis of the Determinants of Fertility Behaviour in South India at the Village Level. In *Fertility Transition in South India*, edited by Christophe Z. Guilmoto and S. Irudaya Rajan, 324–356. New Delhi: Sage Publications.

Clark-Decès, Isabelle. 2007. *The Encounter Never Ends: A Return to the Field of Tamil Rituals*. Albany: SUNY press. (*See also* Nabokov.)

Cole, Jennifer, and Deborah Durham, eds. 2007. *Generations and Globalization: Youth, Age, and Family in the New World Economy*. Bloomington: Indiana University Press.

Collier, Jane F., and Sylvia J. Yanagisako, eds. 1987. Toward a Unified Analysis of Gender and Kinship. In *Gender and Kinship: Essays toward a Unified Analysis*. Stanford, CA: Stanford University Press.

Conklin, George H. 1973. Urbanization, Cross-Cousin Marriage, and Power for Women: A Sample from Dharwar. *Contributions to Indian Sociology* (NS) 7: 53–63.

Daniel, E. Valentine 1984. *Fluid Signs: Being a Person the Tamil Way*. Berkeley: University of California Press.

David, Kenneth. 1973. Until Marriage Do Us Part: A Cultural Account of Jaffna Tamil Categories for Kinsmen. *Man* (n.s) 8: 521–535.

De Munck, C. Victor. 1996. Love and Marriage in a Sri Lankan Muslim Community: Toward a Reevaluation of Dravidian Marriage Practices. *American Ethnologist* 23(4): 698–716.

Deliège, Robert. 1987. Patrilateral Cross-Cousin Marriage among the Paraiyars of South India. *Journal of the Anthropological Society of Oxford* 18(3): 223–236.

———. 1997. *The World of the "Untouchables": Paraiyars of Tamilnadu*. Translated by David Phillips. Delhi: Oxford University Press.

Dirks, B. Nicholas. 1987. *The Hollow Crown: Ethnohistory of an Indian Kingdom*. Cambridge, UK: Cambridge University Press.

Donner, Henrike, and Geert De Neve. 2011. Introduction. In *Being Middle Class in Contemporary South Asia: A Way of Life*, edited by Henrike Donner, 1–22. London: Routledge

Dumont, Louis. 1953. The Dravidian Kinship Terminology as an Expression of Marriage. *Man* 53: 34–39.

———. 1957. Hierarchy and Marriage Alliance in South Indian Kinship. London: *Royal Anthropological Institute*, Occasional Paper no. 12.

———. 1964. Marriage in India: The Present State of the Question: Postscript to Part I. Part II: Marriage and Status; Nayar and Newar. *Contributions to Indian Sociology* 7: 77–98.

———. 1966. Marriage in India: The Present State of the Question, Part III: North India in Relation to South India. *Contributions to Indian Sociology* 9:90–114.

———. 1980. *Homo Hierarchicus: The Caste System and Its Implications*. Chicago: University of Chicago Press.

———. 1983. *Affinity as a Value: Marriage Alliance in South India, with Comparative Essays on Australia*. Chicago: University of Chicago Press.

———. 1986 [1957] . *A South Indian Subcaste: Social Organization and Religion of the Pramalai Kallar*. Delhi: Oxford University Press.

Dyson, T., and Moore, M. 1983. On Kinship Structure, Female Autonomy and Demographic Behaviour in India. *Population and Development Review* 9(1): 35–60.

Emeneau, B. Murray. 1941. Language and Social Forms: A Study of Toda Kinship Terms and Dual Descent. In *Language, Culture and Personality, Essays in Memory of Edward Sapir*, edited by Leslie Spier, 158–179. Menasha, WI: Sapir Memorial Publication Fund.

———. 1953. Dravidian Kinship Terms. *Language* 29(3): 339–353.

Encyclopedia of Tamil Literature (in 10 Volumes). 1990. Madras: Institute of Asian Studies vol. 1.

Epstein, T. Scarlett. 1973. *South India: Yesterday, Today, and Tomorrow: Mysore villages Revisited*. New York: Holmes & Meier Publishers.

Fabricius, Johann Philipp. 1972. *J. P. Fabricius's Tamil and English Dictionary*. 4th ed., rev. and enl. Tranquebar: Evangelical Lutheran Mission Pub. House.

Fuller, C. J. 1976. *The Nayars Today*. Cambridge, UK: Cambridge University Press.

———. 1992. *The Camphor Flame: Popular Hinduism and Society in India*. Princeton, NJ: Princeton University Press.

———. 1995. The "Holy Family" of Shiva in a South Indian Temple. *Social Anthropology* 3(3): 205–217.

Fuller, C. J., and Haripriya Narasimhan. 2008. Companionate Marriage in India: The Changing Marriage System in a Middle-Class Brahman Subcaste. *Journal of the Royal Anthropological Institute* (NS) 14: 736–754.

Galey, Jean-Claude. 1982. A Conversation with Louis Dumont, Paris, 12 December 1979. In *Way of Life: King, Householder, Renouncer—Essays in Honour of Louis Dumont*, edited by T. N. Madan, 13–22. Delhi: Motilal Banarsidass Publishers.

Geertz, Clifford. 1973. Deep Play: Notes on the Balinese Cockfight. In The *Interpretation of Cultures*, 412–454. New York: Basic Books.

Gillison, Gillian. 1987. Incest and the Atom of Kinship: The Role of the Mother's Brother in a New Guinea Highlands Society. *Ethos* 15(2): 166–202.

Good, Anthony. 1980. Elder Sister's Daughter Marriage in South Asia. *Journal of Anthropological Research* 36(4): 474–500.

———. 1981. Prescription, Preference and Practice: Marriage Patterns among the Koṇṭaiyaṅkōṭṭai Maṟavars of South India. *Man* (n.s.) 16(1): 108–129.

———. 1991. *The Female Bridegroom: A Comparative Study of Life-Crisis Rituals in South India and Sri Lanka*. Oxford, UK: Clarendon Press.

———. 1996. On the Non-existence of "Dravidian Kinship." *Edinburgh Papers in South Asian Studies* 6:1–12.

———. 2000. Power and Fertility: Divine Kinship in South India. In Monika Böck and Aparna Rao, eds., *Culture, Creation and Procreation*, 323–356. New York: Berghahn.

Goody, Jack. 1959. The Mother's Brother and the Sister's Son in West Africa. *Journal of the Royal Anthropological Institute of Great Britain and Ireland* 89 (1): 61–88.

———. 1983. *The Development of the Family and Marriage in Europe*. Cambridge, UK: Cambridge University Press.

Gough, E. Kathleen. 1956. Brahmin Kinship in a Tamil Village. *American Anthropologist* 58(5): 826–853.

Guilmoto, Z. Christophe. 1992. Un siècle de démographie tamoule. L'Évolution de la population du Tamil Nadu de 1871 à 1981. *Les Études du CEPED No. 4*. Paris: Centre Population et Développement.

———. 2011. Demography for Anthropologists: Populations, Castes and Classes in India, in *The Companion to the Anthropology of India*, edited by Isabelle Clark-Decès, 25–44. London: Wiley-Blackwell.

Hann, Katherine. 1985. The Incidence of Relation Marriage in Karnataka, South India. *South Asia Research* 5(1): 59–72.

Harlan, Lindsey, and Paul B. Courtright. 1995. On Hindu Marriage and Its Margins, in *From the Margins of Hindu Marriage: Essays on Gender, Religion and Culture*, edited by Lindsey Harlan and Paul B. Courtright, 3–18. New York: Oxford University Press.

Harman, William P. 1989. *The Sacred Marriage of a Hindu Goddess*. Bloomington: Indiana University Press.

Hart L. George. 1979. *Poets of the Tamil Anthologies: Ancient Poems of Love and War*. Princeton, NJ: Princeton University Press.

Headley, E. Zoé. 2011. Caste and Collective Memory in South India. In *A Companion to the Anthropology of India*, edited by Isabelle Clark-Decès, 98–114. Chichester, UK: Wiley-Blackwell (Blackwell Companions to Anthropology).

Herrenschmidt, Olivier. 2009. "Trop-plein de parents ou aucun parent. 'L'intégration' de l'ethnologue au gré des systèmes de parenté de l'Inde du Nord et de l'Inde du Sud." *Ateliers*, 33, La relation ethnographique, terrains et textes. Mélanges offerts à Raymond Jamous, 2009, [En ligne], mis en ligne le 18 mars 2009. Retrieved on June 8, 2009 at http://ateliers.revues.org/document8208.html.

Hudson, Dennis. 1977. Siva, Minaksi, Visnu: Reflections on a Popular Myth in Madurai. *The Indian Economic and Social History Review* 14(1): 107–119.

Hussain Khan, C. G. 2003. Muslim Kinship in Dravidian Milieu. *Economic and Political Weekly* 38(46): 4902–4904.

Jeffrey, Craig. 2010. *Timepass: Youth, Class, and the Politics of Waiting in India*. Stanford, CA: Stanford University Press.

Jeffrey, Craig, and Jane Dyson (eds). 2008. *Telling Young Lives: Portraits of Global Youth*. Philadelphia: Temple University Press.

Jeffrey, Craig, Patricia Jeffery, and Roger Jeffery. 2008. *Degrees without Freedom? Education, Masculinities and Unemployment in North India*. Stanford, CA: Stanford University Press.

Jones Allison, Charlene. 1980. Belief and Symbolic Action: A Cultural Analysis of a Non-Brahmin Marriage Ritual Cycle. PhD thesis, University of Washington.

Kakar, Sudhir. 1978. *The Inner World: a Psychoanalytic Study of Childhood and Society in India*. Delhi and New York: Oxford University Press.

Kapadia. K. M. 1955. *Marriage and Family in India*. Oxford, UK: Oxford University Press.

Kapadia, Karin. 1995. *Siva and Her Sisters: Gender, Caste, and Class in Rural South India*. Boulder, CO: Westview Press.

Kapoor, N., and A. K. Sen. 2002. Modernization, Religiosity and Marital Adjustment: A Comparative Study of Love and Arranged Married Couples. *Indian Psychological Review* 59: 126–138.

Karve, Irawati. 1953. *Kinship Organization in India*. New York: Asia Publishing House.

Kolenda, Pauline. 1984. Woman as Tribute, Woman as Flower: Images of "Woman" in North and South India. *American Ethnologist* 11:98–117.

———. 1987 [1967] . *Regional Differences in Family Structure in India*. Jaipur: Rawat Publications.

———. 1993. Sibling Relations and Marriage Practices: A Comparison of North, Central, and South India. In *Siblings in South Asia: Brothers and Sisters in Cultural Context*, edited by Charles W. Nuckholls, 103–141. New York: The Guilford Press.

Kroeber L. Alfred. 1909. Classificatory Systems of Relationship. *Journal of the Royal Anthropological Institute of Great Britain and Ireland* 39: 77–84.

Kuper, Adam. 1988. T*he Invention of Primitive Society: Transformations of an Illusion*. London: Routledge.

Lave, Jean Carter. 1966. A Formal Analysis of Preferential Marriage with the Sister's Daughter. *Man* (n.s.) 1(2): 185–200.

Leach, E.R. 1951. The Structural Implication of Matrilateral Cross-Cousin Marriage. *Journal of Royal Anthropological Institute* 81: 23–55.

Lévi-Strauss, Claude. 1969 [1949] . *The Elementary Structures of Kinship*. Translated from the French by James Harle Bell, John Richard von Sturmer, and Rodney Needham. Boston: Beacon Press.

Lukose, Ritty. 2009. *Liberalization's Children: Gender, Youth and Consumer Citizenship in India*. Durham, NC: Duke University Press.

McCormack, William. 1958. Sister's Daughter Marriage in a Mysore Village. *Man in India* 38(1): 34–48.

McGilvray, Dennis. B. 2008. *Crucible of Conflict: Tamil and Muslim Society on the East Coast of Sri Lanka*. Durham, NC: Duke University Press.

McLennan, John Ferguson. 1865. *Primitive Marriage. An Inquiry into the Origin of the Form of Capture in Marriage Ceremonies*. Edinburgh: Adam & Charles Black.

McKinnon, Susan, and Fenella Cannell. 2012. Rethinking the Place of Kinship in Meta-Narratives of Modernity. *Anthropology News* 53(4): 12–13.

Majumdar, Rochona. 2009. *Marriage and Modernity: Family Values in Colonial Bengal*. Durham, NC: Duke University.

Malinowski, Bronislaw. 1937. *Sex and Repression in Savage Society*. London: Kegan Paul, Trench, Trubner & Co., Ltd.

———. 1974. *Human Fertility in India: Social Components and Policy Perspectives*. Berkeley: University of California Press.

Marecek, Jeanne. 1998. Culture, Gender, and Suicidal Behavior in Sri Lanka. In *Suicide and Life-Threatening Behavior* 28(1): 69–81.

Mauss, Marcel. 1990. *The Gift (The Form and Reason for Exchange in Archaic Societies)*. Translated by W. D. Halls. Foreword by Mary Douglas. New York: W. W. Norton.

May, Linda. 1986. Arranging Marriages: Negotiation and Decision Making in South India. PhD dissertation, University of Pennsylvania.

Mayer, Peter. 2011. *Suicide and Society in India*. New York: Routledge.

Mazzarella, William T. S. *Indian Middle Class*. Downloaded on September 11, 2013, from www.soas.ac.uk/southasianstudies/keywords/file24808.pdf.

Mines, P. Diane. 2005. *Fierce Gods: Inequality, Ritual, and the Politics of Dignity in a South Indian Village*. Bloomington: Indiana University Press.

———. 2009. *Caste in India*. Key Issues in Asian Studies 3. Association of Asian Studies.

Mody, Perveez. 2002. Love and the Law: Love-Marriage in Delhi. *Modern Asian Studies* 36 (1): 223–256.

Moreno, Manuel. 1989. Marriage Transactions among the Pallars of Southern Kongu, Tamilnadu. *A Quarterly Journal of Anthropology* 69(1): 13–23.

Morgan, Henry Lewis. 1871. *Systems of Consanguinity and Affinity of the Human Family*. Washington, DC: Smithsonian Contributions to Knowledge.

Mukund, Kanakalatha. 1999. Women's Property Rights in South India: A Review. *Economic and Political Weekly* 34 (22): 1352–1358.

Nabokov, Isabelle. 2000. *Religion against the Self: An Ethnography of Tamil Rituals*. New York: Oxford University Press. (*See also* Clark-Decès.)

Nakassis, Constantine V. 2010. Youth and Status in Tamil Nadu, India. PhD dissertation, University of Pennsylvania.

Narasimhan, Haripriya. 2006. Our Health is in Our Hands: Women Making Decisions about Health Care in Tamilnadu, South India. PhD dissertation, Maxwell School of Syracuse University.

Narayan, R. K. 1954. *Swami and Friends and the Bachelor of Arts: Two Novels of Maguldi*. East Lansing: The Michigan State College Press.

Needham, Rodney. 1973. Prescription. *Oceania* 42: 166–181.

Niklas, Ulrike. 2000. Callikkattu: Embracing the Bull, Tamil Style. In *New Kolam: A Mirror of Tamil and Dravidian Culture*, Vols. 5 & 6: 1–59. Online journal hosted by FASS at NUS www.fas.nus.edu.sg/journal/kolam/index.htm.

Nisbett, Christopher Nicholas. 2004. Knowledge, Identity, Place and (cyber)Space: Growing Up Male and Middle Class in Bangalore. DPhil in Development Studies, University of Sussex, UK.

Nishimura, Yuko. 1998 *Gender, Kinship & Property Rights: Nagarattar Womanhood in South India*. Delhi: Oxford University Press.

Nuckholls, W. Charles. 1993. An Introduction to the Cross-Cultural Study of Sibling relations. In *Siblings in South Asia: Brothers and Sisters in Cultural Context*, edited by Charles W. Nuckholls, 19–69. New York: The Guilford Press.

Orsini, Franscesca, ed. 2006. *Love in South Asia: A Cultural History*. Cambridge, UK: Cambridge University Press.

Osella, Caroline, and Filippo Osella. 2000. Friendship and Flirting: Micro-Politics in Kerala, South India. *Journal of the Royal Anthropological Institute* (NS) 4: 189–206.

———. 2006. *Men and Masculinities in South India*. London: Anthem.

Östör, Ákos, Lina Fruzzetti, and Steve Barnett, eds. 1983. *Concepts of Person: Kinship, Caste and Marriage in India*. Delhi: Oxford University Press.

Ottenheimer, Martin. 1996. *Forbidden Relatives: The American Myth of Marriage*. Champaign: University of Illinois Press.

Pandian, Anand. 2005. Securing the Rural Citizen: The Anti-Kallar Movement of 1896 *Indian Economic Social History Review* 42 (1): 1–39.

———. 2009. *Crooked Stalks: Securing Virtue in South India*. Durham, NC: Duke University.

Parkin, J. Robert. 1996a. On Dumont's "Affinal Terms": Comment on Rudner. *Contributions to Indian Sociology* 30: 289–297.

———. 1996b. Genealogy and Category: An Operational View. *L'Homme* 139: 87–108.

Parkin, J. Robert, and Linda Stone. 2004. General Introduction. In *Kinship and Family. An Anthropological Reader*, edited by Robert J. Parkin and Linda Stone, 1–24. Malden, MA: Blackwell Publishers.

Peterson, Indira. 1988. The Tie That Binds: Brothers and Sisters in North and South India. *South Asian Social Scientist* 4 (1): 25–52.

Pouillon, François. 1996. Marcel Mauss et la Théorie Anthropologique du Don. *Revue Européenne des Sciences Sociales*. Mauss: Hier et Aujourd'hui: XIIe Colloque Annuel de Groupe d'Etude "Pratiques Sociales et Théories" 34 (105): 145–161.

Prasad. Raekha. 2009. Alcohol Use on the Rise in India. *The Lancet* 373(9657) (January 3): 17–18.

Radcliffe- Brown, A. R. 1952[1924]. The Mother's Brother in South Africa. *Structure and Function in Primitive Society*, 15–31. London: Cohen & West.

Raheja, Gloria Goodwin, and Ann Grodzins Gold. 1994. *Listen to the Heron's Words: Reimagining Gender and Kinship in North India*. Berkeley: University of California Press.

Ram, Kalpana. 1991. *Mukkuvar Women: Gender, Hegemony and Capitalist Transformation in a South Indian Fishing Community*. North Sydney: Allen & Unwin.

Ramanujan, A. K. (translator). 1981. *Hymns for the Drowning: Poems for Vishnu by Nammalvar*. Princeton, NJ: Princeton University Press.

———. 1983. The Indian Oedipus. In *Oedipus: A Folklore Casebook*, edited by Alan Dundes and Lowell Edmunds, 234–261. New York: Garland Press.

Rao, Kodanda M. 1973. Rank difference and Marriage Reciprocity in South India: An Aspect of the Implications of Elder Sister's Daughter Marriage in a Fishing Village in Andhra. *Contributions to Indian Sociology* (N.S) 7: 16–35.

Ravindran, T. K. Sundari. 1999. Female Autonomy in Tamil Nadu: Unraveling the Complexities. *Economic and Political Weekly*. 34, 16–17 (Apr. 17–30), WS34–WS44.

Reddy, Govinda. P. 1993. *Marriage Practices in South India: Social and Biological Aspects of Consanguineous Unions*. Madras: Department of Anthropology, University of Madras.

Reiniche, Marie-Louise. 1977. La notion de Jajmani. Qualification abusive ou principe d'intégration? *Purusartha* 3: 71–107.

Richards, F. J. 1914. Cross-Cousin Marriage in South India. *Man* 97: 194–198.

Rivers, W. H. R. 1907. The Marriage of Cousins in India. *Journal of the Royal Asiatic Society*, 611–40.

———. 1968 [1914] . *Kinship and Organization.* London: The Athlone Press.

Rogers, Christopher Martyn. 2005. Tamil Youth: The Performance of Hierarchical Masculinities. An Anthropological Study of Youth Groups in Chennai, Tamil Nadu, India. DPhil in Social Anthropology, The University of Sussex.

Rudner, David West. 1990. Inquest on Dravidian Kinship: Louis Dumont and the Essence of Marriage Alliance. *Contributions to Indian Sociology* 24(2): 153–174.

———. 1994. *Caste and Capitalism in Colonial India: The Nattukottai Chettiars.* Berkeley: The University of California Press.

Sahlins, Marshall. 1972. *Stone Age Economics.* Chicago: Aldine.

———. 2013. *What Kinship Is—and Is Not.* Chicago: The University of Chicago Press.

Scheffler, Harold. 1977. Kinship and Alliance in South India and Australia. *American Anthropologist* 79: 869–882.

———. 1984. Markedness and Extensions: the Tamil Case. *Man* (n.s.) 19: 557–574.

Schneider, David M. 1984. *A Critique of the Study of Kinship.* Ann Arbor: University of Michigan Press.

Sebastia, Brigitte. (2007). *Les Rondes de Saint Antoine: Culte, Affliction et Possession en Inde du Sud.* Paris: Aux Lieux d'être, 'Sous prétexte de médecines'.

Seymour, C. Susan. 1993. Sociocultural Contexts: Examining Sibling Roles in South Asia. In *Siblings in South Asia: Brothers and Sisters in Cultural Context*, edited by Charles W. Nuckholls, 45–69. New York: The Guilford Press.

Shaw, Brent D., and Richard P. Saller. 1984. Close-Kin Marriage in Roman Society? *Man* (N.S.) 19(3): 432–444.

Shulman, David Dean. 1980. *Tamil Temple Myths: Sacrifice and Divine Marriage in the South Indian Saiva Tradition.* Princeton, NJ: Princeton University Press.

———. 1993. *The Hungry God: Hindu Tales of Filicide and Devotion.* Chicago: the University of Chicago Press.

Soman, C. R., S. Safraj, V. Raman Kutty, K. Vijayakumar, and K. Ajayan. 2009. Suicide in South India: A community-based study in Kerala. *Indian Journal of Psychiatry* 51(4)(Oct.–Dec.): 261–264.

Spencer, Jonathan. 1990. Collective Violence and Everyday Practice in Sri Lanka. *Modern Asian Studies* 24 (3): 603–623.

Sreenivas, Mytheli. 2008. *Wives, Widows, and Concubines: The Conjugal Family Ideal in Colonial Ideal.* Bloomington: Indiana University Press.

Srinivas, M. N. 1956. A Note on Sanskritization and Westernization. *Far Eastern Quarterly* 15: 481–496.

Stein, Burton. 1980. *Peasant State and Society in Medieval South India*. Delhi: Oxford University Press.

Tamil Lexicon. 1924–1936. *Tamil Lexicon*. Madras: University of Madras. Available at http://dsal.uchicago.edu/dictionaries/tamil-lex/.

Thornton, Arland. 2005. *Reading History Sideways: The Fallacy and Enduring Impact of the Developmental Paradigm on Family Life*. Chicago: University of Chicago Press.

Thurston, Edgar. 1906. *Ethnographic Notes in Southern India*. Madras: Printed by the Superintendent, Government Press.

Thurston, Edgar, and K. Rangachari 1987. *Castes and Tribes of Southern India*. Vol III, Vol V. New Delhi/Madras: Asian Educational Services.

Trautmann, Thomas R. 1981. *Dravidian Kinship*. Cambridge, UK: Cambridge University Press.

———. 1984. Decoding Dravidian Kinship: Morgan and McIlvaine. *Man*, NS, 19(3): 421–431.

———. 1987. *Lewis Henry Morgan and the Invention of Kinship*. Berkeley: University of California Press.

———. 2006. *Languages and Nations: The Dravidian Proof in Colonial India*. Berkeley: University of California Press.

Trawick, Margaret. 1990. *Notes on Love in a Tamil Family*. Berkeley: University of California Press.

———. 2007. *Enemy Lines Warfare, Childhood, and Play in Batticaloa*. Berkeley: University of California Press.

Tylor, Edward B. 1889. On a Method of Investigating the Development of Institutions; Applied to Laws of Marriage and Descent. *The Journal of the Anthropological Institute of Great Britain and Ireland* 18: 245–272.

Uberoi, Patricia. 2006. Hierarchy and Marriage: Alliance in Indian Kinship. In *Caste, Hierarchy and Individualism: Indian Critiques of Louis Dumont's Contributions*, edited by R. S. Khare, 159–163. New Delhi: Oxford University Press.

———. 2008. Saving Custom or Promoting Incest? Post-Independence Marriage Law and Dravidian Marriage Practices. In *Redefining Family Law in India. Essays in Honour of B. Sivaramayya*, edited by Archana Parashar and Amita Dhanda, 54–85. London: Routledge.

Vaasanthi. 2007. *A Home in the Sky*. Translated from Tamil by Gomathi Narayanan. Chennai: Indian Writing.

Weber, Max. 1949. *The Methodology of the Social Sciences*. Translated by Edward A. Shils and Henry A. Finch. Glencoe, IL: The Free Press.

Westermarck, Edward. 1922[1891]. *The History of Human Marriage*. London. Macmillan.

Widger, Tom. 2012. Suicide and the Morality of Sinhalese kinship. In J. Staples, ed., *Suicide in South Asia: Ethnographic Perspectives*. Special Issue of: *Contributions to Indian Sociology*, 46 (1 & 2): 83–116.

Yalman, Nur. 1962. The Structure of the Sinhalese Kindred: A Re-Examination of the Dravidian Terminology. *American Anthropologist* NS, 64(3): 548–575.

———. 1967. *Under the Bo Tree*. Chicago: University of Chicago Press.

INDEX

The authorized representative in the EU for product safety and compliance is:
Mare Nostrum Group
B.V Doelen 72
4831 GR Breda
The Netherlands

www.ingramcontent.com/pod-product-compliance
Lightning Source LLC
Chambersburg PA
CBHW030735280326
41926CB00086B/1562
9780804790499